HOW TO WIN

MW00439996

Peter Pomerantsev is a Senior Fellow at Johns Hopkins University, where he studies contemporary propaganda and how to defeat it. His first book, *Nothing is True and Everything is Possible*, won the 2016 RSL Ondaatje Prize and was nominated for the *Guardian* First Book Award, Pushkin Prize, Baillie Gifford Prize and Gordon Burn Prize. His second, *This is Not Propaganda*, won the 2020 Gordon Burn Prize. His essay on authoritarian propaganda, 'Memory in the Age of Impunity', won the 2022 European Press Prize. He is a Fellow of the Royal Society of Literature.

'This is an unusual, original work of historical research and critical analysis, written with a literary flourish. Peter Pomerantsev digs deep into the past history of information warfare, in order to help us understand how to fight charlatans and fear mongers in the present.' ANNE APPLEBAUM

'An excellent work of history, carefully researched and beautifully written; and at once a profound study of a central problem of our time. To be read by everyone seeking perspective on all the lies of war and all the wars of lies.' TIMOTHY SNYDER

'Not only will this book excite you and entertain you, it will profoundly unnerve you. Never again will you think about war, truth and disinformation the same. This is history at its most urgent.' BEN JUDAH

'A fascinating wartime biography that is also an inquiry into one of the most urgent issues in modern politics. Highly recommended.' GIDEON RACHMAN

HOW TO WIN AN INFORMATION WAR

THE PROPAGANDIST WHO OUTWITTED HITLER

PETER POMERANTSEV

faber

First published in the UK in 2024
by Faber & Faber Limited
The Bindery, 51 Hatton Garden
London EC1N 8HN

This export edition published in 2024.

First published in the United States by United States by Public Affairs,
a division of Hachette Book Group, 1290 Avenue of the Americas,
New York, NY 10104.

Book design by Bart Dawson
Printed in the UK by CPI Group (UK) Ltd, Croydon CR0 4YY

A CIP record for this book
is available from the British Library

ISBN 978-0-571-36635-4

Printed and bound in the UK on FSC® certified paper in line with our continuing
commitment to ethical business practices, sustainability and the environment.
For further information see faber.co.uk/environmental-policy

2 4 6 8 10 9 7 5 3 1

*For Lee Richards, without whom
this book would not be possible,
and Dasha, without whom there
couldn't have been three*

CONTENTS

THE REAL LIVES OF SEFTON DELMER

He's torn. Ripped in opposite directions. Pulled this way and that, can Sefton Delmer even tell which is the real him?

At the age of ten, he is the only British boy in a German school in the opening months of World War I. It's the first day of term. From the top of a hall packed with German schoolchildren he can hear the voice of the Herr Direktor—his headmaster—up above the crowd on the raised stage. The director's voice is different today. He's normally so calm, but now he's shouting, screeching about the British, those wretched people who have brought this war upon peace-loving Germany and its peace-loving kaiser. The British, that nation of petty traders, are jealous of how Germany is rising, of Germany's new wealth, of its expanding territories. The British have plotted long and deceitfully to encircle us, and now these British assassins have struck. It is a moment for death and glory.

When Sefton greets the other pupils in the changing room, the children who were his good friends just a few weeks ago, they all hiss back at him: "*Verräter!*" (traitor), and the words fill the room like the judgement of a lynch mob. After school, in the Tiergarten, the boys wheel around Sefton, surround him, and the fattest one sets upon him with his fists.

With every morning, assemblies grow more fervent. The boys march round and round the hall, dust rising from the floor as they stamp in circles, crying in unison, "God! Kaiser! Fatherland!" their lungs beating out songs about bloody dawns rising over vast armies, about the sweet yearning to perish on the battlefields just for the joy of seeing Germany's banner flutter victorious.

He has to march with all the others amid the crash of cries, stamps, songs, chants. And although he knows it isn't right to feel this way, he can't help but be filled with enthusiasm, despite himself, by these hymns to German gunsmiths hammering the steel-hard German heart. And he finds his mouth prised open, finds the words take him over, and now he's singing the German war songs even as they celebrate the destruction of his countrymen.

"To tell the truth," Sefton Delmer would admit decades later, "I enjoyed singing the German victory songs. Their lift and lilt gave me a thrill of exultation of which I felt quite ashamed. 'A British boy,' I would say to myself, 'has no business feeling like this about these German war songs.'"[1]

And who, in this moment, is the real Sefton Delmer? Which is his real voice, the one that expresses his "true" identity? The Sefton Delmer who sings along to German war songs? Or the one muttering resistance in English under his breath?

For Delmer, this strain, this splitting of the self, will go on to become the source of his strength and skill. He will grow up to become the nearly forgotten genius of propaganda, a man who understood the secret of how propaganda acts on people, famed for his ability to leave his own personality behind; to cross countries, battle lines and seemingly intractable divides; to reimagine himself as others, become the enemy, climb inside their minds—and then play tricks on them from the inside.

But this quality will also be his greatest vulnerability.

GERMANY. SUMMER 1941. HITLER and his allies rule Europe from the Atlantic to the Black Sea. In the West, Britain is isolated. In the East, Soviet cities are falling one after another. In Germany, the streets and squares of the Third Reich are covered in a forest of swastika flags, the red and black illuminated at night with the glow of torch-lit processions.

Triumphant Nazi propaganda celebrates Victory, Unity, Fatherland and Führer in posters and in the songs of schoolchildren, from loud-speakers and in the headlines of newspapers, on cinema screens, and—most of all—from radios. Ever since they came to power, the Nazis have seen radio as the great force that can bind the country; break down the old divisions, the rifts among classes and regions; unite all Germans; and make real the grand claim of Propaganda Minister Joseph Goebbels that with the arrival of the Nazis, "the individual will be replaced by the Community of the People": die Volksgemeinschaft, populated by Volksgenossen driving Volkswagen and reading the Völkischer Beobachter.[2]

The Führer's speeches were special, festive celebrations, broadcast on radios and blared out from loudspeakers in streets, factories and offices. Every good German was expected to listen. At the sound of a wailing siren, you had to stop whatever you were doing. Whether at home or in an office, on the floor of a factory or in a barracks, life paused. When Hitler spoke, pistons and typewriters across the Reich fell silent. Wardens wearing swastika armbands patrolled the streets, ensuring that everyone was in hearing distance of a radio or loud-speaker so that the whole Volksgemeinschaft would, at one and the same time, be bathed in the Führer's swelling sea of words about Germany. Germany, this community of fate, a people proud to obey a commanding will, resurrected after years of poverty and misery brought on by cold-blooded foreign powers who, despite our hand of friendship, have forced war on Germany, a war begun by the British and by the Jewish newspapers, by Jewish finance and Jewish Bolsheviks, by parasites, by enemies against whom, I prophesy, we will be victorious. We shall fulfill our destiny. We are the salvation of Europe. Sieg Heil!

Radio helped the Nazis. But it also helped people escape from them. Twiddle the dial on one of the more elaborate radios, and you could slip into other worlds on shortwave. Even cheaper medium-wave radios could, with the help of a few choice wires acting as improvised antennas, be used to travel beyond the official stations of the Reich.

The Nazis knew this vulnerability. Tuning in to foreign broadcasts, and especially to the hated BBC, was a crime punishable by hanging. Foreign radios were jammed. Hitler's and Goebbels's speeches repeatedly told about the perfidious lies of enemy propaganda, especially from the British.

Listening to foreign radio stations was something to try only with your most trusted confidants—you never knew who might be listening in. The SD, the *Sicherheitsdienst* (intelligence agency) of the SS, was created to keep every person in the Reich under "continuous supervision". Every week these SD reports, delivered by their myriad agents, were collated into an overall analysis of the "attitudes and behaviours of the Volk", and their radio-listening habits were of special interest.[3]

In July 1941 the SD tersely noted that Germans (especially those in Chemnitz, Hamburg, Berlin and Potsdam) were tuning in to a new clandestine shortwave station called Gustav Siegfried Eins.[4] This secret station was more insidious than the foreign broadcasts. You could legislate and smear foreigners—but here was a seditious voice coming from inside.

Gustav Siegfried Eins opened with the same tune as the main Nazi news show—but instead of the great bells of Weimar, it was played on a wonky-sounding piano. Then an adjutant came on air and announced that *der Chef* was about to speak.

There was something almost dagger-like in *der Chef*'s tone: sharp, maybe drunk, definitely bitter. He swore incessantly, with racial slurs about Yankee-swine, stink-Japs, Russian pig–Bolsheviks and Italian lemon-faces. He called Churchill a "dirty, Jew-loving drunk".

Der Chef loved the army but loathed the Nazi Party. Instead of a Volksgemeinschaft, he attacked what he called "*die Parteikommune*", as if the Nazi Party was a clique unto itself. He blamed party officials for living the high life during holidays on the Dalmatian coast while people at home were being bombed by the Royal Air Force. He respected Hitler, who was the sort of man he had fought next to in World War I, but he accused Himmler, Göring and the rest of being soft on Britain. Hadn't they seen the destruction the British caused in Cologne and Aachen after they launched their first bombing raids in May? When the damn air-raid sirens in Aachen didn't work and whole swathes of this great German cathedral city were destroyed? *Der Chef* had been to Aachen, had seen the weeping German women clambering over the wreckage of their houses trying to dig out their children underneath—and what had the Luftwaffe done in response? Nothing. London should be bombed to smithereens. Those shit Britishers should be blown to shit. But the Luftwaffe was docile. The Nazi Party was full of secret Bolsheviks. They didn't even tell soldiers when their relatives were killed in British bombings. They promoted their SS pals to easy office jobs. They frequented their exclusive SS brothels while soldiers died of dysentery on the front.

Every day, at ten to the hour every hour, for ten full-throated minutes, *der Chef* flew through this fury. He mentioned names of specific Nazi functionaries, their children and their wives. He knew the precise shops where they bought their secret stashes of luxury pâtés and Moselle wines. He even knew which Nazi official's wife just bought a second flat in Vienna thanks to her corrupt connections.

Such details, all the listeners understood, could come only from insider leaks. This meant *der Chef* must have some sort of cover from his higher-ups. There had always been tension between the Prussian military aristocracy and the Nazi Party. Could there be some sort of rebellion brewing? What if the generals were about to turn against *die Parteikommune*? And where was *der Chef* broadcasting from? Some thought it was from a barge bobbing on the Rhine. Others were quite certain he was in France. Or was it Poland? And what, come to think of it, did the name of the station, Gustav Siegfried Eins, actually stand for?[5]

In his diary in July 1941, the writer Erich Kästner, one of Germany's best-known authors—who'd watched his own books burn in the blaze of Nazi bonfires as they incinerated the work of authors who refused to back their party—noted how popular the station was becoming: "More and more people are tuning in to the station called Gustav

Siegfried Eins. . . . What it says about the leaders of the Nazi party is mind-blowing. It's an anti-Communist station, which communicates the position of the army leadership and German nationalists."[6]

It wasn't only Germans listening in to *der Chef*. The US embassy in Berlin was also tuning in, and its service attaché saw *der Chef* as a sign that there was an increase in anti-Nazi sentiment inside the army. The Americans shared their insights with the British.[7]

This was one of the more awkward moments in British–American World War II relations. Prime Minister Winston Churchill was desperately trying to persuade America to join the war. If the Americans believed that *der Chef* was a sign that the Nazis' power was on the wane, might this delay their joining?

David Bowes-Lyon, the queen consort's brother, was entrusted with communicating the truth about *der Chef* to Franklin D. Roosevelt, the US president. Bowes-Lyon came in person to the White House. *Der Chef*, he explained to Roosevelt, was not on a barge bobbing on the Rhine. He wasn't in Poland. Nor in France. Actually, he was a few kilometres from London, in Bedfordshire, part of a covert operation run by the Political Warfare Executive, the British propaganda arm, which Bowes-Lyon represented in Washington.

Every day, the show was recorded in the billiards room of a country house. The windows of the room were shuttered and heavily curtained. Metal microphones stood on the covered billiards table, reflecting a fluorescent strip light above them.

Der Chef was not a renegade Nazi. He was being played by a mild-mannered German novelist of Jewish descent. His adjutant was played by a German journalist, the son of one of Berlin's greatest cabaret impresarios, who had fled the Nazis with his Jewish wife.

At the back of the room stood a vast, bearded man. He was the one in charge. He invented and directed this whole performance. This was Sefton Delmer, the little boy bullied in a Berlin gymnasium in World War I. And in the summer of 1941, Delmer's Empire of Tricks was just getting going.

• • • ▬▬ ▬▬ ▬▬ • • •

How DO YOU WIN an information war? What can you do when those you love—your family, regions, countries—are swept up in a vortex of conspiracy theories and manufactured fears, slip away from you under a quicksand of lies and move mentally into an alternative reality where black is white and white is black?

I research and write about contemporary propaganda, and whenever I present my work, there's at least one person who raises a hand to ask, "But, Peter—what should we do to fight this?" I can sense the whole room awakening, looking at me for an answer. For some, the question can be personal. They have loved ones who, like people bitten by a Dracula of disinformation, have changed so much they can barely communicate with them any more.

But most of the stories I have to share are of unsuccess. Gutsy fact-checkers who, sometimes at great personal risk, strive to establish the truth—but are ignored by the millions of people who don't want to hear the truth. Worthy, well-researched journalism that crumples in the face of suspicion, seeded purposefully for decades, that the media are actually "enemies of the people". The propagandists see this as a war in which information is a weapon you use not to win an abstract argument but to confuse, dismay, demoralise and distract. It is a tool to tap into human fears, vulnerabilities and secret, often violent and cruel desires and twist them to the benefit of the powerful forces they serve. Fact-checking doesn't stand a chance.

And then I discovered Sefton Delmer—and things started getting interesting. Here was a man who fought differently.

During World War II, Delmer rose to become a head of Special Operations for the Political Warfare Executive, running a fleet of secret radio stations in a variety of languages—and much more besides. The little boy confused about where he belonged in 1914 conjured up an ersatz Germany run from the English countryside: "German" stations with disgruntled SS men and angry Austrian priests, stations for German sailors in western France and soldiers in Norway and civilians everywhere. He edited a daily newspaper and oversaw a whole industry of leaflets stimulating desertion and surrender, fake letters, fake stamps and a vast array of rumours, gossip, thoughts and desires, all intended to break the spells cast by the Nazis.

Delmer gathered around him artists, academics, spies, soldiers, astrologists and forgers. Refugees from Berlin's cabaret scene acted and wrote the scripts of radio shows. Ian Fleming, the creator of James Bond, and the novelist Muriel Spark lent their talents to Delmer's operations. Many of Delmer's most important collaborators were Jewish refugees from Nazi Germany pretending to be Nazis in order to subvert Nazi propaganda from inside, dressing up as their own torturers in order to take revenge.

But in the half-century since the war, the memory of Delmer's work had generally been pushed to the sidelines of the public mind. Delmer's (vetted) memoirs were published in the 1960s but are long out of print. Delmer's son, during an interview in the 1990s, mentioned that he thought this amnesia had a reason: the victorious Allies didn't want anyone to think "the war had been won with a trick".[8] This was, after all, meant to be "our finest hour", when our most virtuous qualities shone through, not when we excelled at the darker arts.

Yet Delmer's mastery of propaganda is more relevant than ever as our lives have been upended by digital technology as thoroughly as radio transformed Delmer's. And now we know much more about his tricks. Over the last decade the indefatigable efforts of the archivist and historian Lee Richards have brought to light and organised the formerly classified World War II archive detailing Delmer's work. I first began to explore it in order to understand more about how disinformation works behind the scenes. But as I went through the details of Delmer's plans and the transcripts of the radio shows themselves, Delmer's memoirs and those of his contemporaries, I realised that there was something much more interesting at work here than mere "deception".

During his childhood in Germany, Delmer grew to understand the appeal of propaganda partly because he realised how susceptible he was to it himself, and how it affected Britain as much as Germany. Later, as a star reporter in Berlin during the 1930s, he became a drinking companion of leading Nazis and saw the inner workings of Hitler's campaign to conquer German minds. Delmer was convinced that his German experience meant he could understand the power of their propaganda—and its weakness. After the war, he tried to create a new type of media that could withstand the hate and lies he had seen dominate Germany, and he worried that despite the introduction of democracy, old propaganda habits could return. His focus lay beyond the uniquely nasty phenomenon of Nazism and explored what makes any of us susceptible to propaganda, and what to do about it.

During the war, Delmer and his troupe were in a race against Goebbels in the Reich Propaganda Ministry to understand how media molds us, how it exploits our traumas and desires. The propagandist, like the artist and the psychoanalyst, is on a quest to understand what makes us tick, how we imagine ourselves and those around us—and how to insert themselves into that process. Ultimately, propaganda and its influence over us pose the question of whether we can be truly free. When are you yourself, and when are you a being who has been manipulated by others?

Anyone looking for a simple hero to imitate, some easy lessons we can cut and paste, won't find it in Delmer. He's always provoking us to ask a question: Is he a force for good or evil? The preface to his memoirs even opens with this dialogue:

"I come out of all this as rather a prig, I fear," I said to my wife, when I had read through the manuscript of this book for the umpteenth time.

"What is a prig, daddy?" inquired my daughter Caroline Selina, aged eight.

"Oh, a goody goody sort of chap," said I.

"You're not a goody goody," says Caroline Selina.

"No, I'm a baddy baddy."

But if he's a "baddy baddy", he's one who criticises himself constantly. Although he used disinformation, he also saw its self-destructive consequences. Delmer's memoirs are one long morality tale about how his deceptions boomeranged on him.

● ● ● ▬▬ ▬▬ ▬▬ ● ● ●

THIS BOOK FOLLOWS DELMER'S journey across the propaganda-lands of the twentieth century, from World War I through Weimar Germany and in particular World War II and its aftermath. This is not a regular work of history or biography. As a student of contemporary disinformation, my aim is to understand what he can teach us about the nature of propaganda and how to win an information war. The lessons Delmer has for us are positive, negative and urgent. As I was writing it in February 2022, Russia launched a full military invasion of Ukraine, the country of my birth and where so many of my family, friends, colleagues and loved ones live. President Putin and his battalions of propagandists claimed that Ukraine was not a real country, that it didn't have the right to exist, that it was just "one people" with Russia. It was the latest iteration of a long tradition: Moscow has been invading Ukraine, trying to wipe out or subjugate it, for centuries.

Four weeks later, I travelled to a nearly deserted Kyiv to launch a project recording Russian atrocities in Ukraine, to ensure that the war crimes committed during the invasion didn't disappear under a fresh blizzard of Russian disinformation. On a subsequent trip in April, I joined American journalists when they interviewed Ukrainian president Volodymyr Zelensky.

It was late evening when we arrived. To minimise the risks of bombardment, the lights were off in the Presidential Palace complex, the high windows stacked with sandbags. The windowless meeting room was, by contrast, neon bright. Zelensky was dressed in a khaki T-shirt and trainers. The look was part wartime necessity, part communication tactic: Zelensky represents a state that is at war.

Zelensky thrives on finding a contact with his audience, the way he did for decades as a highly successful stand-up comedian and actor, most famous for playing the Ukrainian president in a comedy. Every country he addressed had a parallel to what Ukraine was experiencing now: the Blitz for Britain, 9/11 for the US.

If there was one audience he thought he knew, it was the Russian one. He had spent years appearing in Russian light-entertainment shows. When Russia invaded, Zelensky sent multiple video messages appealing to ordinary Russians to turn against the war. But he hit a wall. Polling, to the extent you can trust polls in a dictatorship, was showing that the vast majority of Russians supported the invasion.[9] Warmongering TV shows celebrating the invasion were surging in the ratings, their hosts braying how Zelensky would be the last Ukrainian president because soon there would be no more Ukraine. Russian state media was full of calls to liquidate Ukraine's leadership, terrorise its people and annihilate this "fake nation".[10] Many Russians repeated the Kremlin propaganda line that Russia was not the aggressor but the victim of a vast global conspiracy, surrounded by enemies set to invade the Motherland, and "justified" in attacking Ukraine. Many of Zelensky's old friends weren't responding to his calls.

Russians are in an "informational bunker", Zelensky said—psychological as much as technological—refusing to accept responsibility and reality.

I knew what Zelensky was talking about first-hand. I had spent years in Russia, had witnessed the early growth of Putin's seemingly impregnable media system in the first decade of the twenty-first century. Could anything be done to subvert it and the other strains of merciless, frequently murderous, increasingly reality-denying propaganda spawning across the globe—from China to where I live and work in the United States? Sefton Delmer—you "baddy baddy"—what can you tell us?

HOW TO WIN AN
INFORMATION WAR

CHAPTER 1

PROPAGANDA IS THE REMEDY FOR LONELINESS

Sefton Delmer never systematised his ideas about propaganda in any single abstract theory or doctrine. But his memoirs are, apart from many other things, parables of his ideas about propaganda—how it works and how we can fight it—and the stories of his childhood and youth are prequels to his later struggles. His memoirs are the main source for the story of his early years—but it's a retired middle-aged man who is writing them, explaining and sometimes justifying his work, showing how the past informed his craft.

In the summer of 1914, in the last days before the start of World War I, Sefton, or Tom Delmer, as he was always known by his family, friends and associates, was spending the school holidays among the azure slopes of the Harz Mountains. (Although those close to Delmer knew him as Tom, I will continue to call him Sefton, the name he used to brand his books.) Delmer describes the setting as idyllic, almost overly arcadian: sleepy villages with gentle villagers, peaceful rural communities, wells and well-wishers. He will come back to this image over and over in his memoirs: bucolic, open-hearted communities beyond the brutal technology of mass propaganda.

He was on holiday here with his mother and sister.[1] His father, Frederick Sefton Delmer, a professor of English literature at Berlin University, was back in the capital preparing his lectures. Delmer's parents were from Australia, at the time a dominion of the British Empire, and they were potential enemy aliens if there was war between Germany and Britain.

One morning in August, Sefton woke to a new noise: an alien, metallic, rough roar that reverberated up and down the valleys. Outside, the gentle green meadows were suddenly disfigured by troops. The lush woods were pierced with antennas connected to a transmitter powered by an electric generator. World War I was the first time the wireless would be used by an army, and Delmer describes its noise as "the first echo of 20th century war".[2]

Technology and its accompanying propaganda were advancing everywhere through the green hills.

At the village fair there was a new attraction: a tent with a cinema screen, which repeatedly showed newsreels of the assassination of Archduke Ferdinand of Austria, Germany's ally, by a student who wanted to liberate Bosnia from the Austro-Hungarian Empire. Sitting inside the cinema tent, pleasant villagers and well-bred holidaymakers were transformed in the light of the screen, all suddenly baying for war. At the playground, parents of children whom Delmer had been playing happily with just a few days before suddenly turned on him. "Lousy Engländer," they cried, "get away! You deserve a good hiding!"[3]

His mother, alarmed, swept the children to the train station and back to Berlin. They could hear and feel the passengers growing ever more excited at the approach of war as the train neared the city. "This time," the passengers were saying to one another, "we really shall show them." Finally they would be able to take revenge for losses to France in previous wars, finally "our Kaiser will show the world who we are". As he listened, Sefton sensed that their speech was somehow borrowed— cut-and-pasted from the stories about Prussian military adventures that were compulsory reading at all schools. The Delmers didn't dare speak any English on the journey.[4]

Near the capital, the whole carriage gathered round a waiter who had bought a special edition of the *Berliner Tageblatt*. His whiskers quivered with excitement like radio antennas as he read out the official mobilisation order. Germany was at war. The train cheered. "A short merry war!" exclaimed a man with a beard like an upside-down *V*.

By the time the train reached Berlin, the crowds were thick with euphoria and cries of "Deutschland, Deutschland über Alles!" and "Down with England!" Although Britain was yet to even enter the war, Delmer would recall in his memoirs that "Britain was the traitor. Britain was the main enemy. Propaganda had them in thrall."[5]

The scenes were repeating across the country. One of the most famous photographs is from August 6, 1914, in Odeonsplatz, Munich. Among the thousands thronging the square, waving their boating hats in jubilation and climbing on statues of great lions, is a young Adolf Hitler. He is in the middle of the throng, hatless, gleaming-eyed, squeezed in among taller men but bursting through them in a fountain of fervour. "For me these hours came as a deliverance from the distress that had weighed upon me during the days of my youth. I was carried away by the enthusiasm of the moment," he would remember in *Mein Kampf*, and "I sank down upon my knees and thanked Heaven out of the fullness of my heart for the favour of having been permitted to live in such a time."[6]

There is a catch, however. The photograph of Hitler is likely a fake, or at least manipulated. In 2010 a leading German historian of World War I, Gerd Krumeich, studied other photos of the scene on the square and couldn't find Hitler in any of them. He concluded that the image had been cut-and-pasted by Nazi propagandists in 1932, right before an all-important election tour, a tour on which Delmer would accompany Hitler and be granted exclusive access to report on the Nazi propaganda show from behind the scenes.[7]

• • • ▬▬ ▬▬ ▬▬ • • •

THEY CAME TO ARREST Sefton's father at 5:30 a.m. sometime in the second month of World War I. Delmer's memoirs are specific about the time but not the date: memory can privilege some details over others.

The constable rang the door, and when the maid opened it, Sefton could tell that the officer felt awkward. The constable knew the family and when he came to arrest Sefton's father, he kept on using the respectful title of "Herr Professor". Would the Herr Professor kindly get up, pack and come with him to the Alexanderplatz police station? "I am sorry, but these are my instructions. Like everyone else in the street I am most unhappy to do anything to cause the Herr Professor inconvenience and discomfort."

When the war began, Professor Delmer's *Rektor* had offered him a chance to naturalise and become a loyal subject of the kaiser. Delmer refused. That made him an "enemy national", and now he was being put under arrest.

The maid gave the constable coffee as Professor Delmer packed. As a sign of respect, the constable took off his spiked helmet. Young Sefton stood in front of the constable and stared at him. He was transfixed not so much by the arrest but because he had never seen a policeman take off his spiked helmet, that pointy symbol of authority in the kaiser's kingdom. Underneath the helmet the constable had bright, sweaty, greasy orange hair. It was a pitilessly hot month, and the little boy couldn't stop staring at the constable's forehead: the skin was pale where the spiked helmet would usually come down over the front of his head, while all around it was burned by the sun, making for a big white *V* amid the roasted pink of the forehead.

Beneath the authority of the helmet was a normal, sweating, heavy-breathing, awkward human being, but one whose very skin colour had been branded with the uniform he wore. Delmer tells the story from the point of view of his childhood self, but you can sense the adult author implying a more mature question: Where does the private person end and the public role begin?

The constable put his helmet back on as he escorted Delmer through the door: "I am sure this is just a mistake which will be cleared up very quickly. Then the Herr Professor will return home again to his flat."[8]

This turned out to be untrue. Like thousands of other "enemy nationals", Professor Delmer was interned in Ruhleben Prison. The next time Sefton saw his father, the Herr Professor was being led with a column of British prisoners through the Berlin streets, pedestrians teasing and jeering as they passed.

How differently they used to greet the Herr Professor in the genteel neighbourhood where the Delmers lived. On the day that Frederick had been made a full professor, a rarity for a foreigner, many in their home street congratulated him as he rode past on his bicycle, Sefton riding on the handlebars, the breeze mixing with the greetings of the shopkeepers and tradesmen who came out to give them a respectful wave. Before the war, everyone had wanted to be friends with this curious foreign family who spoke such perfect German: Frederick Delmer made Sefton and his sister speak German at home in order to understand the country that they lived in. At the age of ten, Sefton spoke better German than he did English. Even though he was known as *der Engländer* at school, he had been born in Berlin. He'd spent just a few summer holidays in Australia and England. In his short life he'd spoken English at some times with a German accent and at other times with an Australian accent, depending on where he'd happened to have spent his previous summer.

Now, every morning when he went to school, he was under attack for being something he couldn't fully understand.

The physical education class was the worst. The PE teacher, his little goatee twitching with patriotic arousal, ordered the boys to pick up weights and punch the air with them, and as they punched to imagine they were striking a traitor like that "Engländer" over there, a traitor he would beat and expel if he but had the chance. He talked about Sefton in the third person—as if he weren't there.

In the Prussia Sefton Delmer describes growing up in, people glorified and imitated the army.[9] Each country walk with German friends had the air of a military procession, with everyone marching in strict order: men at the front, then children (singing patriotic songs), and finally the women. Now this militarism had taken over: generals were gods. The joint army chief General Ludendorff's bored sneer and know-it-all eyes glared down at Sefton from a poster in the classroom, as if checking the boy's writing for sufficient patriotism. The children wrote essays justifying the war, collected funds for the war effort as homework and were assigned to write stories about how their fathers were fighting on the front. Sefton was relieved of this final duty, and when the Herr Direktor told him that as an "enemy schoolboy" he didn't have to join in the celebrations of German victories, he bit back: "There won't be any victories over the British."[10] But for all his little insolences, the propaganda pushing in on Sefton would envelop him everywhere as he crossed Berlin.[11]

After school, in the great central Tiergarten where the city came to relax, Berliners gathered to pin little envelopes with the donations they'd collected to a huge effigy of General Hindenburg's walrus-whiskered, fleshy face, sticking the donation envelopes into his mighty, spraying moustache. The faces of Generals Hindenburg and Ludendorff were everywhere: on pins, neckties, postcards and playing cards. Walls and windows were plastered with posters of strong soldiers in spiked helmets urging people to donate money for the army.

Passing the cinemas, you would hear cheering from inside as newsreels from the front were celebrated like victories in football matches.

Along the River Spree, street sellers hawked newspapers, their stories celebrating the war as a "holy moment", a "holy flame of anger", a "revelation" that brought forth a "rebirth through war". "What Germany has experienced in these days," stated the *Berliner Zeitung* in August 1914, "is a miracle, a renewal of oneself; it was a shaking off of everything small and foreign; it was a most powerful recognition of one's own nature."[12]

Germany had become unified only half a century previously. It was still deeply divided by region, class and aristocratic clan. But over the last decades, new national newspapers had made it possible for Germans to read the same stories on the same day, see the same photos of the kaiser, desire the same gadgets and scents in the same advertisements, admire the same shots of huge Zeppelins floating in the sky. And as the war started, newspapers became the place where Germans were meant to be fused together in one purpose. They featured photo pullouts that took the reader to the front. Standing in the middle of Berlin, you were transported over to the battlefields, you were among gunners and machine guns, so close that you could almost hear their rat-a-tat. On the next page were letters between soldiers and their loved ones: letters about love, sacrifice and bravery. These were intimate letters that real people had written, blurring the line between the private and the public, creating the sense that this was truly a people's war.[13]

Over the thin, curling river stood the Berliner Schloss, home of the kaiser. He gave his speeches on the balcony—speeches that were then reprinted across the nation—telling the eager crowds how he no longer saw any different parties or classes in Germany.[14] Germany, this young, divided country, which had always been so riven, was truly now one people. The photos of the jubilant crowds at the time seemed to reinforce this: rich and poor, aristocrats and working class together, at least for one snapshot.

Sefton saw the city differently. Rather than a stage of unity, it was an obstacle course holding him back from seeing his father. His mother would try to reunite them, even if just for a moment.

One time they walked to a bridge overlooking the prison. It was an illegal expedition: as foreigners, they were not allowed out of their small quarter of Berlin. When his mother thought no one was looking, she told Sefton to climb on top of the rails, and as he craned his neck and leaned forward, he could peer into the prison yard: "Mummy, Mummy—I can see him. There is a queue of men waiting outside a sort of barracks and he is near the end reading a book."[15] Looking back at his mother, Sefton could see that she had tears in her eyes—but she didn't dare climb on the balustrade herself; it would have been far too conspicuous.

And there was the time in the muddy lane by the barbed-wire walls of the prison when Sefton, his mother and his sister stood for what seemed like hours, drenched by harsh rain and cutting wind, cold hands clutching little packages with tea and jam. A friendly priest had tipped them off that Professor Delmer would be taken down this lane to a bathhouse for delousing. Finally, a door in the fence opened, and there was his father: thin, ill, surrounded by sentries with rifles, but suddenly smiling as he saw his wife and children slipping and stumbling towards him as they thrust the little packages into his hands. The professor had only a few seconds to tell his wife he was being charged with espionage. Then he was dragged off for delousing.

Those were the only two times that Sefton saw his father in the first six months of the war. Six months in which it seemed Germany would be fully victorious.

Every day the local police sergeant on Kantstraße would post new communiqués celebrating Germany's military victories in a glass-fronted box on the street. And with every new victory, Kantstraße would resound with celebration. Flags were unfurled from every window. Not just German flags but also Danish, Greek, Swiss and American ones: even the foreigners wanted to join in Germany's great triumphs. Only the Delmers' window stood empty: alone and dark. "And though I knew it was wrong of me, my small boy's soul hated it, our standing out like that." Despite all the humiliations of being an Engländer in Germany, he wanted to join in with the rest of the street, even as he disapproved of the desire. Once, as the flags were again unfurled, he couldn't control himself any longer, started rummaging around the apartment for a flag, any flag, found one with his father's rowing gear, a British Royal Standard no less, the flag of the British royal family, and was already on his way to plant it into the window box of geraniums when his mother's hand shot out and firmly pulled him back.[16]

●　●　●　━━━　━━━　━━━　●　●　●

WHAT IS THIS URGE that Sefton was fighting? What is this "propaganda" that sucks people in like a whirlpool—from the kaiser's Berlin to today? If we are to subvert it, we need to understand its appeal.

I've already used the word *propaganda* often in the opening pages of this book. Delmer uses it continuously—to label both what the kaiser and the Nazis did and then his own work. Yet he never explicitly defines it. Sometimes he references it as something morally neutral—just any form of mass persuasion. At other times he means some sort of deception.

But in these early descriptions of his childhood, what he calls propaganda is more than just a single campaign or piece of disinformation. The real power of propaganda is not to convince or even to confuse; it's to give you a sense of belonging.

In 1962, a year after Delmer released the first volume of his memoir, the French sociologist, historian and philosopher Jacques Ellul published *Propaganda*, one of the more beguiling books on the subject I've encountered. I like to consider the two works side by side: Delmer the teller of propaganda in action, and Ellul the interpreter.

During World War II, Ellul helped Jews escape Nazis in Burgundy, an act that would earn him the honour of being named a "righteous among the Nations". Decoding the appeal of Nazi propaganda inspired his work, but he casts his search much wider, trying to understand the role that propaganda plays in any modern society.[17] Like Delmer, Ellul refers to different types of propaganda, which, unlike Delmer, he then carefully defines.

Political propaganda is the obvious campaigns all around us: election ads and war slogans, posters and banners.

Sociological propaganda cuts deeper, the television shows and movies, the art and literature that help integrate people into the common myths that keep society together. The United States, for example, argued Ellul, was a nearly impossible experiment of different creeds, languages and religions that had to be integrated together through movies and sitcoms around underlying "myths" such as "the American way of life" or "the pursuit of happiness" or "progress". Any propaganda that went against these myths was unlikely to be effective, for it would go against the grain of how people understood the world. When these myths were swallowed unthinkingly, uncritically, they could turn toxic, casting anyone who questioned them as an enemy.

But this propaganda, argued Ellul, was something that people needed, wanted, yearned for. It wasn't just foisted from above. It was a product of a change in which the bonds of rural and local communities had been ruptured by masses of people moving into big industrial cities, where they were just a cog in a greater machine that they could never quite grasp or control, a change so drastic that people now felt "the most violent need to be re-integrated into a community". As Ellul wrote, "Propaganda is the true remedy for loneliness." And the more we live in a society where we have little control over our lives, the more we need propaganda that gives us a sense of (ersatz) agency: "Man cannot stand being unimportant. . . . Though a mass instrument, propaganda addresses itself to each individual. It appeals to *me*. It appeals to *my* common sense, *my* desires, and provokes *my* wrath and *my* indignation. It gives *me* violent feelings, and lifts *me* out of the daily grind."[18] Propaganda can give you both a community and the illusion of individual agency.

In World War I, German newspapers and cinemas were helping fuse this rapidly industrialising new nation into one propaganda community. What Ellul describes as theory, Delmer tells through stories and symbols. He shows how the rural idyll in the Harz Mountains, where he could at first play with other German kids, is disturbed by the arrival of new communications technology in the shape of military radio masts and the hate-baying newsreels in the cinema tent at the village fair. He shows how stories and education about military heroism and even the militarised way that families went for walks reinforced the underlying myth that Germany was a great military nation, that it indeed was a coherent nation defined by militarism, destined for empire. He contrasts a warm world in the countryside and in the local area where he grew up in Berlin to the shrunken stereotypes of "us" and "enemies" in the warmongering newspapers, his street erupting in jubilation around the communal newsletter they read together.

We have our own ruptures today that leave people yearning for propaganda as a "remedy for loneliness".

The rise of politicians, whether in America or in Europe, who claim to represent the "true people" against real or often imaginary outsiders can be most rapid in what sociologists call "civic deserts": frequently, rural places where the old institutions that bonded communities, the local clubs and town halls, have disappeared and where civic engagement is particularly low.[19]

Or take Russia. This is a country where propagandists believed that their mission was to create a new collective after the collapse of the Soviet Union. When I lived in Moscow, I interviewed one of Putin's early spin doctors, Gleb Pavlovsky, who explained to me how in the 1990s, after the Soviet Union fell apart, the old ways that people used to define themselves—Communist, anti-Communist, collective farmers, workers or intelligentsia—all fell apart. In the flux he invented a new collective for them to dwell in. They were all to be part of one great "Putin majority". As he told me, "I first invented the idea of the Putin majority, and then it appeared!"[20]

There are many societies that have gone through similar changes and that have *not* chosen dictatorship and the destruction of others as their solution. But when Delmer would plot his response to Nazi propaganda, as with any counter-propaganda we may plan today, he knew that no effort would work unless it took into account this need to belong that propaganda satisfies, a need that he knew from his own vulnerability to it. For who could be more lonely and more powerless than ten-year-old Sefton, the freshly fatherless enemy schoolboy abandoned in Berlin? His urge to join in with the German songs, to unfurl the flag to celebrate German victories, is not in contrast to his being bullied, spurned, alienated—it's the consequence of it.

But back in World War I Berlin, a ten-year-old Sefton was, according to the memoirs he wrote over four decades later, noticing that there were weaknesses in the kaiser's propaganda model.

• • ▬▬ ▬▬ ▬▬ • •

ONE PLACE WHERE SEFTON felt safe and secure was in the wine-red soft seats in the stalls of the Deutsches Theater, watching the shows of the director Max Reinhardt and his dramaturge, Arthur Kahane. Kahane's son, Peter, was Delmer's best friend at school and would get him the exclusive tickets. Reinhardt and Kahane were already famous. They had started out with a cabaret, *Schall und Rauch*. All through the night, in a tiny studio, they'd put on sketches that taunted the era's famous stars, poking fun at the way these actors tried to be "natural" with their brooding sighs and pained expressions, satirising the different acting fads popular on the Berlin stage, pointing out the artifice in each.[21] Reinhardt didn't believe in forcing a style of acting onto his troupe. As Martin Esslin, one of his students and later a theatre critic, described, "Reinhardt was convinced that in most people, and most actors, the real personality is buried deep inside under a thick layer of shyness, mannerisms and convention. . . . Accordingly, his conception of the actor's task was never based on the idea that the actor is an impersonator who should assume another human being's personality. For him the actor's task was to use his own personality to the fullest possible extent to express the essence of the character he was portraying."[22]

Sitting safely in the dark red of Reinhardt's auditorium, Sefton watched Maurice Maeterlinck's *The Blue Bird*, a play about crippled children who cross the world looking for the Bird of Happiness, only to find it living in their own garden. He saw Gerhart Hauptmann's *Der Biberpelz*, a dark, despairing comedy that depicts a Berlin underworld of poverty and crime, and in which the characters speak in real Berlin slang.

Meanwhile, the Germany that Delmer saw outside the theatre seemed ever more staged.[23]

The kaiser's propaganda was successful because it gave Germans a sense of belonging, someone to love and someone to hate, someone to include and someone (like Sefton Delmer) to exclude. It tapped into decades of military fantasies and helped articulate a latent desire to simultaneously feel superior to others and to yearn for a cause worth dying for. But there was also something forced about it. For all the melodramatic warmongering, Delmer felt that "looking at it much later, much of this [initial German] enthusiasm was artificial. They had talked themselves into it because it was the right thing, the patriotic thing, to want war."[24]

But what does it mean to "talk yourself into" wanting war? It's as if language, a language that wasn't initially yours, can take you over, talk through you, consume you, control you.

The boys who taunted him were indulging in a form of "boyish play-acting".[25] It was play-acting that tapped into the "romantic and bullying streaks" of the "adult German soul", but it was play-acting nonetheless. The Germans Sefton encountered had more than one role that they played.

The headmaster, Direktor Lange, who would bellow war sermons in morning assembly, was a different person when he spoke to Sefton and his mother in his office. Behind closed doors, he asked their forgiveness for this senseless conflict.

When two schoolmasters returned from the front with missing arms and legs, and were rewarded with Iron Crosses for their sacrifice, the teacher responsible for "patriotic" education, Herr Schlicke, quipped, "Mir is mein Heiles Kreuz lieber als ein eisernes." Literally: "I'd rather keep my spine than be given an Iron Cross."[26] (German uses the same word for *spine* and for *cross*.)

The boys in class were stunned. They'd always heard Herr Schlicke, his face covered in duelling scars, speak in jingoistic slogans, marshalling the classroom as if it were a military unit. Now it turned out that he could also say things contradicting his seemingly heartfelt jingoism.

So who was the real Direktor Lange? Was the real Herr Schlicke the patriot or the punning anti-war agitator? Or perhaps asking for the "real" one is the wrong question. It's the act of linguistic disobedience that mattered, the moment when Herr Schlicke stopped parroting the language of propaganda and instead subverted it with his pun about preferring a real backbone. Puns and word slippages are trapdoors out of the prison of propaganda—and Delmer would always be obsessed with them. We have two ways of having a relationship with the language all around us, Delmer seems to be telling us. We can either be defined by it or rebel and recreate it. Perhaps someone like Delmer, someone unable to join in the communal patriotic ecstasies yet still drawn to them, observing others from outside while yearning to be inside, always aware of how different he could be in different languages—maybe he would be more attuned to how people change themselves and are changed by the roles and words around them.

As the war dragged on and German victories turned into defeats, the kaiser's propaganda started to look like last year's acting fad. On Sefton's way to school, the patriotic posters were scribbled over with graffiti: "Helft uns siegen" (Help Us Conquer) was crossed out to read "Helft uns lügen" (Help Us Lie).

At school, only the butcher's son could still find sausages for his packed lunch. Everyone else had no food to bring from home and had to make do with the school canteen's thin cabbage soup instead.

On the trains, the seats were all sliced open and ripped up: Berliners were stealing the wool padding from inside the seats to stitch into their own coats against the bone-chilling cold.

Outside the stores, plain-clothes police lurked in the long queues for ever-shrinking egg and potato rations, making sure that no one was complaining. Delmer and his mother would stand in such queues for hours. Foreigners always had to be last in line, and the rations were often gone by the time that the Delmers reached the till. Despite the risk, his mother couldn't help but tell everyone how she had heard that in London there were no shortages at all. Butter, chocolate, milk—all of it was available there. Her comments made hungry Berliners angry, and she made sure never to return to the same queue twice.

Delmer's father was finally released in 1915, after six months in prison. Unemployed, he was supported by gifts from former students and spent his afternoons with his neighbours, the Cohns, and their friends, the Liebknechts, future leaders of the German Communist Party who slipped him news of unrest in factories and shipyards, unrest that would later build into the revolution of 1918, which helped bring down the kaiser.

In his memoirs, Delmer related the lessons of these years to his later war work. His mother's complaints in the queues were "first-class subversive stuff"—the sort of sowing of dissent he would later seed in industrial quantities.[27] His father was gathering the sort of research that Delmer would later systematise to know the enemy's vulnerabilities.

But Delmer was also doing something else in his memoirs: trying to prove his family's loyalty to Britain.

• • • ▬▬ ▬▬ ▬▬ • • •

EVER SINCE HE WAS released from prison, Sefton's father had been asking students, colleagues, friends and acquaintances to help obtain an exit visa for the family. But Stadtkommandant Braumüller, chief of the Alien Department in Berlin, had always refused to grant them one. Then, at long last, in May 1917 a well-connected friend, Frau Kunheim, managed to persuade the foreign minister to directly help the Delmers. Braumüller informed Frederick that an exit visa had finally been granted. "I scarcely dared to believe my good luck until I was safely across the frontier in Holland," Frederick would write in a series of articles for *The Times* and other British newspapers about his family's escape from Germany. "To feel the meaning of light one must have first lived in darkness, and to know what the British flag stands for one must have lived in countries where it dare not wave."[28]

Frederick described leaving Germany as exiting some sort of propaganda fog. The fierce grilling he received from the intelligence agents at the British consulate in the Hague, checking his every background detail, reassured him that, in contrast to the claims of German propaganda, Britain was prepared for war. Crossing the English Channel by boat was another revelation: Braumüller had assured the Delmers that German submarines would make such a trip impossible.

Landing at Gravesend, Frederick Delmer wrote in his articles, brought an epiphany:

> There were good will and good nature everywhere, and not the faintest trace of the bullying of the civil population by everything in uniform that I had become so familiar with and had grown sick of in Prussia. . . . How good it is to be back in England! If ever I realized what liberty means, liberty of thought and liberty of conscience, it is now after having lived for nearly three years in an enemy country where there is neither.[29]

Sefton's return "home" was less ecstatic. Right after *der Engländer* disembarked, his feet finally safe inside his motherland, he was greeted with the teasing, taunting laughter of little children all around him. Instead of being embraced by his countrymen, he was surrounded, followed and pointed at by a gang of street kids, calling on yet other kids to come over and laugh at him as well. Ten-year-old Delmer was so disoriented that he turned and ran to the railway station.

He strained to figure out what they were saying.

" 'E's in sawks!"[30]

Socks?

He looked down at his legs. They were in ankle socks. He looked at the legs of the children laughing at him: their socks all went right up to their knees. He was dressed in the sailor's uniform fashionable among Berlin boys: a sailor's blouse, blue shorts and ankle socks. In

England, kids his age wore knee-high socks. All his little life, Sefton had imagined himself a little Englishman. But now his socks betrayed him.

In those first days in England he could think of nothing else but socks and begged his mother to buy him knee-high ones. She had other things on her mind.

The Delmers had nowhere to live. They had no property in England—both parents were from Australia. They had no network of close relatives they could shelter with. A committee for refugees put them up in a greasy bedsit in a street of stuccoed houses whose white facades were grimy and stained with soot.

To make matters worse, Sefton's father was under attack. When Frederick arrived, the British newspapers had jumped at the chance to run his insider, eyewitness, exclusive insights into life in wartime Berlin. He had a whole series of articles on the front pages of the *Mail* and *The Times*, some about the waning power of the kaiser's propaganda. He described the changing scenes in front of the glass-fronted war communiqués:

> In silence they read the report and in silence they turn and walk away. Now and again an individual will point to some telling sentence tucked away in the middle of the report—a village, a trench left to the enemy because it was no longer of any value—and his face will betray an almost imperceptible note of distrust, but he will say nothing.
>
> The womenfolk in the queues are more outspoken, and one used often to hear them say: "We have nothing but victories, and yet we always get farther back."[31]

These observations didn't get the reaction that Frederick Delmer had expected. Letters came in to the editor suggesting he was painting a gloomy picture of German opinions in order to goad the British effort into overconfidence, that he was actually pushing clever enemy propaganda, that his ability to leave Germany was suspicious—had he been sent over to confuse the British leadership and public? Some even accused him of being an enemy agent.[32]

Frederick Delmer's portrait of unhappy Germans went against the image of the enemy that had been cultivated in the British press. Ever since 1914, the British papers had evoked the image of a dreaded, unified, all-powerful Hun. In a single *Daily Mail* piece on September 22, 1914, for example, the kaiser was referred to as a "lunatic", "barbarian", "madman", "monster", "modern Judas" and "criminal monarch".[33] In the following years, stories of German atrocities filled the papers: Germans raping nuns, bayoneting Belgian children, handing out medals for sinking passenger cruise ships in the mid-Atlantic. The stories were not always substantiated. But such articles were hugely popular—there was a demand to see the enemy as pure evil, their population as totally possessed by the kaiser's propaganda.[34]

Frederick was undermining an image, a stereotype that many British people needed to motivate themselves to fight against an enemy. It was another obstacle that Sefton would have to confront in his later war work: How do you deliver truth to people who are resistant to it?

Frederick Delmer was called in for more interrogations at the Ministry of the Interior to ascertain his loyalties. He was, once more, judged to be absolutely sound. But his public reputation was sullied. For long nights he argued with his wife whether to write an article explaining their escape from Germany as his editor wanted—but that could get Frau Kunheim and everyone who helped him leave in trouble: "I remember the anguished debate between him and my mother whether he should accede to the editor's request and tell the story. But in the end loyalty to his Berlin friends supervened." Sefton could see his father's self-confidence deflate: "It was altogether horrible for my father. . . . I could not help catching some of the depression this kind of nonsense cast on him and my brave mother."[35]

All this time, Sefton was still obsessed with the problem of his socks. Alone, he hatched a plan on how to finally fit in. English schoolchildren, he'd noticed, wore shorts and sweaters when they went running with their class for sports. So Delmer dug out his Berlin sailor's shorts, found an old white sweater from his parents, got some gym shoes—and as soon as he was outside on the street ran everywhere, pretending he was an athlete out for training, in his own mind finally

blending in, running, running, across the parks and through the dirt-
ied stucco and red labyrinth of London.

Writing half a century later, Delmer admitted: "The feeling of inse-
curity, which was at the bottom of my sartorial troubles, went a lot
deeper than the affair of the socks. . . . In these first months instead of
feeling at home, as I had expected to feel, I felt a refugee. A little boy
who was not quite sure whether he really belonged where he had always
believed he belonged."[36]

His attempts at fitting in kept failing. At school, the teachers
laughed at his "German" pronunciation of Latin. A fellow pupil found
a newspaper featuring a photo of the Delmers' arrival in England,
and everyone jeered at his wrong socks. In Officer Training Corps the
instructor taunted him every time he dropped his gun: "I thought they
made good soldiers of you in Germany."[37]

Ultimately, Delmer thought that "I had a better time as an English
boy in my Berlin school in the first years of the war than for the last two
. . . in London where I was treated as a bit of an outsider. Maybe this was
partly due to our British way of working up to a real crescendo of hate
and fury towards the end of the war."[38]

The war ended when Sefton was fourteen. And he did eventually learn
to seem more British. He made the rowing team at school and got a scholarship to Oxford: "And I can, as every orthodox Briton should, look back
on my time at Oxford and St Paul's as a very happy period of my life."[39]

But even into middle age, Delmer suffered "persistent and most
depressing dreams" about wearing the wrong clothes, walking around
London in a bath towel or talking to royalty with one shoe missing. He
would never shrug off his feeling of not quite belonging:

> For many years of my life I was secretly ashamed of having been
> born in Berlin. I tried to keep it dark. I did not want to be taken
> for a German. I was British and very much so. But I could not
> keep it dark. Somehow the world seemed always to find itself in
> a situation which would make the man inspecting my passport
> say "Born in Berlin, eh? Would you mind standing back, sir, I'll
> deal with you later."[40]

Yet despite this sense of shame about being born in Berlin, very soon after he graduated from university he moved back to become the Berlin correspondent for the highly popular and not at all high-brow British newspaper the *Daily Express* in September 1928. It seems a curious choice—wouldn't he have wanted to get away from there? In his memoirs Delmer makes the move sound like the result of a simple accident. While visiting his father in Berlin, he spent a day working as an assistant to the owner of the *Daily Express*, Lord Beaverbrook, the Rupert Murdoch of his day, who, impressed by Delmer's intimate understanding of the country, offered him a job.

But there could be something more to Sefton Delmer's motivation, important to understanding both his personality and his relationship to propaganda. My childhood has some small echoes of Sefton's, and I can hazard a guess about what might have driven him. I grew up a Soviet émigré child in London in the early 1980s, during a warm part of the Cold War. My parents had been political dissidents in Kyiv, my father arrested by the KGB. But in my English school I was simply nicknamed "the Russian spy"—few understood where Ukraine was back then—and gently taunted as an enemy. The taunting was not the problem—I was never bullied—but rather the question that it posed about who I was meant to be.

I even had an incident akin to Delmer's socks disaster. I was five and getting changed for PE class. I recall feeling particularly confident that day—my English was improving. And then I remember laughter. Contorted laughter all around me. And everyone pointing fingers. I looked around at who might be the poor victim of this mocking and realised with horror it was me.

"He's wearing tights! That boy is wearing tights!"

In the USSR parents dressed children in cheap cotton tights whenever the weather started to get cold. I'd thought it ordinary. We knew them as *kalgotki*.

I remember choking, my early English stuck in my throat. Finally I stammered out, "These are kalgotki."

But no one knew the word; I may as well have made it up. The whole world that kalgotki came from didn't exist here.

And although I went on to enjoy my school and university "as every orthodox Briton should", I then headed out to Moscow because I had the freedom there to define my own way of being British—much as Delmer could in Berlin. There he was *der Engländer* and could decide what that meant for himself.

Once in Weimar Berlin, Delmer would find that everything that had made him vulnerable as a child—his fluid identity, his cultural ambidexterity—would suddenly be turned into an advantage that would help him penetrate into the backstage of the great, infernal Nazi propaganda show.

CHAPTER 2

THE NAZI CIRCUS

P istol Shots and Screams" ran an early Delmer headline in the *Express*, on May 1, 1929: "A day of thrills. The staccato crackle of revolver shots mingled with raucous shouts of hatred and screams of women. One quarter of the great city after another flared up in civil strife."[1]

In 1917 Sefton Delmer had left a Germany full of rigid order and social hierarchy. He returned to a city in political tumult and in which all the old social order had fallen apart. The monarchy was gone. Germany's experiment with democracy was being strained at the seams by extreme political polarisation from groups that believed the country needed more authoritarian rule. The Weimar Republic was punctuated by attempted putsches and deadly street battles between Communists and far-right nationalists. "Berlin," Delmer remembered, "had everything which the editor of a popular daily yearns for, sex, murder, political intrigue, money, mystery and bloodshed. Especially bloodshed."[2] The blood included that of Delmer's reporting assistant, a forty-six-year-old New Zealander, shot dead by a nervous teenage police cadet during the May street battles.

Every morning, Delmer, the twenty-four-year-old chief Berlin correspondent of the *Daily Express*, would run down from his one-man office to the news-stand to pick up the freshest batch of Berlin papers, all moist from the press and smelling of petroleum ink.

The newspaper stands were packed with a profusion of new tabloids, with their tales of teenage sex clubs whose orgies ended in murder and suicide, and stories of swindlers and government corruption scandals (where, Delmer noted, Polish–Jewish immigrants always seemed to play a leading role). Sales of tabloids were quintupling. The right-wing nationalist *Night Edition* rose from 38,000 in 1925 to 202,000 in 1930. The far-left *World in the Evening* went from 12,000 to 220,000.[3] The Communist papers called for revolution, the official Nazi Party paper *Völkischer Beobachter* (*People's Observer*) harped on, like many others, about Germany's humiliation since the war. *Der Stürmer* had caricatures of hook-nosed Jews lusting after Aryan women, "unnatural" Jews watching pornography, giant Jewish spiders sucking the blood from German business. It made its owner, the senior Nazi Julius Streicher, a millionaire. Many of these—the left-wing and right-wing tabloids, the party papers—had something in common: they hated the more centrist parties' corruption and incompetence, all meant to show that democracy wasn't working. The more high-minded liberal newspapers could rarely compete with these new media, with their mix of the salacious and the furious. They delivered much more than just information to people. They gave someone to love and someone to blame, and in a society in flux, where all the old social roles had suddenly disappeared with the old aristocratic order, a sense of who they were was something that many were desperately looking for, even as they experimented wildly with new roles.

"Looking back on it now," Delmer would write in the 1960s, "I see the mad whirl of this Berlin of 1928 and 1929 as a kind of Pompeian revel on the eve of the Vesuvius eruption. I found my Berliners afloat in a ferment of ultramodernism and get-rich-quick hysteria."[4] Berlin, wrote Delmer, was a city bursting with "the exhilarating avant-garde intellectualism of painters, musicians and theatrical producers exploring new aesthetic worlds", where Max Reinhardt and Arthur Kahane were putting on plays that used the whole city as their stage, with performances in train stations and cathedrals, so that the borders between life and theatre, between real and unreal, were ever more blurred.

This, wrote Delmer, was "the home of the fantastic and the improbable", where old taboos were being broken. On the news-stands you could also find pornography magazines, both straight and gay. Near the Tiergarten the head of the Sexology Institute, Magnus Hirschfeld, was advocating that gay people should have the same rights as heterosexuals. He also studied German sexual habits, publishing illustrated studies on sadomasochistic sex.

Dressed in white opera tails and a silk collar, and carrying a silver-headed cane, Delmer "of the *Express*" was a guest at parties thrown by the super-rich, where tubs of caviar bobbed around in swimming pools and the guests would dive into the water to spoon it into their mouths. Although he was utterly bilingual and could imitate different regional German accents, he would make sure that his German didn't sound too perfect. Unlike during his wartime childhood, being English was now in demand: "I used to allow quite a bit of English accent to peep through in my German—in the hope that it would make me seem more romantic."[5]

After the parties the guests would pile into the cabarets, "where a blind man tinkled a piano or a man–woman sang operatic arias in falsetto". Some cabarets were well known for the transvestite acts, revealing how full of artifice supposedly "natural" female behaviour was: anyone could "act feminine". The cabarets were a place where the seeming solidity of social identities was subverted, and you could revel in reinventing yourself. Berlin's intellectuals saw cabaret as symptomatic of the city's nature. Berlin was "a city that is perennially new", wrote the philosopher and literary critic Ernst Bloch, and "the appeal of the reviews comes precisely from the central power and turbulence of scenes strung loosely together, from their ability to change and to transform themselves into one another". The film and theatre critic Siegfried Kracauer praised the ability of cabaret to convey "precisely and openly the disorder of society . . . in the streets of Berlin one is not infrequently struck by the realisation that all of a sudden everything might split apart one day."[6]

Delmer had spent his childhood and teens in the painful playing fields of being a forever foreigner, where every uniform change between identities came with humiliations and meant finding out that he was not who he thought he was. Now he was in a context where no one knew who they were, and he could delight in putting on different masks.

In summer 1930 a clumsy, giant German appeared in the hotel dining rooms of English provincial seaside towns. He carried an English–German dictionary, spoke far too loudly in a lurid German accent full of harsh Zs, clicked his heels and saluted confused provincial English diners. "You hate very ze Germans?" he asked a girl.[7]

This was Sefton Delmer in disguise, on a reporting assignment to test whether the English had forgiven the Germans for the Great War. In his series of pieces he dropped into small hotels on the South Coast, constantly trying to provoke the English, an early version of today's Borat comedies, where cabaret act meets social research.

Largely, he concluded after his tour, the English treated his absurd, obnoxious German alter ego with politeness, even warmth, and allowed bygones to be bygones.

But moving beyond the past was more difficult in Germany. The Germans, Delmer declared in an *Express* article about the popularity of London fashions in Berlin, wanted "to be English", to dress and behave like the war's victors.[8] But the desire to imitate had a flip side of jealousy and resentment. The cabaret of Berlin was always one costume change away from something sinister.

At a fancy dress ball for Berlin's beau monde, the revelling Arab Slave Girls, Argentine Tango Dancers and Cossacks all suddenly fell silent when a new guest entered the hall. It was Delmer, dressed with a child's German imperial spiked helmet on his head, a toy sword on a piece of string around his middle and a popgun with a cork over his shoulder. The imperial uniform, especially its spiked helmet, was banned in Weimar Germany, a mark of how the country had supposedly overcome its warmongering past. As they took it all in, the guests in fancy dress went from silent to furious: "I think it must have been the pop-gun that did it," reasoned Delmer, a reminder of how impotent the imperial desires of demilitarised Germany had become. "My host only just managed to save me from premature liquidation by one of the angriest and most bizarre mobs it has fallen to me to meet. A member of the ball committee arrived and informed me that I was thought to have insulted the German army and would I please either shed my helmet and pop-gun or leave the house. Gracefully I presented him with both weapons. 'In aid of your next war.' That was too much and I had to leave after all."[9]

The Berlin masquerade itself masked how the old desires for domination still lurked just below the surface, ready to be seduced by a more wild and malign performance.

• • • ▬▬▬ ▬▬▬ ▬▬▬ • • •

WHEN DELMER FIRST SAW Hitler speak, he was unimpressed. It was quite by chance, in February 1929, when he came across a poster for Hitler's performance at the Sportpalast. The poster was ringed in red and black bands—the colours of the banned German imperial flag, which the Nazis had smuggled back into public view on their innocent-seeming swastika banner. The Nazis held only twelve seats in Parliament at the time, but Hitler was already famous for his 1923 failed far-right putsch in Munich. This was the first time he had been allowed to return to the capital since being released from prison.

The Sportpalast was the biggest indoor venue in Berlin and could hold fourteen thousand people. Delmer usually went there to watch bicycle races. Now, when he sauntered in past the storm troopers in brown shirts and breeches, it was half empty. Hitler was already on stage, flushed, yelling—but Delmer could barely make out what he was saying. The microphones were at the wrong level. Slowly the words came into focus. Hitler was yelling about oranges: "We Germans must not eat oranges. We must consume no fruit, no food which we have not grown ourselves."

"A crackpot," Delmer thought—and walked out.[10]

Hitler, Delmer wrote in his memoirs, seemed like just another "miracle man". Berlin teemed with these salesmen-cum-saviours promising to restore German pride while also peddling financial pyramid schemes or magical food supplements that would make your muscles stronger and the nation invincible. Hitler was peddling another "miracle cure": pure racial identity as a solution to all ills.

Later that year, the US stock market collapsed, and the German economy was in despair and disarray. By September 1930, Delmer was kicking himself for having missed the importance of Hitler when the Nazis, now backed by the nationalist newspapers, leaped to 107 seats in the elections, thus becoming the second-biggest party in Parliament.

The second time Delmer heard Hitler speak, he paid more attention. He sat as close to him as possible in the packed hall. He noted the blue eyes almost popping out of Hitler's head, how his starched collar went limp with sweat, how the sweat seeped into his cheap blue suit and stained the damp collar purple, how he stirred the normally prim middle classes in the audience into "aggressive exultation". At the end of the speech the crowd got up to sing "Deutschland, Deutschland über Alles". Delmer refused to sing along or put up his hand in the Nazi salute. "A tiny little fat man beside me wanted to knock me down. 'You just wait till after,' he kept threatening. 'We'll show you; we'll teach you.'"

This was the moment, Delmer tells us in his autobiography, that he decided to penetrate the Nazis' inner circle: "I determined to get to know this miracle man well, study the secret of his appeal, and find out what use he was going to make of it."[11]

• • • ▬▬▬ ▬▬▬ ▬▬▬ • • •

IT'S TEMPTING TO DISMISS leaders and movements with "crackpot" ideas. Delmer was typical in not taking Nazi ideas seriously at first—after all, they seemed so easy to debunk. Paul Radin, a Jewish, Polish-born, American-raised anthropologist who wrote *The Racial Myth*, was one of many in the 1930s who took a swift and clinical scalpel to Nazi ideology: "There never was an Aryan race; the Germans are not, to any extent, Nordic. . . . The whole business of Aryanism is the rationalization of a compensation dream to justify inferiority, or, rather, to explain it away." Radin thought this "madness" could not represent the views of sixty-five million Germans known for their "middle of the road sanity", and was therefore "weak" and "transitory".[12]

But although it's easy to debunk "theories" about "pure" identity, this can miss the many ways they appeal to people. The Nazis' evidence-free claim to "purity" could be alluring in a time of disorienting change. In Weimar Germany, where social roles and norms were transforming as rapidly as new acts in a cabaret review, it promised a simple way of knowing who you were. It cast out all confusion people felt inside themselves. But its very fragility provoked aggression against anyone who questioned it.

Today, throughout the world, whole industries, ways of life, media and professions disappear; the very notion of what is "human" is up for grabs; and propaganda appealing to a "purer identity" can be popular. I saw something similar in modern Russia. The Moscow I discovered in the early years of the twenty-first century was also in a swirl of change. Russians had survived so many political and social systems that flicked through in such blistering progression, from communism to perestroika to shock therapy to penury to oligarchy to mafia state, that many Russians were left with the sense that life is just political cabaret, where every role or position or belief is mutable. The same propagandists who preached the liquidation of Ukraine in 2022, and called for an eternal war with the West, had been supposedly democracy-loving, Western-leaning bastions of liberal journalism a couple of decades previously.

In the run-up to his invasion of Ukraine, Putin offered a crackpot, but what he must have thought alluring, take on who Russians were. As the invasion approached, he broadcast and published rambling lectures about how Russians and Ukrainians were actually historically "one people" whose supposedly single essence had been craftily corrupted by the outside influence of "the West", which had somehow brainwashed Ukrainians into thinking that they are no longer "one" with Russians. Putin harked back to a mythological past when Ukrainians and Russians supposedly emerged from one ancient medieval kingdom, Kyivan Rus, a common myth in Russia despite no serious historians seeing direct lineage between the ethnic groups of then and now.[13] In the propaganda to justify the 2022 Russian invasion, this old myth was given a new twist: any Ukrainians who did not admit to being "one people" with Russia had to be eliminated, so that only Ukrainians who understood that their "true" identity lay with Russia could remain.

Independent Ukraine, Putin and his propaganda machine insisted, was "impure" in other ways too. Ukraine had been "perverted" by foreign LGBTQ rights, which muddled gender roles. Russian media loved to play clips of President Zelensky dancing in high heels and bondage gear (which he had done for a comedy skit on one of his TV sketch shows, where he took on multiple roles in a contemporary cousin of cabaret).

In contrast, contemporary Russian propaganda likes to post images of its president acting out an exaggerated, almost ironic hypermasculinity: riding horses shirtless in the wilderness, swimming across wild lakes. It trumpets Russia as the last homeland of the endangered "real" man. This image can resonate among audiences across the world. In the US, for example, some right-wing movements pine for a "Manosphere" where feminism is banished. This is a sphere with which the Nazis were also intimate.

● ● ●   ━━━   ━━━   ━━━   ● ● ●

As ERNST RÖHM WROTE in his 1928 autobiography, "Manly hate has been replaced by effeminate griping. He who cannot hate cannot love."[14] Röhm was one of Hitler's oldest comrades, having been with him since the days of the failed Munich putsch. Now he was the head of the storm troopers, the fighting units that battled the Communists in street wars across Germany. He had a pug nose and a face disfigured by duelling scars. His writings are a paean to the supposedly declining "masculine" virtues. For him "only the real, the true, the masculine held its value".[15] His homosexuality was also an open secret.

In February 1931, Röhm was inspecting his storm troopers at the Sportpalast. He gave the outstretched Nazi salute as he entered the building—and his men returned the Sieg Heil. Behind him came his aide-de-camp. He too gave a Nazi salute to the sentries as he entered, though in a somewhat louche way. The aide-de-camp was Sefton Delmer.

Acting as Röhm's assistant was a condition of attending the meeting: this was a purely private event, no journalists officially allowed. Everyone was in civilian clothes. But Röhm wanted Delmer to be there. He needed to prove to the British public that the storm troopers were not mere thugs but actually a disciplined fighting force, to ensure that the English and French didn't make too much of a fuss as Hitler came closer to power. Soon he would want to integrate the storm troopers into the official German army, and that would need approval from the victorious powers in World War I.

For Delmer, it was a chance to gain the Nazi leaders' trust. Journalistic access often depends on this quid pro quo: you get an exclusive peek behind the scenes; they get to communicate to the outside world something they need to be known. But you can also hear an actor's delight in Delmer's memoirs: "I squared back my shoulders, turned down the corners of my mouth in correct Ludendorff disdain, and became Röhm's extra ADC. Orderlies rushed up, clicked heels, and saluted with upstretched right arm. I saluted back, rather more negligently with arm half bent, as befitted my rank. The orderlies took my coat and hat. It was wonderful fun." What an odd idea of fun Delmer had—passing himself off as a Nazi. What precisely was fun about it? Just the thrill of getting away with it? Or did a part of him enjoy the role? "We marched down the aisle up to the platform at the other end of the hall. From end to end of the huge sports arena was crammed with Stormtroopers standing rigidly to attention, row upon row, three thousand five hundred of them."[16]

The storm troopers handed Röhm an assiduously polished, eagle-headed Nazi standard, and as the band played, he descended into the rows of storm troopers to inspect them. Delmer followed. And as he passed close by these pale, drawn men, he could see both the power and the vulnerability of the Nazi experiment.

They came from all parts of society. There were students and rich men's sons, workmen, clerks and the unemployed. Some were there from "patriotic" motives, thought Delmer; others came because they were hungry for loot and high positions. The older ones were there to recapture the camaraderie of their war experiences. Many were unemployed.

The Nazis' aim would be to forge a unified Volksgemeinschaft (people's community) from this fractured rabble. Delmer's goal would become to divide them.

Then "a blonde young bully with a low forehead, crinkly fair hair, bright blue eyes and full cherry lips was barking commands. The men jumped, as if whipped . . . at last Röhm returned to the dais. The gleaming swastika eagle standard was presented to him once more— and then he made his speech. 'No one can teach me anything about making a revolution—and if there is any barricade storming to be done, I shall be the one to lead you.'" There was no doubt, thought Delmer, that this was a disciplined group that Röhm could control—which was the message Röhm needed to send to Britain. The storm troopers could be normalised and institutionalised; they would not be starting any chaotic rebellions.

As they drove away, Röhm chuckled. "You make a fine ADC, Herr Delmer. Why don't you come down to Munich and join us in our magnificent new Brown House?" Whatever its dubious morality, Delmer's act had worked; he had passed some sort of test.

"Do you think I could have a talk with Herr Hitler at the same time?"

"Of course. I shall arrange it myself."[17]

• • • ▬▬ ▬▬ ▬▬ • • •

A WEEK LATER, DELMER was on his way down to Munich, crossing the "lovely old towns of Thuringia and Franconia . . . watching the gables of the houses grow steeper and steeper the further south I got. The Brown House, as Hitler had called the edifice which he had built with part of the money his rich industrial backers were now putting up to finance his miracle, was not the aesthetic climax of my journey south. But it was definitely Brown."[18]

The entrance was guarded by storm troopers in black breeches, brown shirts and black caps. As Delmer approached, one barked at him, "Get down off the footpath!" and motioned him towards the gutter. "Pedestrians are not allowed on the footpath in front of the Brown House." Delmer showed the invitation from Röhm, and the sentry immediately sprang to attention, gave the Hitler salute and welcomed him inside: "As I entered the sacred portal, a heavily ornate much be-swastika'ed affair in heavy bronze, I asked myself where else in the world could a political party win votes by bullying the public into the gutter."

Delmer was entering a building whose imitation teak panelling, red Morocco chairs, cream walls and brasses reminded him of pretentious, provincial hotel lobbies. Had the "miracle" man's tastes, Delmer wondered, been influenced by all his travel so he now decked his HQ out like a hotel?

Röhm was there to greet Delmer. Hitler was busy, so he took him on a tour around the building first. It was all calculated to make a grand impression on the reporter: SS men crouched over maps in a mock war-game scenario where they played at invading Poland; other maps showed how many thousands of storm troopers were located in every town—there wasn't a town where their number wasn't increasing.

Hitler, when Röhm finally introduced him, appeared in cheap leather shoes and a double-breasted blue suit. He had sallow skin and overly arranged hair. He was neither mad nor thuggish. Indeed, he reminded Delmer of ex-soldier travelling salesmen he'd seen going up and down Germany trying to sell pills or gadgets, humiliated veterans who were struggling to settle into civilian life. Before Delmer could get a word in edgewise, this travelling salesman launched into his pitch: a tirade about how unfair the French were to the Germans, how terrible the French were in general, unlike the English, of course . . .

"Herr Hitler," Delmer interrupted, "Major Röhm tells me that you are anxious to secure the friendship of Britain?"

And Hitler was off again: claiming that Britain's interests were similar to Germany's, that they were both Nordic peoples, that they should ally, that the only thing Germany wanted was a "free hand in the East . . ."

"There were many occasions on which I talked with Hitler," Delmer recounted in his memoirs, and "every time the same thing happened. I would put a question. He would reply, and his reply would swell out into an oration, as more and more ideas flowed into his imaginative and highly articulate mind. Before anyone could pull him up, he would be shouting as though he had the Sports Palace crowd before him, not just a solitary British reporter."[19]

But as quickly as the oration swelled with passion, it was shut down, almost like a machine whose power is switched off, when Hitler took his leave of Delmer and departed for his next meeting.

However, Delmer had enough for his exclusive.

"Herr Hitler Talks to the *Daily Express*" ran his front-page head-line on May 4, 1931. The article left out Delmer's observations about the Brown House's tackiness and the bullying sentry. But it did commu-nicate to the British public Hitler's offer of a British–German alliance. It also made clear that Delmer thought Hitler was destined for great things: Delmer predicted that Hitler's rise meant that Germany would soon join the ranks of the other fascist powers in Europe. "I don't want no softies in my movement," Delmer quoted Hitler. "I want fanatics and idealists."[20]

The article must have pleased the Nazi leadership: later that year Delmer got another exclusive one-on-one with Hitler. This time they met in a Berlin hotel room.

"I realised in a flash the secret of his power," Delmer boasted in his article, squeezed in next to a much larger advertisement for Craven Cig-arettes. "There was nothing in his tale of financial woe different from what all German politicians and statesmen have been saying for the last twelve years. But from his personality there issues the same aura of personal zealotry . . . and into his slightly prominent blue eyes came that staring, fanatical gaze which has mesmerised millions of men and women into fanatical allegiance."[21]

In order to ingratiate himself further with the Nazi elites, Delmer invited them to his parties. He made sure to also invite plenty of danc-ing girls and Hohenzollern princes to make the fascists feel as impor-tant and relaxed as possible. He even bought a giant Bechstein piano for Hitler's press attaché, Ernst "Putzi" Hanfstaengl, to play on with his enormous hands, bobbing his head in time to his bouncing chords. Ernst Röhm would pass out drunk, face down on the dinner table. Her-mann Göring would play with Delmer's pet parrot, laughing as the par-rot pooped on his white dinner jacket.

And while Delmer was busy wooing the Nazis, they were also busy wooing him.

Röhm invited Delmer to a transvestite bar, where "one of the 'girls,' a huge creature with a very prominent Adam's Apple and a distinctly blue chin under a layer of powder, began to talk about what appeared to be a very enjoyable party they had been on several nights earlier".

Delmer assumed that this person was a prostitute. Röhm was outraged: "I am not his client. I am his commanding officer. He is one of my storm troopers."

Röhm's aim was to put British minds at ease about the Nazis. He assured Delmer that the movement's anti-Semitism shouldn't be taken too seriously—it was just another act to get more votes. The Nazis, Röhm confided, planned to integrate fifty thousand storm troopers into the German army. He wanted Delmer to communicate this "to his people" in London. Röhm, Delmer had by now realised, thought he was a British spy, and however much he tried to explain that he was not, the more Röhm was convinced he was:

> "Have you managed to arrange a meeting for me yet with the British? Someone I could talk to in the Secret Service?"
>
> "I'm afraid I don't know any secret service men. They're secret from me!"
>
> Röhm would laugh a disbelieving "Ho! Ho! Ho!" and clap me on the shoulder as though it was a terrific joke.[22]

Where did Röhm get this idea? Was it something that Delmer had led the Nazis to believe? Was it the fact that the owner of the *Express*, Lord Beaverbrook, was so politically influential? Or was there something about the way Delmer was always moving between different roles and languages that led the Nazis to believe that he somehow had a second layer, a secret self?

Whether it was their hope he could be a conduit to the British secret services, his articles, the parties, the piano or just the way Delmer's ideal German put Hitler at ease, the Nazis chose Delmer as the only non-Nazi journalist to accompany Hitler in the crucial second round of the presidential election of April 1932.

● ● ● ━━ ━━ ━━ ● ● ●

THE PRESIDENTIAL ELECTION PITCHED Hitler against a living legend, the current president and former head of the army, Hindenburg. Hitler had no real chance of winning. The aim was to increase the Nazi vote share, secure Hitler's standing as a politician of national significance and help him force his way into a coalition government.

The Nazis faced a large obstacle to winning: they were banned from the radio, the most powerful medium of communication with the voters. How to get around this fell to the Gauleiter of Berlin, Joseph Goebbels, who had made the Nazis a force in the capital. Hitler had promised that in a future government he would make Goebbels "minister for popular education. Film, radio, schools, university, art, culture, propaganda."[23] A former playwright, failed writer, doctor of philosophy, and the editor of *Der Angriff*, who had been left with a club foot and a pronounced limp after a childhood illness, Goebbels had swapped academia and the arts for politics, and now had the opportunity to combine the two. But first he had to succeed in this election.

To compensate for not being on the radio, Goebbels organised three thousand party meetings per day. Millions of handbills, brochures and special editions of party newspapers were printed across the country. Goebbels filmed a ten-minute speech, which was projected in the open air in big cities and cinemas. He made a gramophone recording of his speech and printed fifty thousand copies.[24]

The authorities tried to slow Goebbels down, seizing Nazi materials. "Ban after ban. Thus they blunt the point of our attack. Our best posters and handbills are rendered useless," Goebbels wrote in his diary for March 2.[25]

In the first round of the election, on March 13, Hindenburg won 49 percent of the vote to Hitler's 30 percent. Hitler had barely scraped through to a second-round run-off.

"Our Party comrades are depressed and discouraged. Now we need to make some big move," wrote Goebbels. The "big move" he came up with was a "flight over Germany".[26] Hitler would fly across the country giving forty-six speeches in ten days. Although it had been a forced choice for Goebbels, the air tour would play to Hitler's strength of speaking live to crowds. The ageing, ailing Hindenburg wouldn't have managed to pull that off even if he'd tried.

• • • ▬▬ ▬▬ ▬▬ • • •

To THE EXTENT THEY had a coherent theory of how propaganda works, Goebbels and Hitler were informed by the writing of the French sociologist Gustave Le Bon. Writing toward the end of the nineteenth century, Le Bon had observed the behaviour of crowds and concluded that "the part played by the unconscious in all our acts is immense, and that played by reason very small". Le Bon believed that in a crowd the thin shell of individual, rational thinking drops away and people melt into one irrational, aggressive force: "The collective mind is formed. It forms a single being."

The leader whom the crowd looks up to is something like a hypnotist:

> The conscious personality has entirely vanished; will and discernment are lost. All feelings and thoughts are bent in the direction determined by the hypnotiser. The convictions of crowds assume those characteristics of blind submission, fierce intolerance. The hero acclaimed by a crowd is a veritable god for that crowd.[27]

Goebbels told his underlings that the only theoretician they needed to read was Le Bon.[28] Hitler appears to be referencing the Frenchman's ideas in *Mein Kampf*:

> Only a mass demonstration can impress upon [a person] the greatness of this community . . . he submits himself to the fascination of what we call mass-suggestion. The will, the yearning and indeed the strength of thousands of people are in each individual. A man who enters such a meeting in doubt and hesitation leaves it inwardly fortified; he has become a member of a community.[29]

Sigmund Freud, whose works would be banned and burned by the Nazis, expanded on Le Bon's ideas in his work on the ego and "group psychology", which he published in 1921, three years before Hitler wrote *Mein Kampf*.[30] Freud went deeper in analysing the relationship between the orator and the crowd, seeing it as founded in what he called "identification". Josh Cohen, a practising psychoanalyst, author of *How to Read Freud* and professor of literature at Goldsmiths, University of London, explains that "in its first incarnation, identification is making oneself the same as the other. The collective fantasy of merging with the orator. In bringing to the surface the people's hidden spirit and secret yearnings, as though he knew them better than they knew themselves. The orator is the embodiment of the people, but in perfected form."

We often wonder why people follow leaders who are wildly self-centred, greedy and hateful. But that can be the very essence of their power: they allow their followers to indulge in their most cruel and hateful impulses, even as they foster the illusion that they are part of a noble and courageous spiritual mission. "They legitimize, surface, articulate, and elevate all the horrid things we yearn to indulge in."[31]

Hitler's air tour was to be Goebbels's great experiment in crowd psychology, and Delmer would be its breathless chronicler.

• • • ▬▬▬ ▬▬▬ ▬▬▬ • • •

"TODAY HERR HITLER WAS in Berlin, and his reception was a revelation to me," Delmer wrote in the *Express* on April 5. "120,000 fanatical Berliners were waiting to hear him speak. The drive through the crowd in the Lustgarten itself was an experience I shall never forget. The great human ocean which covered the square had been parted off with a cordon of Storm Troopers. And through the wall of cheering men and women drove Adolf Hitler." As Hitler saluted the crowd, "the tempest of answering hails swept the square like a hurricane, and then subsided".[32]

The crowd listened to the Führer's speech in concentrated silence, and then Hitler's cavalcade was off—Delmer speeding along behind him—to give another speech in Potsdam, with Nazi youths standing as sentinels at three-hundred-metre intervals throughout the road, giving the salute as Hitler's car went by.

"Tomorrow morning at 6 o'clock I shall be in Herr Hitler's airplane," reported Delmer as he talked up his exclusive access, "the only newspaperman to accompany the Fascist leader on his whirlwind tour. At the end of the tour I will have a unique opportunity of judging the strength of the Hitler movement."

The next day his report opened with the following:

> My ears are still ringing, but that is not due to the roar of the motors of the great triple-engined airplane in which Hitler, his most intimate staff and myself have been flying for the last twelve hours from one town and from one meeting place to another. It is due to the wild cheering and enthusiastic singing of the overwhelming crowds which have been deafening us all the time we have spent on the ground.[33]

About two hundred thousand people had seen Hitler in one day as he flew between four cities, each "vying with the other in the fanatical fervour of Hitler worship". As the plane swooped down into the Pomeranian agricultural town of Lauenberg, hundreds of peasant storm troopers had to hold back the wildly cheering civilians. The "normally stolid" Pomeranians went wild for Hitler's oratory, with a "scene of such enthusiasm that I have never seen before". In Danzig a crowd of thirty-five thousand was held back by five thousand storm troopers in full uniform, "a magnificent body any of whom would have passed the test to become a London policeman". Fifteen minutes later, Hitler and Delmer were in the air once more—off to another rally. And then: "Sixty thousand Germans are cheering and shouting in hoarse ecstasy while I am telephoning this report from the huge railway station hall here in Nuremberg."[34]

The content of Hitler's speeches struck Delmer as repetitive. He was forever harping on about Germany's humiliation in 1918, how it was "stabbed in the back" by Jews and Socialists on the home front who pushed for revolution and peace just as victory was in sight, how this stab in the back plunged Germany into a Weimar Republic, with its economic collapse, incompetence and corruption, and how he was the German Everyman, the Unknown Soldier, who had experienced every embarrassment himself but would now compensate for it by leading his fellow countrymen out of the slump into a new prosperity, from national impotence to national grandeur, and would take revenge for every humiliation.[35]

But the influence worked both ways: from Hitler to the crowd and the crowd back to Hitler. "The sincere adulation of the crowds mesmerised him," Delmer wrote years later, in an essay for the *Express* on the eve of World War II:

> It made him what they believed him to be—a leader without thought for himself, who was prepared to sacrifice his life, his comfort, his friends for the cause of the Fatherland's redemption; whose one interest in life was to lead the German people into a position of world domination. This, I decided, was it—the answer to the puzzle. This was what the Germans wanted him for. He was offering this illusion hungry people the miracle man it had longed for, the man who would lead it to world domination, whom it could worship and before whom it could creep as it had crept before its warlords and the Kaiser. Hitler himself, like other evangelists before and after him, lived on the emotion and mass hysteria he produced in his audiences, sucking it into himself as he orated, then spewing it out again at them with compound interest.[36]

LATER THAT SAME YEAR an English psychoanalyst, Roger Money-Kyrle, also witnessed Hitler's speeches, and he gave a psychoanalytic spin, increasingly fashionable at the time, to what Delmer had described:

> The crowd was unforgettable. The people seemed gradually to lose their individuality and to become fused into a not very intelligent but immensely powerful monster, which was not quite sane and therefore capable of anything. Yet there was something mechanical about it too; for it was under the complete control of the figure on the rostrum. He evoked or

changed its passions as easily as if they had been the notes of some gigantic organ.

The tune was very loud, but very simple. As far as I could make out, there were only three, or perhaps four, notes.

For ten minutes we heard of the sufferings of Germany in the thirteen or fourteen years since the war. The monster seemed to indulge in an orgy of self-pity.

Then for the next ten minutes came the most terrific fulminations against Jews and Social-democrats as the sole authors of these sufferings. Self-pity gave place to hate; and the monster seemed on the point of becoming homicidal.

But the note was changed once more; and this time we heard for ten minutes about the growth of the Nazi party, and how from small beginnings it had now become an overpowering force. The monster became self-conscious of its size, and intoxicated by the belief in its own omnipotence.

Hitler ended on a passionate appeal to all Germans to unite. The monster became sentimental and far more human than it had been before. But this sentimentality ended on an almost masochistic note. Hitler ceased; and in the deathly silence, the Commander of the serried ranks of uniformed Nazis cried out a single sentence as a sort of Amen: "Germany must live; even if we must die for her." No one asked who threatened Germany; and why the supreme sacrifice should be necessary. That this was so seemed to be beyond dispute. At a single word from its leader, the monster was ready, indeed anxious, to immolate itself.

What was particularly impressive in Hitler's propaganda was the viciousness of the hate that it made people feel against their supposed enemies. This level of loathing, Money-Kyrle thought, in turn inspired the fear of vengeance from the hated enemy. This in turn inspired more hate in order to be able to fight the potential agent of vengeance. And this hate had to be satisfied, it had to be shown to be effective, in order to quell the fear. Such propaganda had future persecutions built into it. It needed to be able to hurt others in order to thrive.

Why was this emotional journey, Money-Kyrle wondered, so powerful? Part of it might have related to the recent historical experiences of many Germans:

> As propaganda, these speeches were an immense success. The first of these themes was the sufferings of Germany. Now it is quite true that Germany had really suffered. She had been humiliated; the depreciation of her currency had wiped out the value of the savings of her people; and she was in the depths of an unprecedented economic depression. These surely are sufficient to explain at least the first part of the response, without looking for unconscious factors.

But such victim narratives, Money-Kyrle argued, were also effective among those who hadn't suffered drastic historical humiliation. He compared it to British propaganda in World War I, with its images of "barbarous Huns" whom it was imperative to destroy; he saw it in religious evangelists who first play on senses of guilt and damnation, then blame all the "bad" feelings on outside "evil" forces: "There must be something in us that makes us peculiarly sensitive to any suggestion that we are ill-treated. Most people, although they seek to deny it, carry an imaginary enemy within themselves; and for this reason they are often over-ready to believe in a grievance of external origin." We are all, Money-Kyrle argued, more than ready to embrace the language of grievance because it gives us the chance to blame external forces for all the things we don't like about ourselves. Orators like Hitler make us feel that we can crush these enemies.

It's just one theory of why we are so vulnerable to grievance narratives, but what repeats from Delmer to Money-Kyrle is that Hitler's power stemmed not so much from his ability to win people over with clever arguments, but from his articulating the feelings that already lay within them and taking them on an emotional journey from feeling humiliated to humiliating others.

"Nazi oratory, as I have tried to describe it," concluded Money-Kyrle, "seems to follow a pattern or theme that is common to many other, and apparently quite dissimilar, types of propaganda. Viewed in an unfavourable light, propaganda often seems to be a method of inducing a series of temporary psychoses, often starting with depression and passing, via paranoia, to a state of manic bliss."[37]

• • • ▬▬▬ ▬▬▬ ▬▬▬ • • •

SKIM THROUGH THE SPEECHES of current leaders from America to China and Russia today, and they will all play the same tunes of humiliation.

In America, Donald Trump's speeches as president started with tales of "American carnage", how America is exploited by immigrants and bled dry by foreign countries, and how he would now be the vehicle through which to execute revenge.[38] The crowds at his rallies reached moments of paranoia and manic bliss that Money-Kyrle would have found familiar.

Other leaders may inspire less manic crowds. Their propaganda plays out slower through decades of repeated messages on television and through education, songs and cinema—but it too revolves around humiliation.

China, its Communist leaders lecture, has to recover from "the century of humiliation"—the nineteenth century, when Western powers dominated it—and now has the right to dominate others.

In Russia, President Putin established his popularity through the claim that he would redeem Russia from the "humiliations" of the 1990s, bring "Russia off its knees" and restore "great power" status. When he still faced relatively competitive elections in the early 2000s, he gained popularity with a merciless crushing of a rebellion in Chechnya, wiping out towns and villages with indiscriminate bombardment. His illegal 2014 annexation of Crimea from Ukraine led to joy in Russia. He won more military victories in Syria and in Georgia, all with minimal casualties for Russia and to maximum media effect, to show that under him Russia was off its knees.

The great paradox is that the Kremlin is the cause of many Russians' historical and current humiliations—just as the Chinese Communist Party has been for the Chinese. Living in Putin's Russia means putting up with endless put-downs. Whether it's the bureaucrats and police who threaten and bribe citizens and businesses, the farce of participating in fixed elections or the cloying fear that you might be arrested if you dare to speak up against the Kremlin—or if some bureaucrat just wants to take over your business. In this system, even tycoons have lived with the uncertainty that someone closer to Putin than they are could take away all their wealth tomorrow. The culture of humiliation goes deep into society. Sexual harassment is routine. A 2017 law decriminalised some domestic abuse against children and women. Extreme bullying is rife in the army.[39]

Putin's propaganda proudly puts him in a tradition of leaders with a "strong hand", most notably the Soviet dictator Josef Stalin, who murdered tens of millions of his Soviet citizens in the gulag, launched a genocide against Ukraine in the 1930s, helped win World War II and is now hugely popular in Russia. The "strong hand" is a common phrase that denotes a leader who will both protect and violently discipline his people. Three-quarters of Russians agree that this is what their country needs.[40]

In the logic of this political psychology, the "strong hand" first humiliates, that humiliation is then celebrated as necessary and even ennobling, and the humiliation is then taken out on others. "No one knows how to suffer like us," the Russian defence minister told his British counterpart as Russia prepared to invade Ukraine.[41] He was referencing how Russians would easily weather Western sanctions, but in reality it was Ukrainians who were about to really suffer. The pose of victimhood is a mask under which to hurt others.[42] When the powerful claim they are being humiliated, they're stating what they actually want to do to you.

Putin's propaganda success as president of Russia has relied on his ability to mete out daily humiliations to Russians and then act as if he feels their rage as they do, as if he alone knows where to direct it—towards the West, towards Ukraine, anywhere except towards the Kremlin. In Putin's televised speeches around the 2022 invasion, he played out both sides of this humiliation drama: he was both grumbling with resentment from perceived slights and the enactor of omnipotence over others. He played both humiliated and humiliator, one moment suffering under the supposed yoke of Russia's enemies, almost slouching down into his chair, the next expressing people's pent-up and unsatisfiable desires for redress through claims to more land, more status and the right to cause more pain.

A few weeks before the invasion, he casually invoked a Russian rape joke to explain what he would do to Ukraine. Conflating Ukraine and Sleeping Beauty, he gleefully put himself in the role of the rapist: "Whether you like it or not, my beauty, you will need to put up with all I do to you." (In Russian, it rhymes.)[43]

· · · ━━━ ━━━ ━━━ · · ·

AS EXPECTED, HITLER LOST to Hindenburg in April 1932—but his vote share rose to its highest level ever: 36 percent.[44]

In the July parliamentary elections, Hitler again flew from city to city. Nazi speeches were pumped out across towns on loudspeakers and megaphones; storm troopers marched down the streets in mass torchlit processions; leaflets were delivered door-to-door. The Nazis won their largest vote and became the largest party in the Reichstag, although they couldn't quite get an outright majority. There was yet another election in November. This time the halls where Hitler spoke were now often half empty: there were limits to the enthusiasm he could inspire.

The closer Delmer observed the "Hitler Circus", the more he felt it wasn't quite what it claimed to be. According to Goebbels, Hitler was a force of pure nature, naturalism itself. "Any kind of pose, any exhibition and attitude is completely alien to his nature," Goebbels wrote in *Der Angriff* on April 4, 1932. "He appears as he is, natural and without any kind of make up."[45] But this wasn't what Delmer observed as he travelled on the plane. On the flight, everyone fussed around Hitler: Goebbels would try to get his attention with some wisecrack; a Nazi reporter tried to excite him with an article. But while others around him chatted and laughed, Hitler sat morose and silent, blankly leafing through press clippings, his chin cradled in his right hand, cotton wool stuffed in his ears: "The man I was looking at now was a tired and not very successful salesman flying with his samples to a client who had no great wish to see him and whom he himself had no wish to see. Was the other Hitler just an act, the product of a terrific effort of will and imagination?"[46]

From his seat inside the aeroplane, Delmer could observe Hitler in his moment of transformation from tired travelling salesman to the Führer who channelled the nation's darkest feelings. The moment that the doors of the plane opened and he emerged onto the stairs for the waiting entourage of local officials, Hitler struck his pose: shoulders back, mouth resolute, hand raised in salute. Delmer recognised the pose: Hitler was imitating General Ludendorff in his World War I prime; he was re-enacting missed glory and arrogance.

Then Hitler widened his eyes to highlight their whites and let the light shine in. This pose Delmer knew well too: the "leutseliges Leuchten", the glorious shining that filled the eyes of German monarchs in Delmer's German schoolbooks, denoting a kindly understanding of the people's needs and a fearless confidence. "As I see it, Hitler's personal tragedy and through him that of his country was that he came to believe in his act. He accepted as truth his own skilfully built propaganda myth that he was the miraculously infallible Führer Lightgod."[47] But at some level it was always an act—not just for Hitler, but also for his audience. How genuine was the "hypnosis" he supposedly exerted?

On the evening that Hitler officially joined the coalition government and became *Kanzler* (chancellor), Delmer was in the crowd observing his ascent to leadership. In the *Express* he described Hitler like a theatre or movie star:

> In the Chancellor's Palace stood Adolf Hitler, arc lights playing on him from the street below, footlights around him in the windows—a Halo of illumination for the man young Germany looks upon as its Messiah. The streets were full of civilians, flaming torches, waving flags, and moving through their cheering midst hour upon hour, the shouting, singing thousands of Berlin's militant youth marched on and on.[48]

Goebbels's diary captures the flurry of excitement that came with the announcement:

> Great jubilation. Down there the people are creating an uproar. . . . The torches come. It starts at 7 o'clock. Endless. Till 10 o'clock. At the Kaiserhof. Till after 12 o'clock. Unending. A million people on the move. Awakening! Spontaneous

explosion of the people. Indescribable. Always new masses. Hitler is in raptures. His people are cheering him. . . . Wild frenzy of enthusiasm.[49]

But as he walked through the crowds, Delmer found that they weren't all that "spontaneous" and that the "enthusiasm" was not all that natural. It reminded him of the performative patriotism of 1914: "The streets of Berlin seemed to be filled with walking Semaphores, as everyone ecstatically 'Heil Hitlered' everyone else to prove what super-Nazis they were. Even though a few weeks back, when they thought Hitler was down and out, they were contemptuously shrugging him off as 'that man'."[50]

When he got home, Delmer found his butler teaching his parrot, Popichka, to say "Heil Hitler". Delmer ordered him to cut it out. But the little anecdote underscores Delmer's view of our relationship to propaganda. We're always somehow parroting it. We're rarely completely hypnotised, or not for long. We are not just brainwashed "zombies" but conscious actors in a performance. People are slightly faking their fanaticism—and their fascist leaders are also somewhat fake.

Delmer can portray Nazis in an almost uncomfortably comedic way. Röhm, the head of the storm troopers, is a "jolly little soldier of fortune with a shot up face". Himmler is a "smiling rather chinless man in pince-nez who I took to be the factotum of the hotel".[51] And then there's Hitler himself, who absent-mindedly munches on a cheese sandwich in a plane between his speeches.[52] The Nazis come across like a grotesque, absurd cabaret. When Delmer sees the kaiser's son, August Wilhelm, give Nazi speeches with his high "falsetto voice" and knock-kneed spindly legs emphasised by his storm-trooper breeches, he then adds that performing "along with the Prince was a robust, down-to-earth Munich plumber. Between the two of them they made a good act—The Prince and the Plumber. United Behind Hitler for the German fatherland."[53]

By describing Nazism as a cabaret, Delmer was also undermining it. Showing it not as something purely awe-inspiring or hypnotic but as a hammy act whose main draw was in helping its followers play out their fantasies of superiority and sadism. Even Delmer's imitating a

Nazi to accompany Röhm shows the Nazis as another flimsy, if sinister, performance.

But if the Nazis could be a sort of act, they were the sort who couldn't countenance any rivals or critics. In his memoirs, Delmer recounts how at the Katakombe political cabaret in the Bellevue Straße he could sense the comedians beginning to fear for their safety:

> A brilliant young satirist . . . used to stutter and stammer the most daring jokes about the regime in three quarter finished sentences which left the audience to complete the treasonable last bit for themselves. "Almost the Tegel Concentration camp for me" the comedian would half-joke, as the audience guffawed. It was like watching a tight rope artist trying to cross the Niagara without a net.[54]

In his articles in the *Express*, Delmer described how the country had changed since Hitler became chancellor:

> Is there much difference between the Germany of today and that of 21 days ago? Come with me for a short walk through the streets of Berlin and we will see for ourselves.
>
> The first thing you will notice are the Black-uniformed youths with death's-heads in their caps, roaring about the streets on motorcycles.
>
> The newspaper stall at the corner of our street too, has a rather different appearance to that which it did three weeks ago. There are fewer newspapers on sale than there were. The reason is a large number have been prohibited by Hitler.
>
> I must not forget to tell you about the telephone. Did you hear that click in the receiver now after I started talking to you? That click is the reason why so many people in Berlin will not talk candidly over the phone. Little birds, they say, are clicking in and listening to all they say.
>
> Turn on the wireless, you will hear the blare of march music.
>
> Go to the cinema, you will see Germans killing Frenchmen and sinking British warships. Talk of war is the fashion. The

bravest men in Germany today are the pacifists. And there are very few of them.[55]

In January, Hitler was off on another election tour. Delmer was, again, invited to accompany him. When he arrived at Tempelhof Airport, he writes in his memoirs, Goebbels was already there, telling stories of "stormtrooper bestialities with the pride of a parent retelling the precocities of his 5 year old". Of all the Nazis whom Delmer met, Goebbels—the "demonic little clubfoot", "a true Jacobin", and his future rival—was the one who most appalled him.

That day at the airport, Goebbels was relating how he had visited a storm-trooper cellar the night before, when they were torturing a Communist. The leading storm trooper had taken off his belt and was using it to lash his victim:

> "And what do you think I heard him saying in between the blows? You'll never guess. It is really excruciatingly funny," and Goebbels cackled some more. "And now we will teach you Atheists to say your prayers. Jetzt werden wir euch Atheisten das Beten beibringen!"
> Goebbels kept repeating the phrase, rolling it around his tongue as though it were a savoury delicacy. What so delighted him, apart from the sadism, was the alliteration of the vowels in "euch Atheisten" and the consonants in "Beten beibringen". A great man for a phrase was Goebbels.[56]

When they got on the plane, Goebbels repeated the joke to Hitler. Delmer enquired whether the victim had been Jewish. Goebbels immediately spotted the trick question: members of the international press were not meant to see the new regime as anti-Semitic. "'No,' he snarled at me like the venomous dwarf he was. 'It was a Communist. We do not beat up Jews—unless of course they are Jewish Communists.'"

This description of Goebbels as the "venomous dwarf" cracking vile anecdotes comes from Delmer's 1960s autobiography. In his articles from the early 1930s, he described him in more neutral terms as "Dr Goebbels" and makes no mention of challenging him. In the *Express*

Delmer recounts how on a trip at the time the doctor was excited about his plans for Hitler's propaganda—now that the Nazis were in the government, the Führer would be allowed on the radio:

> There are much greater things to come. Three times next week the chief's speeches from Nuremberg, Berlin and Konigsberg will be relayed on all German wireless stations. The public squares in all towns will have loudspeakers so that everyone may hear the speech. . . . I retained special permission from the police that everyone should be allowed to place loudspeakers in the open windows of their houses. Germany will be forced to hear Hitler. Has there ever been anything like it in any country before?[57]

On February 27 the Reichstag was set on fire by a mentally disturbed pyromaniac, almost certainly working alone. The Nazis spread the story that the fire was part of a vast left-wing conspiracy. The country, they cried, was in mortal danger. They prompted the ageing Hindenburg to pass the Reichstag Fire Decree: the government now had the right to arrest anyone without charge, dissolve political organisations, ban publications and overrule local laws. Germany was a dictatorship. Many wondered if Hitler would be kept in check by more senior statesmen, but Delmer knew that the Nazis had been plotting a full takeover for years and that they had quietly gained control over the political parts of the Prussian police force, which they would use to build the Gestapo.

His articles expressed increasing distaste for the new dictatorship, but in private Delmer carried on his mission to get as close to the Nazis as possible—and for some it looked like he was getting way too intimate.

• • • ▬▬ ▬▬ ▬▬ • • •

IN A LETTER TO the Foreign Office dated April 7, 1933, the British ambassador to Berlin sent a report about a party at the home of the Berlin correspondent of the *Daily Express*, Sefton Delmer.[58] The report was written by a certain Mr Breen, who was sufficiently shocked by what he saw to report it to the ambassador, and the ambassador to London. Delmer, the ambassador's letter stated, was "probably the only one outside the charmed circle" of Nazi leaders "who can mobilise the Circus in full strength". "The Circus", the letter explained, referred to "the intellectuals of the [National Socialist] movement".

The night that Breen attended, Delmer showed clips of a movie he had shot during the last election campaign. As the night wore on, "Putzi" Hanfstaengl demanded that everyone fall silent, and he announced that he had written a solemn, funereal tune. Everyone cracked up laughing. Was it for the Jews? The Marxists? Someone had a "hilarious" idea: all Jews should be buried to the tune of Hanfstaengl's new funeral march.

Putzi played well into the night, with the Circus singing along to Nazi marches. A perturbed Breen left at 3:00 a.m., while the fascist fun was still going strong. His memo intimates that Delmer was alarmingly accommodating to his guests' whims.

In his own memoirs, Delmer, as if replying to Breen's report, states that he "did get a little tired of listening to eternal repetitions of a march [Hanfstaengl] had composed for the Stormtroops". The parties, he claims, were all part of his reporter's ruse to gain access to the Nazis' inner sanctum.[59]

"This was a story," he writes of his approach, "and a reporter will shake hands with the devil himself on a story."

In another letter from the British ambassador to the Foreign Office in June 1934, Delmer is again mentioned. "Mr Delmer, though a persona grata with the Nazis," wrote Ambassador Phipps, "advised Lord Beaverbrook that Hitlerism was a menace to Europe and urged a preventive war should Herr HITLER become Chancellor."[60]

Delmer was no Nazi appeaser; as early as 1933, he advised a military response. His intimacy with the Nazis had led him to see the extent of their ambitions. Rather than a sympathiser, he was the sharpest of hawks.

But the questions around Delmer's intimacy with the Nazi leadership would always follow him. How had he managed to ingratiate himself quite so closely with them? What did they get out of it? And if it was just a role he was playing, how much of himself did he put in it?

In late 1933 Delmer was told by the owner of the *Express*, Lord Beaverbrook, to take the more glamorous, if less politically charged, job

as Paris correspondent. As Delmer admits, it was one thing to ingratiate and embed himself during the Nazis' rise and thus report on an
opposition movement, and quite another to be known publicly as partying with the country's leadership. He would return in summer 1934 to
catch the "Night of the Long Knives": Hitler's bloody purge of Röhm
and the storm troopers, whom he feared were challenging his authority
and were accused of treachery. As storm troopers were arrested and executed, the Propaganda Ministry refused to give the numbers of the dead.
Delmer published a list of names of people he knew had been killed and
estimated that a total of 108 had been murdered. He was immediately
informed by the secret police that he was being expelled from Germany.
"That was the end of my beautiful friendship with Hitler."[61]

••• ▬▬▬ ▬▬▬ ▬▬▬ •••

IN PARIS, DELMER MARRIED. As a student in England, he wrote that he
had seen a bronze bust by the fashionable sculptor Jacob Epstein of a
girl with "Nefertiti eyes". "You," Delmer told the bust, "are the girl I
am going to marry." In 1934 he saw the same face chatting in a Paris
café. Almost overturning his table he introduced himself and asked
if she was the renowned model. She was, and she informed Delmer
she was actually on her way to see him—a mutual friend had asked
her to bring him a letter from England. Within a few giddy months
of this meeting, where statue became flesh, Delmer relates they were
married.[62]

Isabel, according to her biography, had a slightly different tale. In
London she had a child with Epstein, but signed off all rights to the girl
to the much elder artist and his childless wife. Now she was in Paris
developing her artistic skills, but as the daughter of a deceased British
sailor she had little money to support herself. She first moved to Delmer's
apartment to be his assistant. Delmer proposed marriage partly to miti-
gate the danger of travelling with him and smuggling censored documents across Europe. Isabel remembered that Delmer worried his
"gloomy predictions of the loss of liberty in Europe were getting closer",
and he feared for her safety. "If you say 'I am his wife' to authority, it has
some legal force, whereas the word 'friend' or 'employee' has none."[63]

They were often apart, fidelity seems uncertain, but there was real affection too. Like Delmer, Isabel blurred life and performance: a British newspaper observed how when she went out in public, her haircut, clothes and make-up showed she was "at pains to look and act the part" of the "archaic models" of the famous Epstein bust, which echoed Minoan sculpture. Delmer, Isabel thought, was a "gay and ebullient companion when he allowed himself to forget his frustration with colleagues who continually refused to realise the real intentions of Hitler's Germany to make war".[64]

Their lives, however, lay on different sides of the Seine. He was from the right bank of political intrigue. Isabel was from the Bohemian left bank. She was painted by Balthus and Picasso. Biographers disagree whether her relationship with the sculptor Giacometti was consummated, but both were transformed through knowing each other. Isabel was an inspiration for Giacometti's series of wondering female figures, simultaneously lonely and assertive.[65]

The Delmers' parties brought both worlds together. Delmer described his white-floored, black-surfaced penthouse as his "operating theatre"— Isabel found it vulgar—and it was perfect for entertaining: "Scotland Yard inspectors over in Paris to investigate some Soho murder would find themselves talking to a shockheaded surrealist sculptor," wrote Delmer, along with "Russian aristocrat beauties from the Balenciaga salon" and French politicians. "Isabel handled them all beautifully, never appearing to be bothered, apparently letting things run themselves."[66]

But Delmer's skill at combining different worlds was also causing him problems. As he reported from across Europe, he was often accused of having been soft on the Nazis. Sometimes the impression came from the articles he wrote during Hitler's air tour: they could sound adulatory. Others looked at the official line of the *Express* and Lord Beaverbrook, who wanted to keep Britain out of a war with Germany. In some articles Delmer repeated the *Express*'s line that "there will be no war with Germany".[67] Some rumours about Delmer at the time were more conspiratorial. During the civil war in Spain, Delmer met soldiers who had heard that he helped start the Reichstag fire. In 1934 the speaker of the House of Lords had enquired of a German contact about Delmer's "character" and whether he was a Nazi sympathiser. There's no follow-up to this request, but it just sits there plumply in his secret service files, oozing suspicion.[68]

For some in the British establishment, there was just something not quite right about Delmer.

In a diary entry from 1933, the Anglo-Scottish diplomat and spy Robert Bruce Lockhart records a dinner in Berlin with Delmer. In some ways Bruce Lockhart's career and talents reflected Delmer's: when not working for the government, he was a (perennially out-of-pocket) journalist and author, struggling constantly with his own alcoholism, who made himself the story as he wrote best-sellers about his adventures across revolutionary Russia and Central Europe. Delmer and Bruce Lockhart could, in theory, have been soulmates. Yet after having lunch with Delmer in Berlin, Bruce Lockhart wrote that "Delmer is fat. Jewish-looking. Speaks with a slight German accent."[69]

Delmer may have fancied himself a master of switching languages, identities and accents, but Lockhart thought he sounded odd. The accent is certainly gone by the time of Delmer's earliest radio recordings, but maybe it drifted when he switched countries? And why does Bruce Lockhart use the term "Jewish-looking"? Delmer was a huge, hulking Anglo-Celt—just like the Anglo-Scot Bruce Lockhart—yet somehow Bruce Lockhart thought him from a different tribe.

For all Delmer's delight at moving between identities, maybe he didn't come over quite as convincingly as he liked to think. There was always something not quite "one of us" about him.

Bruce Lockhart's judgement was important: in World War II he would become director of the Political Warfare Executive. He was the sort of man Delmer needed to win over if he was to make full use of his experience. Delmer had witnessed the psychological allure of authoritarian propaganda, how it provided a clear identity in a time of swirling change, how it gave a way to express the need for servility and sadism. He had a sense of its weaknesses too: how people didn't quite believe in it as fervently as Hitler hoped, how they were somewhat "acting" fascist. As a child, he had also seen the vulnerabilities of the kaiser's propaganda.

But would the British establishment entrust him with the power to act on his insights? Delmer had made the Nazis believe that they could trust him. The British Intelligence Services would be quite another matter.

CHAPTER 3

NOT RELIABLE

By July 19, 1940, Austria, Czechoslovakia, Poland, France, Holland, Belgium, Norway and Denmark had all been annexed, invaded, occupied and/or subsumed in Hitler's "New Order" for a Nazi Europe. Hitler appeared undefeatable. Britain was his next target. In the skies over England the Luftwaffe was in daily dogfights with the RAF: Germany's aim was to destroy Britain's air defence before the inevitable invasion. German boats were beginning to mass along the Channel. Britain, isolated and desperate, was mounting air raids into Germany.

At 4:00 p.m. Berlin time, radio wardens across the Reich scurried to ensure that everyone was tuning in to the latest speech. Hitler was to address the Reichstag. The whole country paused whatever it was doing. Was he going to celebrate another famous victory? Another great assault? Was Britain next?

The Reichstag was packed. As well as politicians, the army leadership was present. So was William Shirer, the American correspondent for *CBS News*. As he recorded in his diary, "Under one roof I have never seen so many gold-braided generals before. Massed together, their chests heaving with crosses and other decorations, they filled a third of the first balcony."[1]

But when Hitler started to speak, his message was the opposite of his usual bellicose addresses:

> I prophesy a great Empire will be destroyed which it was never my intention to destroy or even to harm. In this hour I feel it my duty towards my conscience to appeal once more to reason and common sense in Britain. . . . I CAN SEE NO REASON WHY THIS WAR MUST GO ON. I am grieved to think of the sacrifices which it will claim. I should like to avert them, also for my own people.[2]

As far as he was concerned, Hitler continued, he was sated by his conquests. He had taken revenge for defeat in World War I, undone the injustice of the Treaty of Versailles, reclaimed Germany's lost territories, and gained many others. He had always prophesied that he would do this, and now his prophecies had all come true.

When his invasions had begun in 1939, many Germans had been sceptical and scared: there were no celebrations on the streets as in 1914. But when victory came, first over Czechoslovakia, then over Poland and throughout Europe, it only served to show that Hitler saw the future with greater clarity than others, that he could will destiny into reality. Hitler lorded over both space and time.

Shirer was grudgingly impressed:

> The Hitler we saw in the Reichstag tonight was the conqueror, and conscious of it, and yet so wonderful an actor, so magnificent a handler of the German mind, that he mixed superbly the full confidence of the conqueror with the humbleness which always goes down so well with the masses when they know a man is on top. His voice was lower tonight; he rarely shouted as he usually does; and he did not once cry out hysterically as I've seen him do so often from this rostrum. His oratorical form was at its best.

As Hitler spoke, Shirer noted the "beautiful" movement of his "somewhat feminine and artistic" hands and the sway of his body; Hitler used them as much as his voice to express himself. He would turn his head and cock his eyes for irony, "of which there was considerable in tonight's speech, especially when he referred to Mr. Churchill".[3]

Churchill and the British role in the war was the reason Hitler had called this special announcement. He had a message for the British people and their leaders.

If the British gave up their air attacks on Germany, Hitler offered, then he was ready to sue for peace. It was only the warmonger Churchill, the Jewish newspapers and the Freemasons who had dragged Britain into this war. Why bother defending defeated Poland? France was occupied, and there was nothing the British could do about that. Britain was alone—why not join Germany if there was no way it could beat Germany?

Unlike the scene of most special announcements, there was, noted Shirer, "no applause, no cheering, no stamping of heavy boots. There was silence. And it was tense." Deep down—Shirer speculated— Germans desired peace. The silence expressed their hopes.[4]

Goebbels, who had planned the speech's strategy along with Hitler's diplomats, wanted Hitler's peace offer to split the British government and the British public.[5] Appeasers, pacifists, anyone sympathetic to the Nazis would get to make the case against Churchill's belligerence. At his daily briefings to his underlings at the Reich Propaganda Ministry, Goebbels raised the potential for resignations in Churchill's government.[6] He reasoned that it would take the British at least two days to respond.

The answer came within the hour. Not, as might be expected, from the prime minister or even the foreign minister—but from Sefton Delmer, speaking in his perfect *Hochdeutsch* on the German Service of the BBC. He addressed Hitler personally: "You have asked my advice on what Britain thinks before. Let me tell you what we here in Britain think of this appeal of yours to what you are pleased to call 'our reason and common sense'." Delmer paused before delivering his answer: "Herr Führer and Reichskanzler," he said with mock piety, before changing his voice to something much nastier, "we hurl it right back at you . . . right into your evil-smelling teeth."[7]

Hitler, Delmer continued, would soon find himself, like the kaiser in the First World War, "conquering himself to death". Any German of a certain age would have recognised the phrase: it was popular among Berliners in the later parts of World War I, when they had lost all faith in the kaiser's leadership.

Shirer was filing a story at the offices of the Reichs-Rundfunk-Gesellschaft—all foreign journalists had to check their copy with the Nazi censors—as Delmer's speech came through the wireless: "Junior Officers from the High Command and Officials from various ministries were sitting around with rapt attention. Their faces fell. They could not believe their ears. 'Can you make it out?' one of them shouted at me. He seemed dazed. 'Can you understand those British fools?' he continued to bellow. 'To turn down peace now? They're crazy.'"[8]

It wasn't just the message that was so shocking—it was the manner with which it was delivered. BBC announcements were normally restrained. Here the language was borderline Berlin gutter slang—though well spoken, self-conscious and aware of its own theatricality: "Hurl it right back into your evil-smelling teeth!"

The Nazis were flummoxed. They hadn't expected a response so fast or that it would come from Delmer. Goebbels, at his daily conference, where he sat at the apex of a vast oval table in the Reich Ministry, surrounded by the heads of the German press, ordered the radio that broadcast into Britain to repeat Hitler's speech line by line and to make clear in the commentary that rejecting it would be disastrous for Britain. He ordered they stress that "for the British listeners this is a matter of life and death".[9]

It wasn't just the Germans who were taken aback. In Parliament the honorable member for Ipswich protested the fact that the answer to Hitler had been given by a "person of no importance" (some MPs heckled this description), not by the prime minister.[10]

The minister of information, Duff Cooper, responded that "Mr Sefton Delmer, whose name is well known in Germany, where he was a foreign correspondent for many years, took care that nothing he said should commit the government."[11] Delmer's speech was a commentary rather than an official reply, he explained. The official response came on July 22 from the foreign secretary. Hitler's peace offer was rejected as it contained nothing about the rights of occupied countries to self-determination: "We shall not stop fighting till freedom, for ourselves and others, is secure." Germans, the foreign secretary argued, had "given their consciences to Hitler so the people have become machines".[12]

Nazi officials instructed the German press to treat Britain's rejection as a crime and attack Britain with all the fierceness they were capable of.[13]

"Britain will not see reason until she has suffered the first blows," Goebbels told his underlings. "At the moment she simply has no idea of the situation facing her."[14]

Operation Sea Lion, Hitler's plan for the invasion of Britain, advanced. Two thousand barges were gathered in the Channel and the North Sea. Landing manoeuvres were held. On August 1 Hitler signed the order for air strikes against Britain.[15]

In between his talks on the BBC, Delmer was still reporting for the *Express*, dashing over to observe any signs of Hitler's approaching armada from the cliffs of Dover, chasing after downed German aeroplanes in the hope of interviewing pilots. Having reported from Berlin, Paris, the Spanish Civil War and the invasion of Poland, he was by now one of the most famous foreign correspondents of his day, a sort of outsized Tintin of Fleet Street. In his memoirs he's always aware that being a "war reporter" was just another slightly absurd act, so he crafted a curious mix of front-line correspondent and buffoon as a role for himself. He covered the Spanish Civil War together with that paragon of manly war reporting, Ernest Hemingway. Whereas Hemingway had perfected his adventurer look in "shabby but comfortable old buckskin boots, grey flannels and a wind-fastened wind cheater", looking out at the world with "cat-like eyes", Delmer describes himself travelling across revolutionary Spain looking "super-bulky, a sort of grinning fat boy of the Lower Fifth, in the dirtiest of shrunked and frayed grey flannels over a khaki shirt and a wide brimmed straw hat".[16]

When covering Nazi ally Hungary's invasion of Ukraine (or, to be precise, Carpatho-Ukraine) in 1939, Delmer describes how he "cautiously advanced to a nice fat tree about twenty yards from the Hungarian front line in the ditch. I was feeling splendidly heroic watching the battle from behind the tree. Here I was, the intrepid front-line reporter, 'the *Express* man on the spot', getting the news from the jaws of death. In my mind's eye I could see the fat-leaded type of the headlines." He was slapped out of his self-regard by an old peasant woman who came over and brought him a chair to sit on from her cottage, utterly relaxed about the supposed danger. "My glamour picture of myself as the hero reporter was irretrievably smashed."[17]

Now that the war had come to Britain, Delmer's talks on the BBC German Service excited him much more than reporting—here was a chance to really help the cause, to use his knowledge of Germany to undermine the Nazis. All of his past was coming together to have meaning, purpose, patriotism. When Cooper asked him to lecture on the German BBC, it felt "like being given a knighthood".

Delmer was no longer just reporting—he was subverting. As the invasion approached, the Germans issued their troops guidebooks about what to expect from England and the English when they landed. Delmer used his talks to deliver a little primer of phrases German sailors would find useful in their attempt to invade the island:

> We English, as you know, are notoriously bad at languages.
> And so it will be best, meine Herren Englandfahrer, if you learn
> a few English phrases before visiting us.
> 　　Now repeat after me:
> 　　"Das Boot sinkt . . . the boat is sinking.
> 　　Das Wasser ist kalt . . . the water is cold.
> 　　Ich brenne . . . I burn.
> 　　Du brennst . . . you burn."[18]

The references to burning were no coincidence. The British secret services were spreading (false) rumours across the continent that they had a secret weapon that could set the sea on fire. British agents whispered the lie a little too loudly in the bars of Swiss hotels; triple agents dropped the "fake news" to their German handlers. This story of the burning-water weapon became so pervasive that when the RAF bombed German ships in France and charred corpses washed up onshore, German sailors became completely convinced that they were victims not of regular bombs but of the infamous weapon. In times of panic, fantasies become real.[19]

But Delmer was not privy to the details or development of such psychological operations—instead, he had to take direction. "Sefton Delmer, in his talk at 1030 PM," ran a note from the meeting of the Political Warfare German Region Committee from July 1940, "should attack the 'New Order' (avoiding the words 'Neue Ordnung' and 'Neues Europa'). If Hitler speaks before then, he should deal with that."[20] Anything sensitive, like the response to Hitler, had to be cleared with the more senior editors who sat on the secret committees that decided information policy. And not everyone on these committees was impressed with his performances. Frederick Voigt, who was a government adviser on psychological operations into Germany and who had been the *Guardian*'s correspondent in Berlin, thought Delmer "ridiculous and useless".[21] This would not be the last time that Voigt would try to undermine Delmer.

Delmer desired to get behind the scenes and direct the propaganda strategy. Ever since the war began, he had been asking to join the intelligence services and aid in Britain's psychological warfare operations. Wasn't he perfect? He knew the Nazi elites and understood the country and its people. "But would the mysterious THEY give me a chance to do a secret job? Would THEY be ready to make use of me?"[22]

For every time he asked his well-connected friends to help him join the secret services, even though he heard he had come close, some shadow of suspicion fell across him, and he was ultimately rejected. He never knew precisely what it was, but he felt that his very closeness to the Nazis, what should have been seen as an advantage, made him suspect, that being born in Berlin, the thing that gave him the deepest insights on the Germans, "militated against me".

Instead of him being welcomed in as "one of us", stool pigeons were sent to test him. Random minor officials reached out to ask whether he knew how to get in touch with fascist leaders—an obvious trick that would show he was still suspiciously close to the Nazi leadership: "MI5 officers got into oh so casual conversations with me on leave trains and tried to catch me out as a German agent."[23]

In his broadcasts to Germany, speaking in German, Delmer liked to identify himself with Britain. He started sentences with "We here in Britain" and "We English". But for all his self-identification with Britain, he wasn't trusted by his own government. Ever since he'd been an enemy schoolchild in Berlin, he'd imagined himself on secret missions for His Majesty's government. Being part of the "secret" war meant that you really, truly belonged. He didn't. Instead, he felt he was being forced to relive his father's experiences after he came to Britain in 1917.

His frustration was not only personal—it was professional as well.

After his initial excitement at giving his talks, Delmer thought the BBC German Service's strategy all wrong. He believed that the service was full of worthy intellectual émigrés who still wanted to convert ordinary Germans to their high liberal or Socialist ideals. Listening to them, Delmer muttered in his memoirs, was like "Maida Vale calling Hampstead": one part of émigré London talking to another.[24] What was the point of talking to like-minded people and preaching to the converted? How would that ever help get under the psychic skin of those under the sway of Nazi propaganda?

From the late 1930s, the official British propaganda policy was to engage "the Good German": appeal to the supposed mass of democratically minded, decent, upstanding, peace-loving ordinary citizens who resented Hitler.[25] After all, such an audience had existed during World War I, when a revolution had eventually brought down the kaiser. But as the Nazis captured one country after another with minimal casualties, as Hitler's popularity, or at least his aura of invincibility, seemed only to increase, so the search for "the Good German" seemed to Delmer ever more hopeless: "In my view all this attempt to convert Germans to rebellion against Hitler by argument and appeal was a waste of breath and electric power. The Germans, I was convinced, would only begin to listen and react to that sort of thing when they had realised the war was lost and it was better for them to abandon Hitler than to fight on."

According to analysis that Delmer quotes in his memoirs, the BBC's output was dominated by programmes that broadcast "ideological humanitarian appeal" (21 percent), "argument" (32 percent) and "revolution or active opposition" (35 percent). This, he thought, would never work.[26]

Delmer had seen the psychological power of early Nazi propaganda. You needed to tackle people's connection to the Nazis at its root: the need for belonging, the sadism and the simplified identity that the Nazis offered. One needed to climb into Germans' relationship with the Nazis—not lecture them from outside.

• • • ▬▬ ▬▬ ▬▬ • • •

As in Delmer's day, media that claim to "defend democracy" can fail to reach audiences that don't already agree with them.

When Russia launched its full-scale invasion of Ukraine, in February 2022, the final vestiges of independent media in Russia left. Even the BBC Russian Service left. Independent media had long been banned from the TV, accused by state media of being traitors, "liberasts" (liberal pederasts) and "demschiza" (democratic schizophrenics). They were now legally labelled as "foreign agents", and many were paid visits by security forces. Calling the invasion a "war" rather than what the Kremlin termed a "special military operation" became a crime punishable by prison. Up to a million Russians, many of them the audience of non-state media, left as well.

The vast majority of Russians who remained told pollsters that they were for the war. In dictatorships, such sociology has to be taken with a grain of salt. It can be hard to talk of "public opinion" in a society where there is no "public" in the sense of a political culture where having a personal political opinion is encouraged, valued and protected. But the reasons why people would go along with the war were deeply rooted: the belief that Russia had a "right" to subjugate Ukraine was hardwired through the "sociological propaganda" that ran from the Russian Empire through to the Soviet Union and Putin's Russia; the idea that Russia was surrounded by threatening enemies was intertwined with the feeling of being "Russian" for many. Resentment and the desire to humiliate others could be profound.

"What one might term 'support' for the war is better understood as an acquiescence born of many factors: apathy, lack of sympathy,

self-interest, avoidance of cognitive dissonance and so on," concluded
Jade McGlynn, a research fellow at King's College London.[27] In her
study *Russia's War*, she uses a mixture of interviews, polling and analysis of online discourse to define these varieties of support as "active
support" (20 percent), "passive ritual support" (20 percent), "loyal neutrality" (28 percent), "apathy" (22 percent) and "active opposition" (12
percent).[28] The Kremlin could employ different narratives for different
groups: from the more aggressive "military might" angle for active war
supporters to the more vague "my country right or wrong" approach
for loyal neutrals.

The Kremlin varied its message according to its audience. The problem for most of the exiled independent media, including the BBC, was
that they largely appealed to the "active opposition" audience. There
could be spikes in interest when there was a big story. Some pre-war
polls showed that 22 percent of people might use one or two independent media occasionally, so there was a larger potential audience lurking out there, but that only 6 percent would do so regularly, suggesting
that most weren't sufficiently motivated to engage intensely.[29]

In democracies we have none of the censorship or danger that
truth-telling media in dictatorships face, and we have far less excuse
not to reach audiences under the sway of propaganda preaching
lies and hate. As I write this, in the United States up to 40 percent of
Republicans believe false stories about the 2020 election being stolen
from their candidate, the Republican former president Donald Trump,
despite there being no evidence of voter fraud.[30] The country is preparing for a new election when nearly half of its people don't trust the
process. But are we going about the best way to reach them—if we are
trying to reach them at all?

In the United States, some media play on the same needs, fears and
desires that the most powerful propaganda has historically drawn on.
Fox News, which has pushed the story of the election being stolen, tell
their viewers that they are victims of "liberal elites" and "mainstream
media". Their mission is less about sharing evidence than, in the words
of media and journalism professor Daniel Kreiss, offering their audience the hope that they will be "restored to their rightful place at the
center of the nation". Such "media are about identity, not information".

Trust, in this environment, becomes partisan: viewers trust the media that represent their political identity, and they distrust the others. Poll after poll shows how Republican voters trust Fox but actively distrust the sort of media who claim they are defending democratic institutions and value accuracy, such as the BBC, National Public Radio or the *New York Times*.[31]

However, Kreiss writes, journalists continue hoping that "citizens are rational deliberators, weighing the information that media provides to make informed decisions at the polls".[32]

When we talk about how media are meant to operate in a democracy, we often use metaphors like the "marketplace of ideas", where the best information will somehow win out in some version of rational choice. We can rely on assumptions that simply "exposing" the truth will be enough to hold the "powerful to account", like shining sunlight on a vampire. Yet what happens when leaders and their followers actively reject the truth if it undermines their political identities? When the powerful are no longer frightened of the truth? Do we need a new type of media dedicated to understanding and overcoming that?

Meanwhile, adapting to different audiences is something that the enemies of democracies do all the time. They don't do it, of course, to bring diverse audiences into a common public square, but to exacerbate our divides still further. Russian foreign propaganda channels have spent many years telling the right in America and across the world that Russia is fighting against LGBT rights in Ukraine— and then telling the left that Russia is fighting "Western imperialism". They will tell white supremacists that Russia is the last bastion of "true" European values and white power, and then preach to the countries of Africa that the Russians are the friends of the colonised peoples of colour.

Back in World War II, Goebbels was likewise ahead of the Allies in finding the right message to manipulate the right audience.

● ● ● ▬▬▬ ▬▬▬ ▬▬▬ ● ● ●

ON SEPTEMBER 7, 1940, the skies over the Thames estuary suddenly turned dark as vast squadrons of German bombers and Messerschmidts flew in arrow-shaped formations, one after another, from Europe towards London. Hitler, unable to defeat the RAF after months of air raids, had turned the Luftwaffe's firepower towards British cities, his aim to break the British will. This was the first week of the Blitz. It would last nine months.

The Nazi planes arrived over London after twilight. The impending attack was heralded with the dance of searchlights in the darkling sky and then the curling, undulating holler of the air-raid sirens. Europe's largest city stopped. People dropped what they were doing. Some hurried to small, stuffy air-raid shelters or raced down into the tunnels of the Underground. Others hid in their homes, in the safest space, underneath the stairs. Apart from the searchlights, London was dark, its millions of lights blacked out.

In the next weeks Londoners would learn to track the air raids with their ears: the crackling ack-ack guns in the distance; the ever-approaching, ever-louder drone of German bombers; the clatter of shrapnel on the road and on the rooftops; the exploding hail of incendiary bombs; the breaking glass as the attack came closer. You were always waiting for the big bang—the bomb that drops too close, sending an earthquake through the shelters, making the concrete shake and stairwells tremor. A Home Intelligence report noted how in the first week, "Factors which contribute to the strain on morale are, of course, as much psychological as material. Listening tension (e.g. anticipation of planes and bombs) is one to which little official notice has been paid. Few people are using ear pads or understand that the diminution of noise can do much to lessen their state of anxiety."[33]

To ease the "listening tension", Londoners huddled around their wireless sets. As you sat hiding in the thundering dark, trying to measure with your ears whether the bombs were coming nearer, radio became the only connection to the world. You might be trapped and passive, but at least you can twiddle the dials and escape: find music, the BBC, America.

On the first day of the Blitz alone, 430 were killed, mostly in the East End. These poorer parts of the city were both where the most important factories and warehouses were found and where the fires spread fastest because houses and people were so tightly packed together.

On September 11, Churchill made one of his less well-remembered speeches on the radio in an attempt to unify the nation. He spoke deliberately, slowly:

> These cruel, wanton, indiscriminate bombings of London are, of course, a part of Hitler's invasion plans. He hopes, by killing large numbers of civilians, and women and children, that he will terrorise and cow the people of this mighty imperial city.
>
> Little does he know the spirit of the British nation, or the tough fibre of the Londoners.
>
> This is a time for everyone to stand together, and hold firm, as they are doing.[34]

The Home Intelligence reports remarked that people thought Churchill sounded tired.[35]

That evening, as the Blitz bore down on London once again, some were using their radios to tune in to something a little less grandiloquent than Churchill's speeches.

At 8:10 p.m. on September 11, on 213 Medium Wave, 1417 kc, it was time for another edition of *Workers' Challenge*. The show had been running since the summer, every night at ten past eight, nine and ten. It starred East End cockneys talking about their experience of the war. On September 11, 1940, one of its regular stars, Bill, discussed the latest air raids with his friend, Jack. Jack was concerned about rumours that the air-raid sirens were going off too late, not giving the workers enough time to flee the factories and take shelter properly. Bill was convinced that this was no accident, that the factory owners were doing it on purpose:

> "The nobs are afraid their profits will drop, so they don't care a monkey's bugger about what happens to the workers!"
>
> "Oh, stop pulling my leg, Bill," answered Jack. "I knows you like to take a rise out of me once and again, but no kidding,

mate, do you think there's something going on between the bosses and these mess ups when there's an air raid?"

"Now listen here, Jack mate, use your noodle for once. A couple of weeks back the alarm was delayed for a quarter of an hour before the raid started, while the last one wasn't started at all. So what do you think?"

"But I still can't see where the bosses come into it. Though it does look a bit fishy, I'll admit."

"Why you bleedin' twerp, it's as easy as ABC. A delayed alarm means more production from the workers, and more profit for the bosses. And besides, they don't care about Jerry dropping a few more bombs on the factory, as long as they're out of the danger zone."[36]

With Jack slowly coming round, Bill now started his tirade on what had to be done. The workers have been "bloody mugs". But that can change. The workers make the munitions for the army, the air force and the fleet. They can halt these hellish air raids if they rise up against their capitalist bosses and their lackeys in government, halt production and stop the war.

This was pretty typical fare for Bill. He was constantly agitating against "the so-called bosses of ours" who were "all swine who've taken a Yid bribe", while claiming, "This movement is British. Come out into the streets and put it into action! Workers of Britain unite—you have nothing to lose but your chains!"[37]

But *Workers' Challenge* did not actually represent a "British move-ment". Bill, Jack and the other characters who appeared on the show were broadcasting from studios nestled in a well-guarded villa in Ber-lin, part of Germany's covert radio operation, the "Büro Concordia". The "cockneys" were played by British prisoners of war recruited from Stalag XXA Camp in eastern Prussia. They had joined the *büro* after being offered far more preferable living conditions: they could wear their own clothes, were provided with tobacco and alcohol, and had the option of visiting a brothel once a week. Of the thousands of prisoners available, eight agreed to join.[38]

In 1940 the "Workers' Challenge" station was one of four "British" stations run by the *büro*. "Radio Caledonia" lamented how Scotland had been pulled into England's war with Germany, calling for "a Scotland free of international entanglements, conducted not in the interests of Jews and capitalists, but the Scottish people".[39] "Christian Peace Movement" was meant for conscientious objectors, and over at the New British Broadcasting Service (NBBS) you could tune in to upper-class gentlemen talking in a BBC-like style but with very un-BBC-like content. In the poshest of tones, NBBS called on its loyal listeners to "hang Churchill and his Jewish bosses; let's make peace and cut our losses".[40]

Some NBBS presenters were dedicated British fascists, others just "peace-loving" English teachers who were working in Berlin at the outbreak of the war.

The stations were directed by Goebbels himself. On the night of Hitler's offer to Britain, for example, he had expressly directed the "workers' transmitter" to "call for the formation of action committees against Churchill. As a catchy slogan each single transmission should be prefaced by 'The Empire is ruled by a Fool; Churchill is a Fool.'"[41]

William Joyce, an American–British fascist who had fled to Germany, oversaw scripts and recruited staff. However, he could never go on air himself: that would blow the whole operation. Millions in Britain knew his voice too well. He already hosted the official Reich's English-language radio broadcasts. He was better known as Lord Haw-Haw, a tribute to his (in Goebbels's words) "aggressive, superior and insulting tone".[42]

Haw-Haw put out amusing yet alarming lies that the British "Ministry of Misinformation" had ordered women's hats to be lined with tin (to defend from falling bombs), warning that "Tonight our bombers will be coming over Stamford Hill—so you have that pleasure to look forward to."[43]

A BBC Listener Research Department Poll in 1940 showed one in six Britons tuning in to Haw-Haw's show *Germany Calling*. Some may have tuned in because they found him so grotesque that he was funny, but these were still alarming figures.[44]

By late 1940, Joyce's official broadcasts, along with the "secret" ones he oversaw at Büro Concordia, were starting to make parts of the British government fidgety. Not only were they targeting British morale; they were also issuing instructions for direct action. In the event of a bombing, the Büro Concordia stations told their listeners to flee the city for the countryside, the precise opposite of British government instructions. They explained how to make pamphlets and posters and where to plant them: throughout 1940, printed sheets supporting the NBBS were found planted in telephone boxes, inside library books and at aircraft factories.[45] The real number of NBBS "agents" was unclear, but the radio station was skilfully giving the sense that it had people everywhere. The presenters claimed that "NBBS is the headquarters of a vast organisation, with branches wherever there is a short wave wireless set. With co-operation from our listeners, we can resist Churchill's attempt to ruin the country."[46]

You can sense the rising alarm in the debates at the Ministry of Information during 1940. What should they do about the Büro Concordia? Should they jam the stations? This went against government policy, and in any case the German stations were on wavelengths too close to British stations to jam easily, and the Germans had far more transmitters than the British.

Or should they launch a huge publicity campaign revealing the German sources of the stations? But that risked giving them even more publicity. The director general of the BBC, Sir Frederick Ogilvie, already regretted that by having used the BBC to attack Lord Haw-Haw's broadcasts, he had given the "traitor" a vast amount of free advertising.[47]

The seeming success of Haw-Haw and the Büro Concordia brought up questions about the efficacy of Britain's own propaganda. These questions had been cresting for a while. On September 30, 1939, the *Daily Telegraph* wrote that the BBC German Service programmes "are lacking in character", "that they are too uniform in type" and that they ignored "the great possibilities for conveying the warmth and colour of human personality and emotion in delivering the news broadcasts to foreign countries". Delmer's own *Daily Express*, in an article written before Delmer joined the BBC, announced that "Britain is losing the war of the wavelengths" and contrasted the BBC's "musty dignity of a second-hand bookshop" with the "Goebbels rules" for radio propaganda, which demanded that the broadcast "rivet their attention from the opening sentence. Use every trick you know to keep them listening."[48]

Although there were no reliable data on the BBC's audience figures in these years, the Gestapo estimated that in 1941 the BBC had about a million listeners in Germany, from a population of eighty million.[49] This was much lower than Haw-Haw's numbers.

Was it finally time to try something—and some*one*—different?

• • • ▬▬▬ ▬▬▬ ▬▬▬ • • •

BOODLES, 28 ST JAMES STREET, is the second-oldest private gentlemen's club in London. It's unpretentious on the outside: there's a little white stucco at the entrance, but the rest of the eighteenth-century building is naked brick. Inside it's more opulent: oak panelling and plush purple carpets, with paintings of its largely aristocratic members up and down the walls.

This meeting in September 1940 was particularly clandestine. The three men had made their way up to the card room, checked that it was empty, and only when they were sure they were alone settled on chairs by the fire and began to speak.

One of the men was Sefton Delmer. Another was Leonard St Clair Ingrams, a financier who had known Delmer from his time as a correspondent in Weimar Berlin. Ingrams was nicknamed "the flying banker": before the war, he would fly to meetings across Europe piloting his own Puss Moth aeroplane. In 1940 he cruised smoothly from financial to intelligence services, from one part of the British establishment to another, and joined the Special Operations Executive (SOE), the covert agency dedicated to acts of subversion and sabotage in Nazi-occupied territories, tasked by Churchill to "set Europe ablaze".

He had brought Delmer to meet Valentine Williams, a *Daily Mail* journalist and future Hollywood scriptwriter, second in command of British covert propaganda operations. Williams looked cuddly, with his floppy ears, curly black hair and eyes close around his nose. He was the sort of man who made you feel good by laughing with you—until you realised, thought Delmer, that he was also getting you to open up and unmasking you at the same time. Now he was talking in a whisper, probing Delmer with questions to see if he was the right fit for his department. We don't know the details of the conversation, but as Williams was the likely author of a recent secret strategy document that argued British broadcasts should not moralise at Germans but focus on personal doubts and feelings, he and Delmer quickly found common ground.[50]

At the end of the conversation, Williams asked Delmer to come and join his outfit. Ingrams vaguely explained it would involve sitting on the "secret committees" that advise the BBC—just the sort of thing Delmer had been hoping to join.

"It will take a little time," Valentine whispered. "You have to be vetted, you know. You must be patient. I'll let you know when it's all fixed."

Once again, Delmer's "reliability" would be tested by shadowy forces: the mysterious THEM would judge if he belonged. But now that he'd met with the deputy director of SOE 1, in the high-society sanctuary of Boodles, Delmer finally seemed set to join the "secret war".[51]

•••▬▬ ▬▬ ▬▬•••

WHAT SOURCES WOULD HAVE been used to vet Delmer? His MI5 file has been declassified, but there are few documents in there from 1940. However, there are many more from 1941, which give some sense of the sort of information collected on him.

Going over the materials makes for painful reading. We often wonder what people are saying behind our back, but when we find out, it's not always pleasant. You can't control your own story; it's always partly created by others. When you're accused of something that you haven't done, it's not just the injustice that strikes you but also the sense of helplessness, the feeling that anyone can say any vile lie about you and you can do so little back. You can try to correct the lie, but with tomorrow will come another and another until you're buried under them.

Delmer's lack of respect for his émigré German colleagues at the BBC was repaid in spades. The "shadow of suspicion" that had begun from the early 1930s had metastasised.

Karl Otten, a German writer exiled in Britain, told MI5 that Delmer was well known as an appeaser: "Everyone at the BBC knows that Sefton Delmer is a fifth columnist. . . . [Delmer] has openly avowed to [Otten] that he considers the Nazi regime to be the best form of government for Germany and that it would be most unwise to root out all the Nazis if Germany were defeated."[52] This accusation would have particularly hurt Delmer: after the war, he would do much to weed out "former" Nazis.

Another source, simply identified as "MA", reported that it was well known in Berlin that Delmer was an admirer of Nazi methods during his time as a journalist in Germany.

MI5 didn't necessarily take such statements at face value. Otten, the file noted, was bitter at having been fired unceremoniously from the BBC and had slung similar mud at Delmer's other colleagues.

An agent who self-identified as simply "Blimp" dismissed the criticism of Delmer being too close to the Nazis as "typical refugee talk of course: anyone who had wined and dined with Nazi officials must be a Nazi himself, whether it belonged to his duties to wine and dine with them or not".[53]

And from the MI5 files, it's clear that Delmer always had his supporters too.

"I know Delmer well," noted P. E. Ramsbotham, the future third viscount of Soulbury and a senior MI5 member. "There is a lot of nonsense written about him in this file."[54]

There's also another entry in the Delmer MI5 files that grabs my attention. It's not about Sefton Delmer but about his father, Frederick. It's dated 1918, and it's from an interview the British secret service conducted with Braumüller, the chief of the Alien Department in Berlin, who granted the Delmers their exit visa from Germany in 1917. Braumüller told the British agent that Delmer never wanted to leave for England but wanted instead to travel to neutral Switzerland. He claimed that Frederick told him that he didn't want anything to do with England and the English, and that he considered himself to be Australian.[55]

Braumüller was bitter at Frederick for having written unkindly about him in his English articles, and there could have been many reasons why Frederick was playing up his Australian identity: he was, after all, trying to get his family out of Germany. But it still highlights how Sefton Delmer's own avowed Britishness always stood on eggshells.

● ● ● ▬▬ ▬▬ ▬▬ ● ● ●

WHILE DELMER'S IDENTITY WAS being analysed behind his back, he and Isabel held a party at their flat among the seventeenth-century spires and courtyards of Lincoln's Inn Fields, halfway between the offices of the BBC and the *Express*. During the London Blitz their parties were smaller than in Paris—but more dramatic. They made a point of partying through the air-raid sirens and the bombs. One such evening, as the guests moved on to brandy, "what seemed like an end-of-the world explosion sent us all sprawling. The building heaved as in an earthquake. The lights were gone. Smoke and brickdust covered everyone and everything. After a few numbed seconds I went over to the entrance hall and opened the door."

Delmer opened the front door—and found himself staring into nothingness: the stairwell had been blown away. The building had been hit by a bomb. A few metres closer, and they all would have been dead.[56]

In Delmer's memoirs he recounts how the guests lit candles, opened more champagne and went on talking through the night "as if nothing had happened": a model of unfussed sangfroid. Isabel remembered other details. Ian Fleming somehow got down the absent stairs and disappeared right away, terrified for his car: "When I read the James Bond stories I understood Bond was Ian's fantasy, skilfully told. Ian thought himself Bond."[57] Most of the party were rescued by the arrival of the fire brigade and their long ladders.

The next day the police came to the Savoy Hotel, where the Delmers stayed the night. There'd been reports, they explained to Delmer, that his guests had been speaking foreign languages—and supposedly signalling to the bombers with some searchlights. In the paranoid early months of the Blitz, with Hitler threatening invasion, anything "foreign sounding" was viewed with suspicion. The flickerings of candles and cigars were mistaken for secret signals.

The police ordered Delmer to provide a full list of his suspicious guests. This he enjoyed, reeling off his connections: Martha Huysmans, daughter of the Belgian prime minister; Prince Bernhard of the Netherlands; Ian Fleming, personal assistant of the director of Naval Intelligence; Leonard Ingrams of the Special Operations Executive.

But for all Delmer's fame and friendships, Ingrams would have more bad news for him: he'd been rejected by the secret services yet again. The MI5 files mention that there had been "doubts of his reliability".[58]

Williams and Ingrams were, according to Delmer, disgusted. Though Delmer had an unsurpassed understanding of the enemy's propaganda and its people, though he could see clearly what British counterpropaganda was doing wrong, the mysterious "THEY" just couldn't seem to see how much he could contribute.

Some of Delmer's memoirs of the time are shot through with irritation, as if expressing his frustration at not being able to do his patriotic duty as others avoided fulfilling theirs. In the London Underground, he was dismayed at the growing number of people who had moved there permanently to shelter from the bombs, not even emerging during the day to do their work. Who were these cowards lolling about on mattresses, getting in the way as he headed about his business, some copulating publicly on the platform? American journalists were broadcasting about how courageous the British seemed in facing down the Blitz, but as he passed along platforms crowded with subterranean refugees, Delmer wasn't quite so sure about the "Blitz spirit".

The secret services did have some uses for him. Once a month he would meet with a carrot-headed young Oxford graduate from what Delmer assumed was MI5 (it was actually MI6), who would ask him to do the odd sordid job: go drinking with other journalists to see which of them might be a German spy, check out which German journalists might be ready to betray the Reich. But beyond such minor snooping, Delmer was not being let anywhere near any propaganda decision-making power.[59]

The one bright spot in this autumn of rejection was a new home. Some distant relatives of his father heard that the Delmers' apartment had been bombed and allowed them to use the "Valley Farm", a sixteenth-century cottage with a thatched roof and oak beams, framed with a low row of elms that led down to the slow-running River Stour, which winds from Essex into Suffolk, sheltering the farm from the road and also from the passage of time. This is the part of England depicted in the paintings of John Constable, who, in his arcadias of hay wains and water mills, evokes England's idealised version of itself, an icon of remaining rural idyll sheltered from relentless industrialisation. The Valley Farm was not just a sanctuary to escape the Blitz; for Delmer, it symbolised leaving his German childhood behind and becoming thoroughly part of England. Isabel, however, felt she never belonged there.[60]

The idyll did not last long. When Hitler began to plan the invasion of Gibraltar, the *Express* ordered Delmer down to Lisbon. His handlers were excited too—whatever he could glean about the Germans' plans he should report to them. They didn't explain how to contact them; they would explain when the time was right.

Almost as soon as he would arrive, however, Hitler would abandon his plan to take Gibraltar. Instead, Delmer got to probe developments in Germans' attitudes—and just how deep Hitler's hold on them had become.

• • • ▬▬ ▬▬ ▬▬ • • •

AN AMERICAN JOURNALIST DESCRIBED flying from England to Portugal during the Blitz as akin to "flying in a sarcophagus". The windows in passenger planes were blacked out so that any potential spies on board would not be able to report on air defences. Passengers travelled in a gloomy cabin. Flying to Lisbon direct would have been too dangerous because the route passed right over German-controlled airspace, so the planes flew way out over the Atlantic in a wide zigzag, minimising the chances of being hit.[61] Commercial planes were still attacked. In 1943, Flight 777 was set upon by eight German Junkers 88. There were no survivors among the seventeen passengers and crew.[62]

In his memoirs Delmer breezily mentions a five-hour flight running "the gauntlet of Luftwaffe interceptor planes in the Atlantic" before sliding down onto the Tagus River in neutral Portugal.

Emerging from the dark of the seaplane must have felt like passing into a brilliant, bright, sparkling new life. Unlike London, Lisbon in 1940 did not suffer from blackouts. The city's casinos and restaurants were teeming. Neutral Portugal was awash with spies, playboys, refugees, more refugees, gamblers, weapons smugglers, war profiteers and writers. The abdicated king of England, Edward Windsor, along with his retinue, occupied a set of suites overlooking the Atlantic. Lisbon was one of the last outposts of European high life in the depths of the war.

The Palacio Estoril Hotel was the favoured spot of Allies; the Reich's agents, the Abwehr, preferred the Atlantico. The Abwehr trained prostitutes to extract information from English sailors and hatched a scheme to abduct the former king, a Nazi sympathiser, and bring him to Germany to broadcast pro-Hitler speeches to the British. The Abwehr were themselves penetrated by British spies. Among them was a Serbian, Dusko Popov, who pretended to be a Yugoslav spy working for the Germans while actually working for MI6 and all the time passing the Germans disinformation about Allied military plans. Popov would be one of the inspirations for Ian Fleming's Bond. Lisbon in 1940, Popov later wrote, was "a very special universe, a tiny enclave of neutrality, where all sides of the war brushed shoulders. It was filled with refugees of all descriptions and all nations. Some were wealthy beyond measure, and they squandered their money like there was no tomorrow—as there might not have been one. Some were impoverished to the point where they would sell anything— which usually meant themselves."[63]

Lisbon was where you could try to escape your old life and start afresh in the new world. A character in the Erich Remarque novel *The Night in Lisbon* gets lucky: in exchange for listening to another refugee's tale of his love affair with a woman left behind in a Nazi concentration camp, he gets a boat ticket to America and the storyteller's passport, which is itself a passport in another man's name. The only demand made of him is to keep telling the story he has heard so that the memory of the lost woman is preserved, so that some constant truth remains as identity papers and ways of life irrevocably change.

For Delmer, Lisbon was the next best thing to being in Germany itself: What could the refugees tell him about the state of the nation under Hitler?

In a grubby boarding house on a narrow backstreet, Delmer located the wizened, seventy-one-year-old Dr Bloch, who had been the Hitler family physician in Linz, Austria, during the Führer's childhood. Delmer wanted Bloch to tell him about any mental diseases that Hitler may have shown as a child.

Bloch had been forced to abandon his profession after the Nazis banned Jews from practising medicine. In old age, he and his wife had had to leave their home for good. Yet they remained utterly enamoured of the Führer and were completely unwilling to give away the patient's secrets. Both the Blochs recalled, delighted, how the Führer's cortège had passed by their house during the Nazi Anschluss of Austria and how, in that moment, as they stared down at the parade, they thought they saw him turn and wave and smile in the direction of their apartment windows. And, can you believe it, they told Delmer, after the Anschluss they had been allowed one privilege not given other Jews: they could still use a telephone! The Führer was a true friend. He'd even personally permitted them to emigrate.

Other émigrés were still "so cowed, that they feared the Gestapo might still catch up with them . . . others preserved a stubborn remnant of their old German national loyalty". Some continued to venerate Hitler, despite all their suffering, "a supreme example of the almost mystic hold which the conquering hero-figure of Hitler had over Germans".[64] Again, Delmer was convinced that trying to get Germans to lose faith in Hitler quickly, let alone surrender their patriotism, was going to be a futile struggle. However, the Nazi system had other flaws. Delmer's notebooks filled up with details about which German Gestapo officers accepted bribes from refugees to leave the country, the latest jokes about officials, the corrupt perks enjoyed by party bosses. All these notes would later serve as the first raw material for his broadcasts.

Hitler was, for the moment at least, invulnerable. But the whole Nazi Party edifice—that could be attacked.

In the evenings, Delmer parked himself at the bar of the Estoril. Here too he was surrounded by potential stories. One English business-man with spectacular rabbit teeth held special interest. He was buying precious metals from the Portuguese just so the Germans couldn't get their hands on them and use them in their U-boats. Delmer had been working on the story for a while when, one particularly boozy night, the man asked him up for brandies in his room. They were accompa-nied by another hotel guest who, it turned out in a somewhat strange coincidence, had known Delmer's father in the prison at Ruhleben.

When the drinks were poured, the businessman dropped his facade and said he was a colleague of the carrot-headed spy in London. He wanted Delmer to share any interesting information he might have learned from his interviews with refugees.

Delmer is almost too self-effacing about his value to the Secret Intelligence Service (SIS) in Lisbon: "While my reports at *The Express* were read by about twelve million people before being used to light a fire, those I delivered [to MI6] were distributed to several hundred per-sons, read by no one, and then incinerated as secret waste."

You can usually tell that an English person, or someone who knows how to act like an English person, is doing well when they are being so self-deprecating. Although we don't know exactly how Delmer's reports were evaluated, their detailed breakdown of life in Germany, the names of corrupt and corruptible officials and the unhappiness at the conditions in factories could have had all sorts of uses. Even the odd, unexpected presence of a secret service man who had known his father in Ruhleben seems curious: Was Delmer finally getting the thor-ough vetting he deserved?

It was during this sojourn in Lisbon, a city where so many were embarking on new lives, that a telegram came from Ingrams: "Suggest you return earliest possible and resign from the *Express*. Important job awaits you."[65]

• • • ▬▬ ▬▬ ▬ • • •

"How would you like to run an RU, Tom?" Ingrams enquired of Delmer when the new recruit reported to his Mayfair office eight weeks later. Delmer had signed the Official Secrets Act—committing him to never tell anyone about his work on pain of being charged with treason—but it was only now that he was being given a clue about why he had been recruited:

> "What's an RU?" I asked.
> "A Research Unit—didn't you know?"
> "No, I didn't. What do they research?"
> "Do you mean to say you have been with us now the best part of eight weeks, and you still haven't found out what a Research Unit is? A fine reporter you are!"

Research units, Ingrams explained to an increasingly huffy, puffy Delmer, had nothing to do with research. This was the code name for "freedom radios": French, Italian, Danish and other anti-Nazi resistance radio stations that seemed to be transmitting from occupied Europe while actually being run by émigrés based in England, all working under the auspices of the intelligence services.

Delmer was familiar with the idea of covert stations in principle—exiled German Communists and Nazis who had fallen out with Hitler had created ones in France and Czechoslovakia—but he hadn't been aware, or at least claims in his memoirs not to have been aware, of the British operation up until now.

Ingrams explained that there had been two German RUs, appealing to different segments of potential German opposition to the Nazis: a Socialist one run by an exiled member of the Marxist Neubeginn movement, overseen by Delmer's boss at the BBC and the head of all German-language content, overt and covert, Richard Crossman, and a right-wing one run by an exiled former Reichstag member of the conservative "Centre Party". The head of the right-wing one had fallen ill, and the station had closed. "We want you to start a right-wing RU and suggest you take charge of it with full editorial and political control," Ingrams instructed.

Ingrams had one final instruction for Delmer. The head of the SOE, the minister for Economic Warfare, Hugh Dalton, had taken note that the Büro Concordia's Workers' Challenge drew in listeners by using the "foulest language ever". "Old ladies", Ingrams told Delmer, enjoyed listening to it in order "to count the 'Fs' and 'Bs'". He continued:

> Well, my Minister thinks we should reply in kind, and as he is a Socialist, he thinks a right-wing station would be the appropriate one to carry the filth.
>
> Go to it then, Tom. And let me have your paper as soon as you can. It is a great chance for you to show your ingenuity. There are no limits. No holds are barred.[66]

CHAPTER 4

ALL DOUBTS FALL AWAY

Delmer's immediate mission was to create a new radio station. But for this smaller task he needed to crack a larger problem: how to engage German audiences in the first place.

He knew that any efforts would have to dig into the attraction that Nazi propaganda held for Germans. He also knew that he needed to reach out beyond what we might now call the "liberal bubble". But for all his knowledge of Germany, it had also been eight years since he had left Berlin, and Goebbels had been busy during that time.

• • • ▬▬ ▬ ▬▬ • • •

PROPAGANDA WAS AN OBSESSION for many of the senior Nazis—they blamed their failure in it for their loss in World War I. In *Mein Kampf,* Hitler argued that British propaganda had simpler and more consistent messages, stereotyping Germans and the kaiser as monstrous criminals, which motivated their people and their soldiers. British leaflets had successfully undermined the morale of the German army on the front, while at home liberal media and Socialist agitprop promoting peace and revolution had destroyed the monarchy just when victory was in the Germans' grasp. There's no evidence to support Hitler's claim that propaganda was central in Germany's defeat, instead of military or economic failures. Hitler was spreading propaganda about propaganda. But he was not alone at the time in being awestruck by its power. In a similarly evidence-free vein, British newspapers such as *The Times* claimed that "our propaganda shortened the war by a year and saved a million lives".[1] In the United States, renowned public intellectuals like Walter Lippmann were convinced after World War I that humans were unable to deal with the complexity of modern society, that they were easily manipulated by propaganda, that media made things worse by perverting truth into damaging stereotypes. Lippmann argued that optimistic notions about a democratic public sphere where citizens debate the facts and come to common policy decisions were impossible to fulfil. Instead, power had to be handed over to an enlightened elite to make decisions.[2]

The world was living through one of its occasional propaganda panics. The Nazis were determined that on this front they would never be second best again.

Goebbels believed propaganda had one aim—"the conquest of the masses". All methods that furthered this were good, but he was more inspired by contemporary advertising techniques than British World War I propaganda. He believed that with enough hammering away at one insistent message, one set of slogans, one visual pattern, he could mold people's minds into anything he required. As early as 1929, he argued that people are "mostly just a gramophone record playing back public opinion. Public opinion . . . in its turn, is created by the organs of public opinion such as the press, posters, radio, school, and university and general education. But the government owns these organs."[3]

The last time Delmer had spoken to Goebbels was almost eight years ago, as they rushed between Hitler rallies heaving with hysterical Nazi crowds. Back then, Goebbels was already excited: after years of being banned from the radio, now that the Nazis were in power he had the chance to get Hitler into every home. When Hitler began his rise in the 1920s, his speeches could be heard only by those who would physically attend his initial beer-hall meetings and then his larger rallies. In the first year of Nazi power, Goebbels broadcast fifty Hitler speeches on the radio.[4] Now you were as close to Hitler on your settee in the living room as at a march in Nuremberg. The Nazis mass-produced a cheap, sleek radio set, a *Volksempfänger*, to summon this Volksgemein-schaft into being. By 1941, 65 percent of Germans owned one of these "people's receivers".[5]

As with his early speeches, Hitler could still play the humble, humiliated German everyman anyone could associate themselves with. "What am I?" he asked the German audience in March 1940, then answered: "Nothing but your spokesman, proclaiming your rights."[6]

But now he was not merely promising them supremacy; he was delivering it with every fresh conquest. Here was the humble corporal, the unknown soldier, turned Great God of War leading Germany to one startling Blitzkrieg victory after another. He was imbued with a nearly mystic gift of prophecy: every time he launched a new offensive, people might doubt it, but he invariably won.

The Sicherheitsdienst of the SS (the SD), whose intelligence agents were forever covertly taking careful notes of people's reactions, reported in early 1940 how people thought that "when the Führer speaks, all doubts fall away".[7] Although the announcement of war with Britain caused consternation, people believed that if Hitler willed England to fall, it would be done. The SD noted how Germans believed that "the Führer had never held out a prospect of something which had not happened".[8] It described "with what childlike trust the most ordinary people in particular look up to the Führer and his leadership of state. . . . The people always want to see how the Führer looks, whether he is serious or laughing. . . . The words of the Führer are gospel for the people."[9]

Goebbels's propaganda sought to put Hitler above politics, on a plane both parental and almost divine. His birthdays were the high-est of all celebrations. Every building in the Reich, from palaces to peasant huts, flew flags and ribbons. At the Chancellery in Berlin, adoring, meandering queues of devotees lined up to sign the birthday book. The radio took you like a personal guest to Hitler's own birthday table, where messages of congratulation were read out from across the world.[10] Joyful subjects of captured nations paraded through the streets

from Norway to the Balkans, announcing their love for and gratitude to the Führer, who showered down amnesties to POWs as tokens
of his divine magnanimity on this great day. Adoring speeches were
read out on radio from across the Reich, from Volksgenossen great and
small, tumbling like roses from the radio, so many that they spilled
into the following days. In that sleek little Volksempfänger you were
joined into one soundscape of common feeling with the Führer and the
Volksgemeinschaft.

"The German radio," boasted Hans Fritzsche, the always elegantly
dressed director and lead presenter of the Reich's radio, "has managed
to unite at certain hours, and for certain moments, Germans all over
the world, welding them into one single listening community with one
common purpose. A Führer speech, relayed by German wireless, unites
Germans across the world into a community."[11]

Jews were not allowed to own a radio. But such was the profusion of
loudspeakers in every corner of the Reich, every restaurant, park, factory and public building, that as he walked through his home town of
Dresden, the Jewish literature professor Victor Klemperer found Hitler's voice following him everywhere: "I could not get away from it for
an hour. First from an open shop, then in the bank, then from a shop
again."[12]

Since the Nazis came to power, Klemperer had lost his home and
his job. But he'd kept his life, thanks to being married to an ethnic
German, an Aryan. He spent the years of Nazi rule doing odd jobs in
factories, being interrogated and beaten by the Gestapo, and keeping a
diary where he tried to figure out how ordinary, usually pleasant Germans became so spellbound by Nazi propaganda.

The marriage between Nazi propaganda and the radio was, Klemperer thought, no accident. As he observed the "forests of radio masts"
that sprouted across Germany, as he craned his head and gazed at the
"perforated steel constructions [that] rise up into the haze and seem to
disappear", he took notes in his diary, trying to work out the nature of
this still-new medium: "In general pay attention to the role of radio!
Not like other technical achievements: new contents, new philosophy.
But: new style. Printed matter suppressed. Oratorical, oral. Primitive—
at a higher level."[13]

If writing and reading books made you sit and think in more formally rational debate, then radio could appeal to something more instinctive. Radio, this utterly oral medium, was where the Nazis could further spread their new language. Words like *Führer, Volksgemeinschaft* and *Volksgenosse* entered Germans' everyday vocabulary and redefined their relations to themselves and to one another. When you described the world in terms of superior *Übermenschen* and inferior *Untermenschen*, you felt part of a special caste, looking down at those below, even if you had never amounted to much yourself. When you described yourself as "Aryan", you got to feel similarly superior.

Klemperer, who had always considered himself a German patriot, watched with horror as his friends and neighbours began to repeat these words and, as they repeated them, fell into their logic—as if the language itself was shaping them, not them shaping the language. It was a specific type of language, too short and shrivelled for the complex thinking you find in thick books, especially the sort of "decadent" books the Nazis set ablaze in their great public book-burning fires. It was useless for introspection and intimate conversation. However, it was perfect for public speeches. It was declarative, a language to scream your allegiance through rather than to turn inward and reflect with. The sort of language that would work effectively in today's social media.

This language was designed to seep into every part of life. Political content was only one part of Goebbels's formula to fuse the Volksgemeinschaft. "The first law," he told the Reich's radio managers in March 1933: "Don't become boring!"[14] Nazi radio was also full of musical request shows and big-band upbeat melodies. Even anti-Semitism was more "effective" when delivered through "entertainment". The glossy costume drama *Jew Suss*, a movie about an ambitious Jew scheming and raping his way through eighteenth-century German court politics, was significantly more popular than the quasi-documentary *Eternal Jew*, with its montage of mass insect infestations intercut with close-ups of destitute Jews.[15]

For the film and literary critic Siegfried Kracauer, who had fled Berlin for Paris in 1933 and when the Nazis took Paris fled to the US, Goebbels's aim was more than merely to represent the Volksgemeinschaft through mass media; it was also to get people to participate, as in some vast costume-drama production where they were both audience and actor, each playing their part and applauding themselves in the inexorable march of history—a history that Hitler had both predicted and made real—through myriads of marches, common endeavours to build and clean up common spaces, communal dinners in support of soldiers and communal holidays sponsored by the Nazis.[16] People began owning cameras en masse, and the newspapers encouraged them to photograph themselves taking part in the Nazi festivities— early versions of selfies. Soldiers were given special booklets in which to write their diaries, which had photo-sized spaces reserved where they would stick in photos of themselves at the front—a precursor of how we use social media now to blend our private moments with a greater crowd. When he reported from the German march on France, Shirer was surprised at how many soldiers were carrying their own cameras: "I saw them by the thousands today, photographing Notre-Dame, the Arc de Triomphe, the Invalides. They bare their blond heads and stand there gazing."[17]

As the war progressed, Goebbels's aim was to turn the Nazi conquest of Europe into something that felt less like a dangerous war and more like a glorious interactive radio drama about almost risk-free conquest.

Working first with the British government and later the Americans, two exiled academics, the Austrian psychoanalyst Ernst Kris and the German sociologist Hans Speier, were tasked with analysing wartime Reich's radio hour by hour and detailing how Goebbels tried to achieve his aims.

Every evening from seven to eight, the Volksgenossen were expected to listen to *The Hour of the Nation*. It opened with the tolling of the grand bells at Weimar Cathedral. Then came "the news", with its stories about racially pure party members and courageous Hitler-Jugend combating bestial Bolsheviks and the conspiracies of global Jewry.

At 7:15 p.m., suppertime for most Germans, came the "Front Report". Narrated breathlessly, the "Front Report" took you, the listener, right to the front lines of Hitler's seemingly unstoppable series of conquests, cutting swiftly between scenes recorded all along the front. When the *Wehrmacht* invaded a new country, there was often a radio team with its armoury of microphones travelling with the most forward-surging troops. You were with the soldier as he moved into Czechoslovakia and France, clearing mines with sappers, capturing foreign forces and shooting down their planes. Blitzkrieg after blitzkrieg victory was won almost bloodlessly, and you could live all this vicariously, imagining yourself the daring hero while sheltered in your living room, warmed by the oral furnace of the Volksempfänger.[18]

Soldiers were the heroes in the "Front Report". But although they were interviewed and often named, Kris and Speier noted, they all seemed to blend in with one another. Little was told about the soldiers' past apart from their home region (to show how the whole country fights together). The soldier was more a symbol than a person: "brave because he belongs to a soldierly race, successful because he was led by the best officers in the world, and superior to all others because he was the bearer of the national socialist idea". The soldier was a machine, well oiled, beautifully designed, inseparable like a centaur from his German Panzer, which, the presenter told you, was "ready for attack, ready for a mighty push forward, [for] these tanks carry with them the new romance of fighting".

The "Front Report" reversed the accusations of atrocities that had so damaged Germany in World War I—now it was the Allies who were the monsters. As the British retreated through France in 1940, the "Front Report" lamented that "our soldiers do not mind bullets. They know it is not every bullet that hits. But when we see these defenceless people machine-gunned [by the British]—we feel a pain in our hearts." Wehrmacht soldiers on the Western Front were chivalrous and chic. When they bombed a French village with heavy artillery, they purposefully avoided hitting its historic church. When soldiers took a town, they washed and visited the hairdresser salons before getting to know the locals: "They marched down Paris avenues, surrounded by adoring French citizens, looking radiant and disciplined."[19]

Soldiers' deaths were rarely mentioned. The "Front Report" described SS men and party members as bearing the brunt of the fatalities: Nazis were always ready to lay down their lives for the Volk. When death made an appearance on radio, it was utterly heroised. On May 5, 1940, as the Nazis conquered Norway, the commentator related the end of the heavy cruiser *Blücher* in the icy waters at the fjord of Drøbak Sound:

> Suddenly the stern rose upright out of the water. There I saw a German soldier standing straight, his hand lifted in the German salute. All of us on the island spontaneously broke out into the Sieg Heil and Deutschland über Alles. Never in our life will we forget those minutes when the *Blücher* sank, and when a German soldier, death before his eyes, saluted his Führer and the country.

But even this glorious death was quickly softened: "It is a strange circumstance that just now we learned that every man who went down with his ship has been saved after all."[20]

Luftwaffe pilots over Britain were similarly both brave and blessed: "When the observer took off the pilot's helmet, streams of blood came down, but the wound turned out to be insignificant."[21]

Luftwaffe pilots were in charge of their emotions: "Only after a specially eventful day, as for instance, when they successfully bombed the Spitfire and Rolls Royce works and got special mention in the High Command, are they a little unbalanced by pride—but only by a little."[22]

"The listener," concluded Kris and Speier, "lives in war which is extraordinarily easy or extraordinarily total. If they suffered at times it was with iron hearts, for their suffering was always full of historical meaning and pointed to a future measured in centuries."[23]

You could and should tune in to the "Front Report" daily. However, the "special announcement" was a much rarer and more exalted piece of listening. It signalled the celebration of some great victory. Radio presenters would spend the whole week heralding that there was a "special announcement" pending. When it came, almost always on a Sunday, the radio emitted a tremendous blast of trumpets. Not just any old blast of trumpets but a hundred-strong brass band, as mighty as the blaring that brought down the walls of Jericho. All other programmes were broken off mid-flow. Hans Fritzsche read the special announcement, intoning which new city, capital and/or country had been taken.

The brass orchestra played the national anthem and Nazi songs, and then came a solemn request: "We shall now have a total air silence." A silence in which to let the vastness of the victory sink in. The "special announcements", explained Fritzsche, "are the voice of history."

Klemperer was visiting the State Bank in Dresden when the "special announcement" heralded the Anschluss with Austria: "I innocently opened the door leading to the main banking hall of the Staatsbank and started back until I was at least partially hidden by the half-open door. The reason being that inside everyone present, both behind and in front of the counters, was standing stiffly erect with outstretched arms listening to a declamatory voice on the radio. I remained half-hidden in order not to practise the salute along with everyone else."

At the front of this entranced crowd saluting a disembodied voice, spellbound by the power of the radio, Klemperer spotted a family friend, a well-educated woman who had always been pleasant to her Jewish friends and never had a bone of malice in her body: "She was in a state of total ecstasy, her eyes sparkled, she was not simply standing to attention like the others, the rigidity of her posture and salute was more of a convulsion, a moment of rapture."[24]

• • • ▬▬ ▬▬ ▬▬ • • •

THE ROLE OF FACTS in this system was secondary. All in all, Nazi propaganda wasn't meant to win people over with evidence and arguments as in some sharp debate in a "marketplace of ideas". It was doing something else entirely. Even the news, Nazi propaganda manuals openly declared, "does not aim at being objective, free, and independent, as is the ambition of the liberal gentlemen of the press".[25] It was there to reflect the "spiritual foundation of National Socialism", to conjure a great battle between dark and light and to give you a place within it. Nazi news was not part of a "public sphere" where evidence, information or even disinformation was weighed and debated, proven and disproven. Its aim wasn't an encounter with reality—but an escape from it.

Describing the allure of such reality-denying propaganda, the German–Jewish philosopher Hannah Arendt, who had fled Nazi Germany and eventually immigrated to the US in 1941, described how

Germans, lost in an "an ever-changing, incomprehensible world . . . are obsessed by a desire to escape from reality because in their essential homelessness they can no longer bear its accidental, incomprehensible aspects. . . . What convinces masses are not facts, and not even invented facts, but only the consistency of the system of which they are presumably part."[26]

Instead of "evidence", whether fake or real, what people were looking for was a larger sense that they were special, that they were surrounded by enemies, that they were part of a common destiny. Fealty to the leadership became a value in itself. The Nazi leadership could often change their policies—at one moment the USSR was an ally; the next moment Germany was at war with it—but such inconsistencies didn't matter, thought Arendt. In a world where Germany was portrayed as being surrounded by malign, deceptive, endless conspiracies, the leader's duty was to lie:

> The totalitarian mass leaders based their propaganda on the correct psychological assumption that, under such conditions, one could make people believe the most fantastic statements one day, and trust that if the next day they were given irrefutable proof of their falsehood . . . they would protest that they had known all along that the statement was a lie and would admire the leaders for their superior tactical cleverness. . . .
>
> The essential conviction shared by all ranks, from fellow-traveler to leader, is that politics is a game of cheating and that the "first commandment" of the movement: "The Fuehrer is always right," is as necessary for the purposes of world politics—i.e., world-wide cheating—as the rules of military discipline are for the purposes of war.[27]

• • • ▬▬ ▬▬ ▬▬ • • •

ON APRIL 4, 2022, the prime-time current-affairs show on Russian state TV opened with a report on how the country's leadership was calling for an emergency meeting at the United Nations in order to inform the world that "there has been a brutal provocation by the Ukrainian Nazis in the city of Bucha, Kyiv region. The Ukrainian central government, Zelensky and the so-called civilised West, are trying to create a fake."[28]

I was in Bucha a week later, standing in a brown field by a white church. The field around us was filled with neat rows of long black polythene bags. At first glance I thought the bags might contain food or military equipment—there were so many of them and laid out in such neat order.

This was no fake atrocity: thirty-three days of occupation. Of the civilians who hadn't fled in time, 1 in 10 were murdered. There were 458 bodies, with 419 bearing markings that they had been shot, tortured or bludgeoned. People shot in the head for looking at a soldier the wrong way. Executed for target practice as they rode on their bicycles. Raped and locked in their cellars. Liquidated for daring to speak Ukrainian.[29]

We were being taken round the site by Brigadier General Oleksandr Gruzevich, who had helped lead the defence of Kyiv. Over the past two weeks he had been directing combat against Russian paratroopers landing in the local airport, guiding squadrons of Ukrainian soldiers through the woods to destroy static Russian tank columns with rocket launchers. But even as he fought Russians, he still thought he understood them. After all, he had studied with them in the former Soviet Union and shared student digs with them at the Military Academy in Omsk, Siberia. He struggled to take in the scene at Bucha: "The nation has degraded. They've been fed so much brain-destroying propaganda. This"—and here he signalled at the black polythene body bags—"is created by the propaganda."

Ever since Russia had invaded Ukraine and annexed Crimea in 2014, Brigadier General Gruzevich had tried to reach out to his Russian fellow students from the academy. He couldn't recognise them anymore: they told him that Russia was the victim of aggression, not the perpetrator. In the following years, Putin's propaganda had only intensified. Ever since the invasion of February 24, Ukrainians across the country tried to call their relatives and friends in Russia, telling them they were under bombardment, that Russian artillery was pummelling their cities. After Bucha was discovered, President Zelensky appealed again to the Russian people on video: "What did the Ukrainian city of Bucha do to your Russia? How did all this become possible? Russian mothers! Even if you raised looters, how did they also become butchers?"[30]

But however much Ukrainians appealed, their Russian friends, or now former friends, and relatives refused to listen to the evidence, and they told their Ukrainian relatives, the ones sitting under bombardment, that they were wrong, that the evidence of shells and body parts exploding all around them was a myth, or they were exaggerating, or that the Ukrainian army was bombing its own citizens, or that if it was happening, it was a necessity. The specific excuses could change in line with Russian propaganda that in one moment claimed that atrocities like Bucha were a fake and in the next moment celebrated Russian strikes against civilians as "necessary"; they claimed in one moment that Russia just wanted to dispose of the "Nazi" government and "liberate" Ukrainians, and in the next they claimed that most Ukrainians were Nazis and had to be wiped out. Some of the excuses were wildly absurd but were still pronounced seriously. Russian state media's most popular current-affairs presenter, Vladimir Soloviev, claimed that Zelensky's use of the word *butchers* in describing the events at Bucha showed why Western spy agencies had selected the town to stage their fake atrocity: they wanted similar-sounding words for better headlines about a "butchery in Bucha".[31]

Did the Russian relatives really "believe" this? That's the wrong question. We are not talking about a situation where people weigh evidence and come to a conclusion but rather one where people no longer seem interested in discovering the truth or even consider the truth as having considerable worth. Supplying the people with facts, reasoned arguments and evidence of war crimes—in short, with reality—was the absolute opposite of what they seemed to want. Polls in Russia concluded that Putin's supporters thought that "the government is right, solely because it is the government and it has power".[32] Truth was not a value in itself; it was a subset of power.

One consistent motif of the propaganda, however, was how it took away the burden of responsibility. Russia, Putin and his officials repeated, had been forced into the war: "We were given no choice." This propaganda sat right next to other messages that celebrated

Russia retaking "historic" lands, called for burning and drowning Ukrainian children (the presenter who said this was suspended but soon reinstated), compared the invasion to "deworming a cat" and demanded that Ukrainians be "liquidated".[33]

The propaganda allowed you to both relinquish responsibility and enjoy dominance. This was part of the psychological deal the Kremlin offered people. You can identify yourself with the sense of supremacy, but you don't need to carry any moral burden.

Travelling along the areas liberated from the Russian forces was a journey into a raw wound of tortures, casual executions and mass graves. Driving past craters in the road from shells, past broken bridges and blackened tanks with the burned embers of bodies whose outlines you could just make out, we came to the village of Yahidne. The villagers were crowding around vans that were handing out food and drink. Almost the whole village, 350 people, had been held captive by the Russians in a cellar under the local school. A whole village stuffed into a cellar for a month, three toilets among all of them. Dozens had died from lack of medical attention. The Russian commander had said he would give out medical supplies only if the prisoners sang the Russian anthem. No one did. Some of the older people had gone mad. Anyone who tried to resist was shot. When the villagers buried them, the Russians shot at them for fun, and they had to jump and hide in the graves where they were burying their friends.[34]

I walked around the cellar and found the remains of Russian propaganda newspapers: they told the soldiers they were fighting "Nazis" in Ukraine, that they were liberators, repeating the language blaring out from Putin's television daily. They used the term "Nazis" in the same way as Klemperer described Nazis calling Jews "Untermenschen": by labelling Ukrainians Nazis, the Kremlin made them beyond the pale, subhuman, and allowed for their mass murder. And at the same time, it took away the original power of the term. When we want to accuse the Kremlin of being "like the Nazis", the word has lost its significance through the Kremlin's own repetition of it, which in turn makes their behaving like actual Nazis all the easier. The language that defined evil, that was meant to help lock it up in the prison of the past, had grown weak with repetition, so now the worst of the past was here, taunting us by using the very language that was meant to hold it at bay.

Had the soldiers believed any of this language? They had definitely used it as an excuse for sadism. They could see perfectly well that there were no "Nazis" among the Ukrainians, that, unlike what the Russian propaganda said, they could freely speak the Russian language. But they had continued to act as if there were "Nazis" there in order to enable their atrocities. We sometimes describe aggressors as "brainwashed" by propaganda that dehumanises their victims, so much so they are "hypnotised" into committing atrocities. But what if the "dehumanising" propaganda rather legitimises cruelty, makes it ordinary, and the aggressor sees the victims' humanity all too clearly?

Putin's and Goebbels's propaganda is different in many ways: the current Russian system has no pseudo-scientific Nazi race-based (or Soviet class-based) ideology; there are fewer jackbooted mass marches, fewer ecstatic crowd scenes, no torch-carrying party rallies, more cynicism. It relies more on keeping people passive than motivated. But the newer propaganda has also made naked the underlying mindsets that were always lurking under the ideology of the old, like a skin that's been taken off to reveal the bloody pulp and pulsating muscles underneath: the needs it feeds and the pleasures it provides, the way it delivers a remedy for loneliness, stills a spinning world, feeds you a simpler, superior identity, consumes your potential to be you, burns away the humanity of others, makes murder ordinary.

So, Sefton Delmer, what are we going to do about it?

CHAPTER 5

INTO THE RIDICULOUS

At half past two on May 23, 1941, a small black limousine pulled into the drive of a two-storey red-brick house with arched gables and a conservatory in the village of Aspley Guise, Bedfordshire, on the outskirts of the Woburn Abbey estate. It was the sort of house that might be home to a local vicar or perhaps the headmaster of a local school—but now it was home to Sefton, Isabel and Delmer's first collaborator on "covert propaganda". Today was the debut recording of Delmer's new RU, his attempt to crack the seemingly impregnable edifice of Nazi propaganda.

Delmer emerged from inside and got into the car, accompanied by a man with a thin, long face, curious eyes and a noble-looking nose. The black limousine set off across the vast estate.

Welcome to Woburn Abbey—home to Britain's secret information war against the Nazis. Since 1550, it's been the ancestral seat of the dukes of Bedfordshire. Over the centuries the dukes had built up the original Tudor buildings to include a vast, white, winged Palladian palace, the second largest in England, with more than ninety rooms (including apartments reserved for frequently visiting royalty), walls plastered with paintings by Canaletto, Gainsborough and van Dyck, and surrounded by twenty-eight acres of landscaped gardens and three thousand acres of forests filled with deer and small South American ostriches and Javanese muntjacs that exposed their behinds to passers-by.[1] Over the centuries, different dukes of Bedfordshire had been prime ministers and trusted emissaries of the British Crown. However, the current incumbent was different: he wrote articles in far-right journals urging peace with Hitler and authored leaflets sent to British soldiers with titles like "Have Britons Brains". The only reason that Britain's fourth-richest man had not been interned was that the secret services considered him inept. The duke must have been somewhat disappointed that before his death in 1940, his father had lent the estate to the British government for its propaganda operations.[2]

By early 1941, the Woburn operation had been running for a year. In the main house, heavy Victorian furniture was jumbled with typewriting tables and steel filing cabinets below portraits of the Russell family by old masters. Below them were departments dedicated to dreaming up rumours that would be spread through Axis countries— such as the "burning-sea" weapon story—departments designing leaflets to drop over enemy lines and departments forging Nazi documents, money and stamps. Émigrés from across occupied Europe wrote and edited newspapers to support resistance movements. French, Italian, German, Czech and Danish "resistance" stations were already up and running, although Delmer was about to utterly transform the field.

Robert Bruce Lockhart, who became head of the Political Warfare Executive (PWE) in 1941, thought that the staff included "many freaks, some genuine antiques, several fakes and a few geniuses".[3] The composition was "extraordinarily varied ... journalists, business men, advertising experts, school masters, authors, literary agents, farmers, barristers, stockbrokers, psychologists, university dons and a landscape gardener. ... On account of the shortage of men we relied for staff mainly on women who were in the majority. Two were expert propagandists who ran their own section with men under them."[4]

The staff could dress in civilian clothes, and they lived in small houses across the estate. Different groups of émigrés were forbidden from communicating with each other. Gin and claret fuelled the work late into the night. The secrecy, segregation and "continual preoccupation with enemy conditions combined to create a rather unreal mental atmosphere, one of the strangest the writer has ever experienced, there was more than a touch of madness about it", wrote David Garnett, the secretary of the PWE.[5] He was also a modernist author and member of the Bloomsbury Set; his first book was about cocaine addiction, and his second was a surrealist tale about a man who is suddenly transformed into a fox. Garnett would later write the official history of the PWE, which the government would then block from publication for fifty years because it revealed far too much about the blunders and backstabbing at Woburn.

For behind this eccentric, arcadian facade lurked many jealousies—and Delmer was about to be thrust into the middle of them.

Hugh Dalton, minister of Economic Warfare until 1941, described the staff at Woburn as "a mixed lot, with much talent and much temperament. . . . Most of them were continually active, and some were sleepless prima donnas. I found the atmosphere highly charged with personal rivalries."[6]

The rivalries were not just personal but also ideological: different factions had different ideas about how to engage enemy audiences. Many still put their faith in the "Good German". The "Sender der europäischen Revolution" (Station of European Revolution), the only operational German RU before Delmer's arrival, called for a left-wing revolt against Hitler. Its catchphrase was:

> *We call on the masses to political and social revolution!*
> *We fight for a Europe of peace!*
> *We win in a spirit of Freedom!*[7]

The exiled German Marxists at the Sender had important backers: Richard Crossman, head of all German-language propaganda put out by the British government, oversaw their work.

But Delmer didn't want to target any type of political idealism—that wasn't where he thought the system's vulnerabilities lay.

"I want no softies in my movement," Hitler had told Delmer in their very first interview at the Brown House in May 1931. "I want fanatics and idealists who are willing to risk their all for their cause." For Hitler, the "ideal" of National Socialism was to give yourself up for the higher cause of the Volk. As he wrote in *Mein Kampf*, "True idealism . . . is essentially the subordination of the interests and life of the individual to the interests and life of the community. . . . This feeling alone makes men voluntarily acknowledge that strength and power are entitled to take the lead and thus makes them a constituent particle in that order out of which the whole universe is shaped and formed." Hitler's aim was that "the individual renounces representing his personal opinion and his interest".[8]

People's motivations, however, were often a source of disappointment to the more ideological Nazis. Consider denunciations. The Nazis demanded that Germans report on one another for even vaguely seditious comments—which they duly did in vast numbers.[9] But according to the SS, only 24 percent made their denunciations for ideological reasons—most did so to get back at neighbours and colleagues they didn't like or whose homes or jobs they coveted. Some SS leaders were dismayed. They wanted the people to denounce in the name of ideology, not self-interest.[10]

It was the lack of idealism, rather than other virtuous ideals, that Delmer wanted to tap into. Hitler, Delmer told Ingrams, had once told him that "there is an inner pigdog in every man". "Pigdog" (*Schweinehund*) was a common enough insult in German at the time, a reference to one's weaker self. Instead of democratic aspirations, Delmer wanted to target this German pigdog: "We must appeal to the inner pigdog inside every German in the name of his highest patriotic ideals, give him a patriotic reason for doing what he would like to do from self-interest, talk to him about his Führer and his Fatherland and all that sort of thing, and at the same time inject some item of news into his mind which will make him think, and if possible act, in a way that is contrary to the efficient conduct of Hitler's war."[11] And for all the power of Goebbels's propaganda, the pigdog was sticking out its snout from beneath the veneer of Nazi "idealism".

As Britain refused to break under the Blitz, and as British bombers began to penetrate the skies over Berlin, the SD detailed how people were getting anxious that the war would never end. By November 1940, the SD reported that "personal economic worries" now gave rise to "discontented and sceptical thoughts".[12]

The target of the discontent was Nazi bureaucrats. Wehrmacht soldiers were seen as heroes—partly thanks to how they were portrayed by Goebbels's radio propaganda—but people's ire was taken out on the party members, who stayed safe on the home front while soldiers risked their lives. Whereas soldiers brought glorious victories and sacrifice, party members were responsible for enforcing the frustrations of daily life: they made sure that everyone was inside during blackouts; they decided which farmers would be called up and which not. You can sense people's irritation in the SD reports. Already in 1939, farmers in Franconia labelled Nazi Party functionaries as "shirkers". In 1940, in Würzburg, crowds would come and greet returning sailors and soldiers, but the same people didn't show up to events that the party held.[13] In Lower Franconia, people were "tired" of "ideological education" and were largely interested only in the Wehrmacht. By April 1941, the Würzburg SD relayed that Hitler was adored but that the Nazi Party bosses were seen as "little tin pot Gods alongside the Führer"; people were fed up with the "glorification of persons who would otherwise practically be nobodies".[14]

Delmer wanted to give a new label to this self-serving elite. Just as the Nazis had introduced terms like *Untermenschen* to define the enemy, Delmer would label this venal version of the party the *Parteikommune*: a community out for itself and at odds with the people. This approach was Goebbels's greatest fear. "If the English were to make a difference between the German people and ourselves, they could undoubtedly gain more," he worried in his diaries.[15]

Delmer had plenty of material to work with. In early 1941, rumours about Nazi corruption were rife: there were stories that Julius Streicher, editor of *Der Stürmer*, had fled across the border with 30 million *Reichsmarks* and that a senior Gauleiter had crossed the Swiss border with 22 million Reichsmarks confiscated from dissolved monasteries.[16] The Nazi Party had come to power complaining about corruption, so why were they, some Germans wondered, now living it up in plush hotels while ordinary people had to struggle? Why did the party build such absurdly grand buildings when many lived in poverty?

In a letter to Ingrams, Delmer wrote that "for talks, one of the best subjects is corruption of leaders. We should serve up inside dope which is new and true. Talks should strike a tough note frequently, should be rude and robustly abusive."[17]

Delmer's purpose in complaining of elite corruption was not to end it, but to further encourage this practice so detrimental to the Nazi system. "The station aims to strike at the roots of totalitarianism with individualistic sentiments," the director of country house HQ at Woburn, Rex Leeper, would explain later that year. "In order to accelerate the corruption of Germany it seeks to poison the souls of individual Germans by guiding their attention, under the pose of right-mindedness, to the pleasures and benefits of avarice, crime, greed, the lusts of the flesh and all the rest."[18] Delmer hoped that by having "a super patriotic platform from the new station we ought to be able to get across all manner of subversive rumour stories under a cover of nationalist patriotic clichés".[19] A strategy document in the declassified PWE archives summarised the aims for GS1—the code name for the new RU:

- We want to spread disturbing and disruptive news about the Germans which will induce them to distrust their government and disobey it, not so much from high-minded political motives as from ordinary human weakness (for which, however, we shall be delighted to provide a high-minded political excuse).
- We are making no attempt to build up a political following in Germany. We are not catering for idealists.
- Our politics are a stunt. We pretend we have an active following to whom we send news and instruction. The purpose of this is to provide ourselves with a platform from which to put over our stuff.
- We therefore make no attempt to provide our listeners with a political programme.
- GS1 by its organisation is able to get plenty of news from everywhere inside Hitler Europe, news which tends to show

directly, or (preferable indirectly), that every man for himself is the axiom every intelligent German should be following.[20]

The format of the radio station was also like nothing that the British had tried before. Delmer's idea was that as Germans surfed their shortwave radios, they would suddenly encounter what sounded like the "insider conversations of a clandestine military organisation". So instead of pushing content onto audiences aggressively, Delmer was allowing them to feel they had stumbled onto something quite by chance:

> Our listeners are intended to feel they are eavesdropping on the private wireless of a secret organisation, whose members presumably know what the programme of the organisation is. What the listener knows of this programme he picks up by studying the news that we put over. He finds that we are anti-Communists who once thought Hitler pretty good, fought alongside him in fact, but are now appalled at the corruption, godlessness, profiteering, place-hunting, selfishness, clique rivalries, party-above-the-law system which the party has instituted.[21]

Instead of strong-arming people with opinions, Delmer was titillating their curiosity. For thinkers like Arendt, the Nazis had undermined the very sense that you could ever discover truth, that truth even mattered. But Delmer thought that the Nazis' propaganda grip was not quite total. One needed to kindle the audience's desire to think for themselves again, to fall in love with finding facts. Even the name of Delmer's broadcaster, GS1 (Gustav Siegfried Eins), was designed to make people wonder. What did it stand for? *Generalstab* (General Staff) 1? Or maybe *Geheimsender* (secret transmitter) 1? In actuality, GS1 didn't stand for anything; it was just there to stimulate enquiry.

The soldier sending these subversive messages was going to be "of the old Prussian school, who would use the transmitter to give members of the organisation his caustic and salaciously outspoken views of what was going on . . . while being spiced with plenty of inside information. The station, in fact, would seek to be a nightly demonstration of a growing split between the conservative elements of the army and the radicals of the Nazi party."[22]

The nameless leader of this organisation would be known simply as *der Chef,* the title that Delmer heard members of Hitler's entourage call him during the flying tours. *Der Chef* would speak like a foul-mouthed Prussian soldier and have all his racism and resentments too. Churchill he would insult as a "drunk Jew". Delmer was rather proud of insulting Churchill this way. No German would ever suspect, he thought, English propaganda of insulting its own leadership quite so strongly. In Joyce's Workers' Challenge the Nazi ideology, its anti-Semitism and Hitler worship, still shone through. That was part of the reason why its ratings, as well as those of the other stations at Büro Concordia, had ultimately collapsed. When the Home Intelligence Service reviewed their figures in 1942, they found them minuscule. The number of people listening to Lord Haw-Haw had similarly plummeted with the horrors of the Blitz—his guffawing at the sufferings of the English wasn't funny any more.[23]

Delmer wouldn't make the same mistakes. He demanded speech as genuine as the underworld swindlers in Reinhardt's production of *Der Biberpelz.* But he needed a speaker who could deliver it with the necessary vitriol. And here Delmer had a problem. His companion in the limousine was to play *der Chef.* And as Delmer was about to discover, it was one thing to write *der Chef*—quite another to make him speak.

• • • ▬▬ ▬▬ ▬▬ • • •

AFTER A TWENTY-MINUTE DRIVE, the limousine delivered Delmer and his companion to their destination. Delmer had expected some sort of studio. Instead, he found himself by "what looked like a London stockbroker's more than comfortable country retreat. Rhododendron bushes, spreading chestnuts and a few venerable monkey puzzle trees hid a lawn from which came the click of a croquet mallet."

Inside, Delmer and his companion entered a book-lined drawing room where a blonde woman was playing Mozart on the piano. When she noticed them, she stopped. "G.3?" she enquired brightly. "We have everything ready for you, if you will follow me." She led them into the billiards room. The table was covered. The windows were draped with curtains as heavy as the ones resting on a theatre stage before a performance: "Three chromium plated RCA microphones twinkled at us invitingly under a trip of ultra-modern fluorescent lights. One microphone was suspended from the ceiling, a second topped an adjustable stand, the third stood on a very business-like desk with two chairs in front of it."[24]

The man meant to play *der Chef* was Peter Hans Seckelmann, a Berliner who had earned his way as a journalist and writer of detective novels. He was also a talented tennis player (in 1982, in his eighties and living in Zurich, he won the Swiss Senior Tennis Championships). He had arrived in England in February 1936 with his Russian wife, Margrit Melnikova Schneidermann, and announced he wanted to stay permanently because he was angered by the treatment of Jews under the Nazis. In London he worked as a literary agent and the representative of a German publishing company. His MI5 file describes him as "anti-Nazi, quiet, serious, sensible". The agent who interviewed him says, "He impressed me extremely favourably. Although he claims to be Lutheran he is I think clearly of Jewish origin . . . he is quiet spoken, not in the least bombastic, and has a delightful personality. I feel quite sure that he considers himself no longer to have any ties with Germany at all. He seems to be one of the very few Germans who are not only loyal to us, but who have severed all connections with Germany."[25]

When the war began, Seckelmann joined the Pioneer Corps, the military unit open to émigrés, where he rose to the rank of corporal and risked his life digging up and defusing unexploded German bombs. Not content with this job, he volunteered to be parachuted behind the German lines with Special Operations 2 (SO2), where he caught the attention of Leonard Ingrams, who passed him on to Delmer, whose ears were enticed: "His voice seemed to me just right for Der Chef as I envisaged him, virile and resonant with just the right trace of Berlin drawl which I had found so often in the speech of Junker officers of the Kaiser's guards regiments."[26]

His drawl may have been right—but that didn't mean this "quiet, serious, sensible" man, whom everyone described as "gentle" and "polite", could instantly transform into the steaming anger of *der Chef*. Delmer wanted him to be a foul-mouthed monster of resentment.

Our first transcripts of the show appear in September 1941. They were recorded and then quickly, crudely translated by US State Department monitoring teams that followed Nazi media and were convinced this was a genuine German station. The transcripts are littered with guesses about the supposed location of the station (France? Germany?), and the rude words are often demurely replaced with stars or even comments like "there follow a string of obscenities" or "uses a vulgar expression".

On September 9, the first State Department transcript we have, *der Chef* lamented the decrease in butter and meat rations, attacked the minister in charge of rations as incompetent and complained: "It's a pity we can't cut our meat from the buttocks of the SS."[27]

On September 16 he complained that "France is filled with saboteurs and spies. No submarine can leave the port without the knowledge of those shit Britains and shit Americans. The shit Gestapo is sleeping in the day and drinking in excess and fornicating in the night together with the spies and saboteurs." And then he went after the head of the Gestapo in Paris: "It starts with Otto Abetz. Abetz, don't think we don't know about your Mademoiselle Nicolle Bardeau about this [uses a very vulgar word] whom he supports in the Rue de Barry. We know everything, even the price of the apartment and the Rolls Royce. Yes sir! She needs an English car, this [uses a very vulgar expression]."[28]

Delmer delicately says that in the early shows, the "corporal had not been able to get the hang of what I wanted".[29] Robert Walmsley, a senior PWE civil servant who headed the division dedicated to analysing the impact of Nazi propaganda on Germans, put it more bluntly: "The 'corporal', probably one of the most successful 'voices' in Europe, filled Delmer with such despair that on the twelfth day he was on the point of giving him up altogether."[30]

Delmer never revealed the details of this torturous process. Ellic Howe, a PWE specialist in forgery, tells us that "der Chef's broadcasts resembled small scale theatrical productions and even minor details of presentation were discussed and rehearsed".[31] One imagines Delmer and Seckelmann rehearsing: Delmer goading, coaxing, forcing, despairing and becoming more irritated as he tries to squeeze Seckelmann's innate gentleness into his vision of *der Chef*. Sometimes I imagine them in the billiards room, at other times striding and arguing as they cross the Woburn estate among the rabbits and muntjacs showing their behinds.

Der Chef's disgust would have to shade into revulsion when the material turned to what Delmer referred to in his notes as "sexual corruption": such as stories of how the SS were pawing and pestering soldiers' wives on the home front.[32] When the Nazis took over the monastery of Münsterschwarzach to use as a military hospital (a fact), *der Chef* spun out a lurid tale of sexual depravity (a fantasy):

> Two hundred SS men marched into the monastery and took possession of it in the name of a committee which rescues children. Father Winnibild has been put under arrest and has not been seen since. A bawdy house was made out of the monastery for the SS men and their whores. The serene gaiety of the rooms incited these lewd beasts to parodies on things which are sacred to millions of Germans for centuries. The holy mass gowns are used as sheets and the women wear precious lace tunics made out of choir robes with nothing underneath them. These pigs. Like this they go into the chapel and drink liquor out of the holy vessels and what happens then . . .

Here the transcription breaks off, the State Department official seemingly too shy to give details of the orgy. Then it continues:

> By this Godless harlotry the German monasteries are defiled. How can honest German soldiers fight and risk their lives in a destructive battle when these blasphemers at home do whatever they like and take over one cloister after another for their filthy purposes.[33]

Der Chef was outraged at all the corruption and perversion, but he was always returning to these topics in the way that tabloids show disgust at depravity and thus give their readers the excuse to enjoy it.

Here was Delmer's approach in miniature: acting appalled at something that was actually titillating to his audience, while at the same time breaking the taboo on insulting the SS and deepening the rift between the party and the army, the party and the people.

When British bombers hit Magdeburg (already an indictment of the German air defence), *der Chef* reported that they hit the canalisation system and how, because of the party's incompetence, typhoid spread. Seckelmann would have needed to find just the right level of anger at Reischle of the Margarine Union, who had been making margarine out of machine oil from decayed fish and causing dysentery. *Der Chef*'s Germany was an inverse of the cohesive Volksgemeinschaft: a world where different government departments fought against each other and forgot about the people, and where the healthy Nazi body, and by extension its body politic, was infected by burst sewage systems spreading disease and margarine made out of rotten fish.[34]

Johannes Reinholz was the first new speaker to join Delmer and Seckelmann. He was a journalist who had fled Berlin with his Jewish wife in 1939. In Germany he had written for the conservative newspapers of the Prussian military aristocracy, the sort of environment that *der Chef* would have emerged from. He was also the stepson of one of Berlin's most famous cabaret impresarios, the Jewish Rudolf Nelson, whose songs were famous for their sexual innuendo. In "The Shop Girl" Nelson sang of a sexual encounter in a woman's fashion store with a female sales assistant who undresses as she passes through the rows of clothes: "Past the blouses and the dresses, past the petticoats and past the undergarments, and then and then came she."[35]

Reinholz, this son of kinky cabaret and Prussian militarism, now took on the writing of the scripts. He also played the role of "the adjutant" who introduced *der Chef*. Soon, more stars of the German cabaret scene would join Delmer. Perhaps this is one way to characterise *der Chef*: the last great Berlin cabaret act, subverting the Nazis from abroad.

Delmer believed that the act was coming together: Reinholz's "metallic baritone and his clipped accent, pregnant with generations of heel-clicking, goose-stepping, command-barking Pomeranian forebears gave just the right military tone to the station. And when he announced 'Es spricht der Chef . . . The Chief speaks,' I could almost see Hitler himself walking gravely and stiffly up to the microphone in the small interval the corporal allowed to elapse before, solemn and deep-voiced, he went into his act."[36]

Howe wrote that "working with Reinholz gave the corporal a confidence he had lacked when he was on his own with Delmer". A relieved Delmer wrote, "Now, at last, he began to get the knack of how to handle his voice at the microphone. With every transmission he was growing more and more into the role of 'Der Chef'." Finally, the corporal volunteered to write his own script, "a masterpiece, caustic, witty, even moving. Those salty, vividly impudent Berlinese phrases I had hoped for after my first conversations now at last began to blossom forth in all sorts of unexpected places."[37]

• • • ▬▬ ▬▬ ▬▬ • • •

EVERY MONTH, DER CHEF's naming and shaming became more specific: "Mrs Schmidt of Vienna, Maxing Street 47, has informed the police that the following things were stolen from her pantry: three dozen sausages, five Westphalian hams, two pails of Danish butter, 450 preserved eggs." At a time of mass rationing, this detailed list of luxury food was designed to make audiences both lick their lips and rumble with jealousy. "Mrs Schmidt is not an ordinary woman. Oh no! She is the wife of the Minister Dr Paul Schmidt [uses a very vulgar word]."[38]

The names and even the foodstuffs were all, or almost all, real. In midsummer 1941 Delmer's team had been joined by Max Braun as head of intelligence. Braun had been the leader of the Socialist Party in Saarland, where he had resoundingly lost a referendum to Hitler in 1935. He had fled to France, where he led the Socialist Party in exile, then to Casablanca, and on to Britain, where he joined Delmer's team. He still dreamed of a better Germany. He didn't believe that Germans, as some in the British establishment argued, were somehow destined to be fascist. He still believed that millions of Germans were secret opponents of Hitler, although they had been silenced by terror, and millions of others were in favour of the Nazis only on the surface. While in England he wrote a manifesto for a vision of post-war Germany: demilitarised, with a new education system, integrated into a larger European order, respectful of its neighbours and forgetting any aspiration for a "greater Germany".[39] He must have known this was a far-off dream, but it was a vision that was uncannily accurate about what happened after the war. However, it's not a vision that Braun would ever be able to see: he died in July 1945. His work at Woburn would be his last battle for a better Germany, and he was utterly ruthless and meticulous in using all his knowledge and skills to undermine the Nazi propaganda.

Braun started his day with a cold bath and then pored over reports from agents of the Socialist Party that gave detailed accounts of the mood in Germany and among trade unionists and factory workers up until 1940.[40] He combined these reports with stories from national and local German newspapers, and assembled a catalogue with thousands of personal biographies, from the Führer down to local Nazi officials. The more facts Delmer amassed, the more truthful der Chef's screeds were. When he added fabrications, he insisted that it had to be done with utmost care. Whereas the Nazis wanted to obliterate the difference between truth and lies, Delmer's careful approach to fibbing accepted the primacy of facts, respected reality even as he twisted it. "Never lie by accident, only deliberately" was the creed of his operation.[41]

A lot of the time Delmer didn't need to lie: the truth was damning in itself. Intercepted private letters from Germany to America were another source for Braun's files. Genevra Wolft-Limper, the American-born wife of a German industrialist in Cologne, simply adored telling her friend, Mrs Ruth Stradling of Nevada, all about the lavish parties she and her husband hosted and visited. Der Chef revelled in outrage as he revealed how Nazi comrade Herr Wilken-kampner treated his guests to a magnificent sugar-baked cake in the shape of Cologne Cathedral—just as ordinary Germans had their sugar rations cut.[42]

Delmer also had access to another source. After German prisoners were taken captive by the British, they were imprisoned in camps where microphones hidden in the walls recorded their conversations. The intelligence agencies thus gleaned important information about military operations. They then passed the transcripts to Delmer, who would plunder them for the latest gossip, details of daily life and turns of phrase and attitudes.

The recordings gave Delmer the details that made *der Chef*'s shows feel so genuine. Though we don't know the specific extracts he read and used, the available archives reveal much that would have delighted him.

> "I paid 60 francs in a brothel at Brest," one POW complained to another.
>
> "Go on with you! At Brest, at GRÜNSTEIN'S, on the corner there, you don't pay more than 25 francs—that's the usual charge."[43]

They also confirmed that many soldiers were sceptical of the party but were still virulent anti-Semites, just like *der Chef*:

> "At any rate, I have still no idea of where the Nazis are going to land us in the end. That swine with his brown shirt!" one soldier told another in a typical exchange recorded in early 1942, before adding: "Our racial policy is excellent, also the Jewish question, and the entire legislation for preserving the purity of German blood. That law is really first-class."[44]

The POWs rarely mentioned the Volksgemeinschaft. The Wehrmacht was their community. They delighted in detailing the order of military hierarchy, the organisation of their units, how their wonderful weapons worked, their promotions and awards. Delmer's mission to pitch the Wehrmacht against the Parteikommune was on point.

But Delmer wasn't just interested in causing rifts. He believed in propaganda that changed behaviour. "[GS1] has never incited directly to action," Delmer explained to his superiors. "It has spoken only in such a way that the idea of action is planted in the mind of the subject without letting him see that he is being influenced at all." For example, Delmer's programmes had tried the following:

> · To make people take habit-forming sleeping drugs in air raids. It was described how the SS—who ought to know—took

Veramon tablets before going to sleep (Veramon is habit forming).

· To induce panic buying of clothes. GS1 described how people were already rushing to buy clothes because they had heard that large numbers of extra ration cards were being printed.[45]

Garnett described this focus on behavioural over attitudinal change as "revolutionary": "Delmer and Ingrams had always favoured the kind of propaganda which aims to induce action on the part of the listener. What he believed seemed to them of quite secondary importance if he could be made to act in the desired manner."[46]

Der Chef would act appalled at some behaviour that many people were doing, such as buying up clothes on the black market, thus normalising it even as he condemned it, and making his listeners feel that it was a safe thing to do. Most people, Delmer reckoned, want to stay in the collective rather than stand out and take personal risks.

Some of the early efforts to influence behaviour were, shall we say, ambitious. On August 16, 1941, Delmer reported that *der Chef* had run a story "about a pyromaniac who is using the British bombing as a cover for setting houses on fire himself for his perverse sexual enjoyment. Object of this is to encourage pyromania." It's unclear whether this had any success.[47]

And although Delmer may have been a pioneer in prioritising behavioural over attitudinal change at Woburn, he certainly wasn't alone. One of the reports from the "SIBS" (rumours) department from the same year explains that "the following SIBS are designed to encourage suicide. . . . Suicide is notoriously catching, and reports of particular methods used lead to imitation."[48] The British spread rumours that bridges over the Rhine were being patrolled by police after dusk because of the increase in suicides, and how after the bombing of Aachen a woman threw her children on the smoking ruins of her house and threw herself after them.[49]

When I first read these underhanded encouragements to suicide among civilians, I paused in shock. Irrespective of whether such specious methods were effective, did "we" really do such things? Of course

we did. And in our firebombing of German cities we went much further. This was a war to the death against a genocidal enemy. No holds
were barred.

● ● ● ▬▬ ▬▬ ▬▬ ● ● ●

THE BRITISH INTELLIGENCE SERVICES could not do detailed polling in
Germany to measure *der Chef*'s "ratings", but they tried to piece together
the success of their propaganda through what they called "come backs",
combining "evidence of reception" from different sources: prisoners of
war, British spies who talked to German officials, opened letters and
journalists in Germany. There were forty such "come backs" from
the first year of the radio programme's existence. Thirty-six of them
assumed that the station was in Germany.[50] The others suspected that
the station was in England but then dismissed the idea: "We listened to
him regularly until end of last year," the *Times* correspondent in Swe-
den reported, "and like others, came to the conclusion that it emanated
from a group of naval officers . . . it was once said he was an Englishman, but I personally cannot believe that."

Der Chef, judging from the intelligence agencies' sources, was an
instant success. As early as 1941, a "reliable" German source from Swe-
den affirmed this:

> This station is extraordinarily interesting, and there is no doubt
> that it is being freely listened to and has a great effect. For the
> Allies and all opponents of the Nazi regime it is simply price-
> less. It destroys in the German people their confidence in the
> Party apparatus, partly even their confidence in the military
> leadership. The organiser of the station must be in touch with
> the German army and in touch with oppositional Army circles.
> He must have an extensive apparatus and a pretty good internal
> German information service. The language of these broadcasts
> is of the kind met with in the lowest pot-houses, and that fre-
> quently broadcasts contain certain pornographic accounts of
> the orgies of Nazi bosses, may offend aesthetic ears, but the fact

is the broadcasts are listened to everywhere, above all by the Wehrmacht. One may say confidently this station is the most listened to in the whole of Germany.[51]

I assume that this means the most-listened-to non-Nazi station—but it's still a great compliment—and it's repeated by other sources:

> A German refugee in Scotland reports that GS1 was much listened to in Germany. German travellers reported that it could be regarded as one of the most popular stations. A German business man described recently how its bulletins are spread. Nobody is willing to admit he listens to GS1, but one is constantly being asked by acquaintances "have you heard the story that . . ." and then follows the news that GS1 broadcast the previous morning.

"This type of broadcast is unbelievably effective in attracting German listeners," wrote the US naval attaché, unaware that the station was actually British. "The obscenity is more than Rabelaisian." Captured German soldiers were impressed with the amount that *der Chef* knew about goings-on inside their units.[52]

Der Chef's carefully implanted pieces of disinformation took on lives of their own. An early *der Chef* story claimed that faeces were being used in the production of margarine. Soon enough, German prisoners were mentioning this as if it were reality.

Delmer was especially delighted to read in a Kiel newspaper about a run on clothing stores as women cashed in their clothing coupons. Six weeks previously, *der Chef* had started a rumour that party officials had secret information there was about to be a shortage of woollen textiles, and now their wives, these "traitorous whores", were exchanging their coupons for clothes before ordinary Germans could. To Delmer's "great satisfaction", the editor of the newspaper repeated *der Chef*'s rumour, bemoaning that "if everyone behaves like this, there will be nothing left for anyone, and the clothing coupons will be valueless".[53]

Der Chef had rapidly become popular with German audiences. But what is it they heard? For although we have many transcripts of *der Chef's* shows, we have very few recordings.

Whenever I read the texts, I'm always rolling them through my mouth, playing with the different ways they could have been performed. The language is so over-the-top, the bawdiness so burlesque, it's hard not to read them almost as satire. But it wasn't meant as pure satire. The German Service of the BBC had shows with absurd Nazi characters who openly poked fun at the regime. But with *der Chef* the listeners were meant to consider him to be genuine, and indeed often did so.

One of the few recordings we have is from November 19, 1941, when Bruce Lockhart recalled, "the King and Queen made an official visit to Woburn. . . . A special show—a kind of March of Time of our propaganda activities—was staged for their benefit. Their Majesties stayed for over three hours and seemed to enjoy the proceedings. Their visit was a great stimulus to the Woburn organisation and undoubtedly gave a fillip to our propaganda."[54] In this recording we not only hear *der Chef*, but Delmer also explains what he was trying to achieve with the style of the performance—which carried as much meaning as the message. It also shows just how different Delmer's approach was compared to the other nineteen stations under the PWE's control at the time.

• • • ▬▬ ▬▬ ▬▬ • • •

THE AUDIO ARCHIVE OPENS with the crackle of the record spinning, a grand blast of trumpets and a drum roll, then a commentator announces: "The Political Warfare Executive Humbly Presents the Free Voices of Europe. A picture in sound of the use of a new force in your Majesty's Service."

Then comes the slightly bored voice of David Bowes-Lyon, the queen consort's brother and the PWE's representative in America: "I'm here to present one of Britain's secret armies, an army that strikes from within enemy lines." Bowes-Lyon introduces each radio show one by one.

First comes Colonel Sutton, director of broadcasting to France. "We are trying to do two things with our French stations," says the colonel, sounding very earnest and very precise. "First to prevent collaboration with the enemy, next to reawaken French morale and inspire resistance." Sutton's four French stations each targeted different sections of society: a trade unionist who appealed to the working class, one for the "the man in the street", a resistance station for supporters of General de Gaulle, and—the one Sutton seems most proud of—an actual Catholic priest who once had a parish in Lille: "He is genuinely devout and believes every word he says." Sutton details how in his daily sermon the priest asks his listeners to get down on their knees and pray with him: "This makes the listener obey the voice, and makes the listener more receptive to the message contained in the prayer. By going down on his knees the listener becomes an active ally of this anti-German priest."

One after another, the heads of the language sections outline their tactics.

The four Italian stations are full of "passionate anti-fascist voices".

The Norwegian one gives an ABC of passive resistance: "Telephone operators have been told to give Germans wrong numbers, waiters to give inefficient service to German officers; chamber maids have been told to give leaky hot water bottles whenever Germans are in the house."

Ralph Murray, who ran five south-eastern Europe stations, struck a darker tone. "In Croatia we are frankly murderous. Threatening the assassination of the Prime Minister Pavelić, for having sold Dalmatia to his Italian paymasters."

In Romania, Murray relates, his station helped campaign against the pro-German president Antonescu. Murray's station called on people to dress in bloodstained sheets and walk through the streets of Bucharest, reminding people of the Romanian soldiers sent to die alongside Germans and exhorting the public to vote against Antonescu, which they duly did. Spectral motifs were common in Murray's work. His Bulgarian radio has a "blood curdling ghost voice" to announce it (when he plays a snippet, it sounds like something from a haunted house at an amusement park).

When it's Delmer's turn to speak, however, the whole tenor changes. If all the other presenters put up a serious facade, Delmer is immediately comedic. He opens with a conversation between a British spy in Stockholm and a "man from the German propaganda ministry", putting on a ridiculous German accent when he speaks the lines of the

Propaganda Ministry employee: "Ze Brrritish are gut at prrropoganda, but not az gut az ze Germans. Why, even ze anti-Nazi prrropoganda iz done better by ze Germans zemselves."

The man from the Propaganda Ministry then goes on to describe how the popular *Chef*, who he is convinced is actually German, must have protection from the highest army officials and how the British should recruit him because *der Chef* is better than any anti-Nazi propaganda the British make. "You and I know," Delmer continued in his usual English, "that *der Chef* is not in fact in Germany, but just a few miles from this house."

Delmer then plays a clip of the programme. When presenting to the king he chose a section with minimal mentions of sex and only a limited number of obscenities. The clip is also a lament. It tells of the destruction of German cities by the RAF, demands that the Luftwaffe respond by bombing London, accuses the Nazi elites of sitting on their arses, of being full of secret Bolsheviks, Jews, traitors, more interested in their brothels than in the victims of British bombs. The anger gains its power from being constantly restrained, with the odd swear words erupting like little violent geysers, just the way that the truth about the bombings and feelings towards the party are bursting through censorship and repression.

When you listen, it doesn't feel quite satirical, but rather ever so gently exaggerated, using Nazi propaganda clichés with attacks on Bolsheviks, decadence and foreign influence.

Der Chef's aim, Delmer explained to the king, was to subvert Nazi propaganda by carrying "Nazi ideology just one phrase further into the ridiculous, where it is harmful to Germany".

"Into the ridiculous, where it is harmful to Germany." What can this mean? Most simply, it means using the hatreds and paranoias of Nazi ideology against the Nazis themselves, seeing Bolsheviks and Jews under every bed, accusing the party leaders of being the things they had incited hate against. Elsewhere in his memoirs, Delmer describes how his aim was to reverse engineer the language of Nazi anti-Semitism back onto the Nazi leadership themselves: "Our stories were peopled with Burgomasters, District Leaders, Local Group leaders and even

Cell leaders. We spread over them a slime of obloquy as foul as that which they themselves had spread over the Jews."[55]

But it also seems to mean a way of saying things, a style. In his presentation, Delmer played the king the honky-tonk piano tune that served as the introductory music to *der Chef*'s programme. This signature tune took the official intro music of the news programme on the official Nazi radio station and then continued it slightly out of tune. This musical touch, Delmer stressed, was emblematic of "taking Nazi ideology into the ridiculous, where it is harmful to Germany". In this musical comparison, pushing "into the ridiculous" seems less about ideological reverse engineering, and more about adopting a style that brings out the absurdity of the original Nazi news tune, but without quite slipping into satire.

Have you ever experienced that sense when you suddenly become aware of the artificial, constructed, mannered nature of the way you speak, the language you are using, how you use that language? Or have you ever glimpsed your reflection in a mirror you hadn't noticed and didn't have time to set a pose to—and noticed just how forced your behaviour is? And in that moment you are paralysed by the realisation that all the times when you thought you were you, you were actually acting without knowing it.

Or have you ever looked back at your old social media posts months or years after you have made them? Posts that perhaps felt so passionately made at the time, and representing your true feelings, but now you realise how artificial they sound?

One of Delmer's insights was how people perform their propaganda roles, how they are acting even when they might seem to be full of passion and "hypnotised". The way people in crowds all imitate one another is even more apparent online, where you can clearly track how key words, sentiments, likes, shares and retweets snowball as people follow and parrot one another. How Delmer would have enjoyed poking fun at the way we imitate others while thinking we represent ourselves on social media: we post pictures and poses and confessions that are meant to express our individuality, but this only brings out how we use the same stock phrases, poses and expressions as others.

In all the propaganda parables in his memoirs, in so many of his articles, Delmer keeps coming back to the performative element in every social role: whether that's "being English" or playing at being a war correspondent or "acting" Nazi. If Le Bon (and Freud) compared mass psychology to hypnotism, a state of mind where you stop being aware of what you're doing or saying altogether, and Goebbels and Hitler's aim was to put that theory into practice, then Delmer's method was to prick you awake by making you aware that there was an element of artifice in everything you do. And in that moment of sudden self-awareness, you could, if you had enough motivation, depart from the power of their propaganda.

This is not the same as satire—which can be so aggressive and overt in its attack, but can also make those under attack feel defensive. Satire can reduce people's fear of an intimidating enemy, make the monster look small and pitiful. This can embolden an opposition that feels weak. But it can also belittle those who, for whatever reason, followed that leader in the first place. *Der Chef*, on the other hand, was gently encouraging you into becoming aware of the ridiculousness of Nazi ideology, without ever openly attacking you.

It was quite a twist that this subtle subversion was being performed by Jews, the victims of the rhetoric, more of whom were joining Delmer's team.

In early 1942 Reinholz was replaced in his role as the adjutant by Frank Lynder. Lynder came from a family of Jewish booksellers in Bremen.[56] His mother, in an attempt to integrate, had him baptised, and Lynder found out he was Jewish only when he was very young and the kids on his street had chased him and screamed "Jew" in his direction as they tried to beat him up. He raced away breathless on his scooter and back at home, a panting mess, asked his mother what a "Jew" was: "Am I one, and is it bad?" She told him to forget it. He never did, and when the Nazis came to power, he wasn't allowed to forget it either. He moved to London in 1937. His mother stayed. Her German friends no longer talked to her, but she was sure she could weather the Nazis: "No one is going to harm an old lady, a woman like me," she told her son as they parted. Delmer hired Lynder partly because his Bremen accent had a "nautical ring to it" and cast him in *der Chef*'s show. So Lynder was playing an anti-Semite, even as he waited anxiously for news of his mother's fate.

What was it like for Jews to work on a show counterfeiting Nazi propaganda? Delmer had once delighted in playing a Nazi while inspecting the SA with Röhm; it seemed to give him a sense of power over them. Did Seckelmann, Reinholz and Lynder experience an even more intense version? From horror when they first put the racist foulness in their mouths, through disgust, and then, weirdly, power, laughter, even the strange pleasure that comes with using your enemies' strength against them?

Whatever their feelings, the PWE's "evidence of reception" indicates that audiences were drawn to their performances. But Delmer's enemies weren't going to let him succeed too easily. For just as *der Chef* was starting to grow its audience, the programme came under attack, and Delmer's continued presence at Woburn would suddenly be in jeopardy.

CHAPTER 6

THAT BEASTLY PORNOGRAPHIC ORGANISATION

At the same time as he was building up *der Chef* in 1941 and early 1942, Sefton Delmer was, as was his wont, living a double life, fighting his duel with Goebbels and German propaganda from two fronts, overt and covert.

Most of the week, Delmer was at Woburn, working on *der Chef* and recording in the billiards room. In the evenings, the dinners at the house went on late into the night, with Delmer brainstorming ideas for programmes, jokes, dirty stories and anecdotes. The German staff members were never allowed to leave the Woburn estate without permission, not even to go to the local pub or to visit the others' houses, as it might compromise their security. They were locked into Delmer's creative process.

Once a week Delmer would disappear from Woburn, this confined space where "no holds were barred", and head down to London to the BBC studios. He was still giving his talks on the German Service of the BBC, but his mission had changed. His job now was to listen to the weekly political sermon preached by Hans Fritzsche on the Reich's radio, then respond with his own as quickly as possible. Delmer didn't believe in the power of opinion pieces on the BBC generally, but this was different. It was a radio fencing match, and that drama drew German listeners over to the BBC.

Hans Fritzsche was no mean opponent. His career had begun in the more traditional national conservative media that competed with the Nazis in the early 1930s. He was already head of news at the national radio when, in 1933, Goebbels persuaded Fritzsche to stay on under the new regime, partly because he wanted someone who could unite different conservative voters. Fritzsche was no fanatic frothing at the mouth. He was sarcastic and generally relaxed, floating elegantly above the ideologies of narrow party politics. Nor did he shy away from the language "of the man in the street". He called Churchill a pig. Duff Cooper, the minister for information, was the "stupidest Minister in the World".[1]

Fritzsche had a whole publicity machine behind him, orchestrated by Goebbels, who built a broadcasting cult around him, just as he had with Hitler on a national scale. There were books by Fritzsche and lecture tours by Fritzsche. Newspapers eulogised Fritzsche's broadcasts. One journalist described him like the mythical Norse blacksmith Wieland, fashioning his words into weapons of perfection (although what the personable Fritzsche really liked, the article continued, was to hold his daughter's hand on walks). The *Kölnische Illustriertre Zeitung* published a poem in Fritzsche's honour:

When Fritzsche talks it becomes silent in every room . . .
    At these moments the radio becomes as much in demand
as light in darkness.
    Are they happy, those Brits, when they listen to Fritzsche
for fifteen minutes?[2]

Fritzsche's talks delighted in debunking British propaganda. According to different estimates by the British government and the SS, between one and three million Germans listened to the BBC in 1943—a more generous figure than the Gestapo's estimate of one million in 1941—although doing so was dangerous.[3] Fritzsche's aim was to dig a moat of doubt between the British and their German audience. He had a research team, a *Schnelldienst* (speed service), which would dredge up any mistake the BBC or British spokespeople made, and he would then riff on these errors to show the superiority of the Nazis. Fritzsche and the Reich's radio revelled in moments when the BBC slipped up and claimed, for example, that the RAF had hit a German railway station that in fact they had missed, or when the BBC claimed the RAF hit Berlin, when their planes hadn't even reached the capital.[4]

But the Nazis didn't just wait for the British to make a mistake. Goebbels liked to plant false stories: that the Nazis had executed ten thousand people in Prague, for example, or that Foreign Minister von Ribbentrop had been fired in a purge. He would then feed these to newspapers in neutral countries, wait for the BBC to pick them up, and then have Fritzsche scold the BBC for telling lies.[5]

The *Picture Post* profiled Delmer, describing him as being like a prime boxer, all bear-like 17.5 stone of him, his coat off, hair thinning, pacing up and down the BBC studios. He had just listened to a broadcast by Fritzsche and was now preparing his reply. He had two hours before his broadcast. He tried one opening sentence, then another, rejected three more, and then, finally, after forty-five minutes,

> his arms outstretched over his head, eyes gleaming, Delmer strides towards the typewriter, towers over the secretary and enunciates with incredible gusto a tortuous complex of words. He repeats the sentence, rolling the words into his mouth, until at last he achieves the right rhythm.
>
> Countless Germans listen to him because he talks to them as human beings in a voice that might belong to one of themselves.[6]

"Fritzsche, Fritzsche, you forgot something," Delmer teased in one of the few recordings of the show that survive, facetiously wondering why Fritzsche hadn't mentioned the failed RAF raids on Germany in his last broadcast.[7] Could it be because Fritzsche didn't want to admit to Germans that the RAF usually succeeded? When Fritzsche looked up at the night sky, what else did he see there apart from glimmering stars? In these nights of deadly RAF raids, the night sky didn't reveal just your horoscope.

Avoiding the truth about Allied bombardments was an Achilles heel of the Reich's radio. Fritzsche's listeners would write in letters complaining that while the Reich's radio star taunted the supposedly meagre results of RAF bombardments, the truth was that their cities were being devastated.[8] The BBC, unlike the Reich's radio, was honest about Britain's setbacks, a deliberate editorial policy to win trust. Delmer listed British defeats in North Africa, displaying a candour that must have been impressive to German listeners.[9] But this self-criticism also meant he could be trusted to tell the truth about the German lack of success on the Eastern Front—Hitler had claimed that victory would be secured in 1941, but there seemed no end in sight: "For eleven Tuesdays one after another I sit here and wait for your take on how the Winter war in Russia is going, Fritzsche, and you never speak about it, you never speak about it."[10]

Listeners' letters warned Fritzsche that with the Russian campaign going so wrong, "it was making it easy for Delmer to make you into a laughing stock" and that he had better give up his show.[11] A British "evidence of reception" report claimed that these anti-Fritzsche BBC programmes helped make Delmer "the most popular broadcaster in Germany".[12]

Goebbels was keeping careful track of Delmer's attacks on his pet presenter. The Reich's minister for propaganda was stuck in the classic dilemma: debunk Delmer directly, and he augmented his stature; ignore him, and he let his messages proliferate unopposed. He chose the latter. Goebbels ordered "that the name of Sefton Delmer . . . is not to be mentioned again in the German press or on the foreign language service. With his accurate knowledge of German conditions Delmer tries to invest his very rude insults with an air of great verisimilitude." Goebbels would stick to the policy of not mentioning Delmer in the media, even as he worried about his success to his underlings: "Delmer has got Fritzsche on the run [auf dem Kieker]," he said in a daily meeting, but "we should not do him the honour of responding".[13]

Delmer's success was a symptom of a bigger problem for Goebbels: his supposedly all-powerful propaganda was starting to show its first strains as the invasion of Russia went from bad to catastrophic. In order to prepare the nation for a long struggle, the "Front Report" adapted the image of the soldier. No longer bathed in the glorious sunshine of easy early victories, the radio now prepared the country for a long struggle: "The chivalrous German soldier had to adapt to a new enemy, an army of Mongolian and other Asiatic elements forced into action by the kicks and pistol butts of the Commissars. These men did not fight according to the decent rules of war."

The dashing hero of the early Blitzkrieg now had "the long and hard experiences of fighting . . . [which] marked his features. His soldier's eyes were clear and resolute as ever, but they seemed to have become darker and wiser. His uniform showed signs of wear, which always commands respect of anyone who understands. Comradeship is closest in the infantry; not only good days but bad days link us together, blood and sweat."[14]

Delmer and his team smelled propaganda blood. The BBC could deliver the dry news about RAF bombardments, but Woburn could give stories that took Goebbels's heroic soldier image and turned it against the party. *Der Chef* celebrated the stoic stand of First Lieutenant Meyer, who single-handedly, while variously wounded, held off a huge Russian infantry attack:

> He did not notice that the hot barrel sagged the flesh from his bones. The cold made him insensitive. He stuck his last cigarette into a man's mouth who lay there with a head wound and who soon died. Eight times Lieutenant Meyer asked for reinforcements and air protection. No reinforcements could be sent. Meyer died, the last man standing in his battalion, covering the escape of his men alone as they trudged across the snow.[15]

How much of this story is true, and how much embellished, has been impossible to ascertain. However, the aim was clear. Under the guise of celebrating German heroism, Delmer's aim was to underline heavy losses in the Russian campaign and stimulate desertion.

Even more worrying for Goebbels was that the SD was reporting people having their first doubts about the infallibility of the Führer.

In October 1941, Hitler had promised that the Soviet Union was "already broken" and "will never rise up again".[16] Since that promise, the Volksgenossen tuned in to the radio expecting, hoping, yearning to hear Hitler's prophecies come true. Weren't Russian soldiers meant to be poor and badly equipped? They pined for Hitler's voice, to "draw new strength from his words". The SD described how people wanted to see him in newsreels, how there was never enough of him: "A smile of the Führer, his look itself gives us strength and courage again."[17]

But as the promise of quick victory melted, Hitler was appearing on the radio ever more rarely. When he did, he was more subdued than usual: "The terrible cold forced us to wage a defensive battle," he explained in early 1942. In order to reinforce Hitler's argument about the weather, the Reich's radio was suddenly full of meteorological reports about icy conditions, with instructions to cover water pipes from the cold snap.[18] These were desperate, if clever, propaganda measures.

Goebbels needed scapegoats. The Reich's radio blamed the military setbacks on the generals, whereas Hitler's inspiration helped German soldiers endure the Russian winter.

Der Chef, by contrast, defended generals, such as that "genius of military science, the Field Marshall Von Bock", who had been dismissed after failing to take Moscow, and pinned the blame for losses on the "filthy Parteikommune": "It becomes more and more clear that we could conduct this war much better if we could not depend on the Sheisskerle [*sic*] from the clique of Die Kommune."[19] He tore into SS men who were avoiding the toughest fighting:

> In the Norwegian territory the women stink and the men have filled themselves so full with drink that one does not know the other. Their balls should be scraped. These men are wearing

the German uniform, but they drag the German name in the mud. They should send them to the east. There they would have to stick their ass in the mud, without whisky, without water, without sleep, without relief, and without protection against airplanes they would know what war really means. All the pigs of the Waffen SS should be sent there. There everything else but their penis would get stiff. There they would get an idea how hard the German soldier has to fight for his good name, while the SS clique does not give a shit about it.[20]

While the party and the SS lived it up in Paris, *der Chef* described the terrible conditions of field hospitals on the front, with nurses dying every day because of the dirt and disease. His mentions of lice are so frequent that I started itching reading them.

The German body was being exhausted by the Nazis:

In France one can see them, the typhoid sufferers, their hair cut off close, with hollow faces, and ragged uniforms; they are treated like lepers, in the ground, in the run down Scheiss casements of the French fortifications.[21]

Sickness was everywhere:

It is not only typhus which attacks the homeland, but also Paratyphus, diarrhea, and the many intestinal and stomach diseases which people contract by bad food, canned food, low grade meats and in air raid shelters. The supplies for coal, fats and soup are available, but die Kommune sit upon their supplies.[22]

The Nazis were fixated on athletic, Aryan bodies, their movies, posters and communal exercises celebrating physical health as a metaphor for the pure Aryan body politic—while all disease was expelled outwards, associated with the "dirty Jews", who, in Nazi propaganda, were portrayed as carrying illnesses, as vermin or maggots. *Der Chef* was bringing the disease back inside, forcing Germans to face their own ugliness and to see the Nazis as its source.

The SS, *der Chef* claimed, was giving German workers ephedrine to work harder:

First you are subject to headaches, then you feel faint, you are sleepy, yet you cannot sleep, it excites you and at the same time puts you in a depressive mood. And when such a workman after a shift of eleven hours, sits on a kitchen stool, and his soup becomes cold because he has no desire to eat, he is sleepy and deadly tired. He wants to sleep but isn't able to sleep. So he returns to the factory, goes to his machine, stamps and stamps, and suddenly he throws his tools away because he is unable to work any more. But the crappy SS are waiting outside and let the man die.[23]

Delmer exploited how Germans felt about their bodies in other ways as well. In early 1942, German soldiers in Crete awoke to find a pamphlet had been slipped under their doors. On the cover was a bleak, black-and-white photo of the corpses of German soldiers abandoned in the icy forests of Russia. The photo was accompanied by a line from a patriotic World War I song: "Lieb Vaterland, magst ruhig sein . . ." (Dear Fatherland, put your mind at ease). Turning the page, the soldiers would have expected to read the next line: "Fest steht und treu die Wacht am Rhein" (Firm and true stands the Guard on the Rhine). Instead, they read a line with the same rhythm and metre, but quite a different meaning: "Fest steckt's und treu der Italiener rein" (Firm and true sticks the Italian his dick in).[24]

In front of them was a bright, multicoloured watercolour—a visual contrast to the monochrome photo on the front. This gaudy picture showed a naked, pink-skinned, blonde woman lowering herself onto the erect penis of a dark-haired, olive-skinned man. The focus of the drawing is on the woman's pleasure: her thighs tilt to the soldier's crotch; she has a little smile of anticipation as he pulls her down.

The message was simple: while you are on the front, your girl is sleeping with foreign workers back home.

The artist was Isabel Delmer. She had, at first, been expected to run the household at Woburn, which was "hardly attractive to me". Her talents were soon put to better use when she joined the leaflet team. "Fancy being employed by the Government to create pornography." She relished the challenge and thought her "picture painstakingly realistic of a foreign worker making love with a bright blonde German girl" effective. An SOE note stated that "in order to ensure its automatic circulation, it has been given a definite onanistic value". With its combination of death, jealousy and arousal, the leaflet appears to have been designed to get into the minds of German soldiers through a swirl of strong, contradictory yet interconnected feelings.[25]

The Greek resistance members, who had been slipping Isabel's pamphlet under the doors of German soldiers, considered it such a success that they ordered thousands more: they reported that the leaflet made the Germans' "flesh creep".[26]

At the start of 1942, der Chef was also producing some of his most pornographic and sexual content. A recurring story was about the SS's "Immaculate Community", a secret society of sexual depravity: "The SS Immaculate Community organize prostitution, [it's] all organized by the yellow, atheist dog Himmler. Monasteries, the places where monks used to pray, are being used for the most disgusting orgies where their priestess of lewdness, a common whore, stands naked in front of the altar . . . [From transcriber: the end of the sentence is unintelligible because der Chef speaks with such indignation that the words choke in his throat]."

The outraged Chef played a record that the Immaculate Community had allegedly sent to students: religious organ music was followed with instructions to young Germans on how to have sex: "Naked you must be, my Sisters. Softly, softly, softly feel the warmth of the body."

"This is the work of Himmler's Immaculate Community," der Chef announces, appalled, "which is operating without punishment when our German men suffer at minus thirty-two degrees of cold, down in the dirt."[27]

The Immaculate Community was a fiction. But it was true that the Nazis were so obsessed with racial purity that they published manuals on how to have a happy sex life with other Aryans, and at Matthias Göring's Institute for Psychological Research and Psychotherapy, men were "cured" from homosexuality by being forced into sex with a female prostitute—and sent to concentration camps if they didn't perform.[28] Delmer was again pushing the Nazis' ideology "into the ridiculous", using their obsession with enforcing Aryan sex against them.

His propaganda approach was increasingly at utter odds with others at Woburn. In the same week that Delmer broadcast his sex tales of the "Immaculate Community", the Sender der europäischen Revolution was exhorting Socialists not to lose heart: "You remained a Socialist because you knew that this fascism can solve none of the great questions which face mankind today. You remained a Socialist because you believed in progress and the German working class."[29]

Often, the type of sex that *der Chef* described with delighted outrage was strikingly sadomasochistic, not least in his story about a Nazi official, Thienemann:

Take the case of Thienemann, who has been lecturing women in the Weser area to keep away from foreign workmen—when Thienemann has a Polish lover at home who is personally in charge of the bamboo canes, twigs, thin and thick leather straps and cat-o-nine tails with which Thienemann and his guests are strafing her fat and large buttocks. All of them gather in the air shelter which the District Leader Crapper constructed for himself. Mind there are no bombs in this part of the country, but the air raid shelter prevents people outside from hearing the yells of Wanda when the leather cuts deep into her skin.

Thienemann's chauffeur takes her on his back and holds her strongly. The SS swine loves it when the naked woman's body whimpers back, cries and yells under the blows and swears with the vilest words in the Polish language. And when she is properly whipped up to a purple colour, and whimpers and cries from pain, then the old impotent testicles are ready, and Wanda's straight thighs enclose the thighs of the chauffeur and he can feel every push of his lord and master until Wanda bites his arm.[30]

To compile these scenes, Delmer plumbed the works of Magnus Hirschfeld, the German sexologist who had documented the sadomasochistic habits of Germans between the wars. Hirschfeld had been an early campaigner for gay rights. In the 1920s Nazi youth groups beat him nearly to death, and when the Nazis took power, they burned his books and closed his institute. He died in 1935 from a heart attack while in exile in France. Delmer wrote in his memoirs that by using the "fetishisms and perversions" of Hirschfeld's research to subvert the Nazis, he was helping Hirschfeld achieve posthumous revenge.[31]

● ● ● ▬▬▬ ▬▬▬ ▬▬▬ ● ● ●

ACCORDING TO DELMER HIMSELF, these sex scenes were there primarily as listening "bait": as every tabloid editor or advertiser knows, sex sells. "There is a sadism in the German nature quite alien to the British nature," argued an unsigned PWE memo, "and German listeners are very far from being revolted by the sadistic content of some of these broadcasts."[32]

Such essentialist, sweeping statements about "German nature" were not uncommon at the PWE.[33] But setting aside the moot question about whether British "nature" is more or less sadistic than German, or whether any country has a single "nature", the fixation on sadomasochism resonates with contemporary theories about why some people were drawn to Nazism.

In 1941 and 1942, the same time that *der Chef* was broadcasting his tales of whipping and strafing, the German–Jewish psychoanalyst Erich Fromm, exiled at Columbia University in New York, was analysing the allure of Nazism as a form of sadomasochism. For Fromm, the people drawn to the Nazis had never dealt with the burden and responsibility of freedom, and they now yearned to submit themselves to a higher authority, to what Russian propaganda might term a "strong hand". They were masochists in the sense they desired to give themselves up to a higher power: "There is no doubt that suffering, submission, or suicide is the antithesis of positive aims of living. Yet these aims can be subjectively experienced as gratifying and attractive . . . as aiming at dissolving oneself in an overwhelmingly strong power and participating in its strength and glory."

Fromm argued that the authoritarian leader, the sadist, needed the masochists as well. The authoritarian's own sense of who he was remained unsteady. He needed to devour everyone around him and was addicted to the crowd's attention and adoration: "Both the sadistic and the masochistic trends are caused by the inability of the isolated individual to stand alone and his need for a symbiotic relationship that overcomes this aloneness."[34]

Seen from this perspective, Delmer was doing more than merely using sex as "bait"; he was revealing the political psychology the Nazis played on. Whereas Nazi propaganda used fiction to avoid reality, Delmer was using fictions to reveal a truth about them, and thus he cast them "into the ridiculous".

• • • ▬▬ ▬▬ ▬▬ • • •

SUCH PSYCHOLOGICAL SPECULATIONS WERE a far cry from how some senior civil servants viewed Delmer's pornography. On July 12, 1942, Anthony Eden, the minister for foreign affairs, received a letter from one of his more prominent officials. Sir Stafford Cripps had just returned from a successful stint as an ambassador to Moscow, liaising with the Kremlin during the USSR's entry into the war, and was briefly considered, largely by himself, as a potential successor to Churchill.[35] He was now the lord privy seal and a future chancellor of the exchequer. Cripps was deeply Christian, Socialist, vegetarian and teetotal. In Parliament he condemned dog and horse racing.[36]

Cripps's letter was handwritten. This was unusual—official correspondence was normally typed. But Cripps didn't want to traumatise his young female typists with the lurid contents.

The subject of the letter was the "most foul and filthy pornography" put out by GS1. Cripps was especially offended by the

> detailed description of a named German admiral who takes home 4 or 5 sailors with his own mistress. He makes the sailors drunk and excites himself by instigating the sailors to rape his mistress in turn. All this is given in a running commentary which describes in the minutest detail the difficulties of the sailors owing to their drunkenness. Here is a typical sentence from the orgy: "und wenn sie zwischen den Beinen trocken

wird, schütten Sie Butter ein" [and if she gets dry between the legs, they pour in butter]. This is followed by the indignant comment that butter is rationed to the common people.

The climax of the orgy is an even more detailed description of how the old Admiral finally works himself up into a state in which he, too, can copulate with the woman.

What good this is supposed to do I cannot imagine. It could only play up to the most foul and filthy Nazis who we shall never catch—I hope. The decent minded liberals, Socialists, Catholics, Protestants and other resistant sections will be disgusted. I object most strongly to such filth being allowed to go out of this country.[37]

Cripps didn't stop with a letter. He went in to see the foreign minister personally: "If this is the sort of thing that's needed to win the war," he complained, "why, I'd rather lose it!"[38]

He also complained to his cousin—who happened to also be the secretary of the PWE: "I am sorry you belong to that beastly pornographic organisation."[39]

Eden forwarded the letter to Robert Bruce Lockhart, who forwarded it to Rex Leeper, Delmer's superior at Woburn. Leeper's response, in the declassified archives, is lined with worry: "Delmer is a rare artist and a good fellow. I hope very much, that his protest does not mean we shall lose Delmer."[40]

But the Cripps letter was just one part of Delmer's problems.

On April 26 the Nazi newspaper *Das Reich* had a sensational scoop. It was going to reveal the truth about *der Chef*. "'Der Chef is speaking!' The Broadcasts all started with this sentence," opened the article. "Then a Scottish comedian, disguised as Prussian aristocracy, came to the microphone [and launched] into some piece of obscenity as perverse as possible, flourished it in the air to demonstrate its juiciness and then, with a vicious plunge, thrust it into the very heart of the German Party and home politics."

Although the detail about the "Scottish comedian" was wrong, the essence was right: *der Chef*'s cover had been blown. And much else in the article was uncannily accurate: "Gustav worked according to a very simple method. On the left hand of his desk were delectable piles of indecent literature . . . on his right hand lay a bunch of cuttings from German newspapers. This station had long since been located. . . . It was in Scotland, quite far away from Potsdamer Platz!"[41] The article claimed that the programme was being shut down by senior English politicians who, since finding out about the project, were appalled at the way that *der Chef* insulted the British people and the British government. All these details were uncomfortably close to the truth—so close that only an insider could have known them.

• • • ▬▬ ▬▬ ▬▬ • • •

THE PWE LEADERS HAD always been confident that they could disguise the origin of their broadcasts. After being recorded at the billiards-room studio, the records were taken by a special courier to a secret transmitter in the Buckinghamshire countryside, surrounded by War Office signs to "keep out", where radio operators with no knowledge of German played the records, attempting to make them sound as if they were broadcast live.[42] Colonel Gambier-Parry, head of the technical side, had boasted to the king that "radio science presents devices that give the illusion that the transmissions come from occupied enemy territory". He informed the king how German propaganda had previously claimed to have found the transmitters in locations from Central Europe to the Ardennes, even claimed to have arrested the broadcasters—when all the time they were actually in England. Rival British intelligence agencies, unaware of the existence of the RUs and thinking them genuine resistance stations, had reported they were located everywhere from Syria to Le Havre.[43] So could the leak have come from inside? Security inside Delmer's team was tight. POWs were not allowed to leave the Woburn estate; German staff members were barred from visiting houses where the other RUs lived. No one was meant to know about the existence of anybody else.

But despite the elaborate security, Delmer did have enemies. As Garnett recorded in his *Secret History*, "Delmer's ideas were not immediately welcomed."[44]

Robert Walmsley recalls weekly meetings in Leeper's room attended by a group of half a dozen PWE staff, including the head of the German section, Richard Crossman, who also looked after Sender der europäischen Revolution, and Frederick Voigt, the journalist and PWE adviser who had previously attacked Delmer at the BBC: "These meetings often degenerated into long tirades by Voigt against the methods of British propaganda. He was totally unsympathetic to anything but the whitest of white propaganda and seemed unable to distinguish between propaganda to different audiences. At these meetings Delmer used to assume an attitude of innocence and modesty, and Leeper used to enjoy his bland descriptions of the early broadcasts of GS1."[45]

He wasn't bland enough. Throughout 1941, Voigt kept on advocating for Sender der europäischen Revolution and the idealistic approach to political change in Germany, praising it as "a shaft of light, as it were, into the totalitarian darkness", how it was "serious, informative and eloquent" and helped to create the "nucleus of a future German opposition" that would give the British government "leverage" over "Revolutionary movements as soon as they begin to show themselves".[46]

But Voigt was losing these arguments, and his authority. And now he was, allegedly, taking revenge. Delmer and his other colleagues' internal correspondence to Bruce Lockhart furiously pointed fingers of blame at Voigt, who had, Leeper claimed, instigated the attack "for purely personal reasons".[47]

Crossman, head of the German section of the PWE, may have been the main benefactor of the Sender der europäischen Revolution but was nevertheless incandescent. Voigt had "been carrying on a campaign in the press, and, even more, in the clubs and lobbies against the PWE, more particularly its German section". He had widely circulated "a libellous memorandum" disclosing all the PWE's secrets. The PWE was being undermined among allies, its staff were being put in danger and its operations were compromised. This was "political blackmail".[48]

Voigt had allegedly first leaked the secret of *der Chef* to the British press, which didn't reveal his name but was still stinging in its rebuke. "What went out from this station," complained the *National Review* in March 1942, "was horrible and most damaging to our good name."[49]

This article, Crossman and Leeper believed, was the original source for the "scoop" in *Das Reich*.

According to Delmer, it was Voigt's friends at the Sender der europäischen Revolution who made a transcript of one of the most pornographic of *der Chef*'s recordings and had a copy passed to Cripps. The show with the admiral's orgy had been recorded almost six months previously—it was chosen intentionally to undermine Delmer as much as possible.

Delmer despaired. "I would prefer to give up my connection with the Unit if its activities are to be continually endangered by the toleration of gross breaches of security," he wrote to Leeper.[50]

Leeper supported Delmer. In a letter to Bruce Lockhart he commented that the Secret Intelligence Service asked female agents to behave in "perhaps morally questionable ways". He fought for the right to be immoral: "I am not pornographic. I dislike the baser sides of human life as much as Sir S. Cripps does," but he would allow pornography if he could "see a purpose behind it in the fight against evil things. . . . In this case moral indignation does not seem to be called for."[51]

An unsigned PWE document makes a full case for Delmer's station.[52] It argues that the pornography had driven listenership higher and that the "evidence of reception" showed that most listeners thought the station was German, and thus it couldn't really be said to blemish Britain's reputation.

The foreign secretary, Eden, put an end to the matter, writing to Cripps that he had requested the station halt its pornography, but that it needed the freedom to turn Germans against Germans, and German listeners did not realise the station was British.[53]

Der Chef and Delmer had been saved. The Sender der europäischen Revolution was also shut down in June. But the danger of being exposed and unmasked now hung over all clandestine broadcasting.

●　●　●　▬▬▬　▬▬▬　▬▬▬　●　●　●

DELMER'S FURY AT VOIGT may well have been justified—and the article in *Das Reich* could have been partly informed by Voigt's leaks. But the truth is the Germans were also on to the source of *der Chef* without such internal indiscretions. Colonel Gambier-Parry's supposedly brilliant "radio science" was not all that brilliant.

An SS report from October 1941 commented that GS1 contained "very able" propaganda and managed to place the signal as emanating from the area of "Oxford–Cheltenham", just a few miles from Woburn. Ironically, given their rivalry, the first clue the Germans had was when one of the broadcasters had mistakenly played Sender der europäischen Revolution on the same wavelength as *der Chef*, giving away that they were part of one overall operation.[54]

• • • ▬▬ ▬▬ ▬▬ • • •

ESSENTIALLY, DER CHEF MANAGED to keep his identity secret for about half a year. Such is the fate of so many information operations that rely on a mask for impact: they are vulnerable to being revealed, and it is usually only a matter of time before they are.

With social media, creating "sock puppets" like *der Chef* is easy. Anyone can play at being a Delmer, or a Goebbels, and rustle up their own RU or Workers' Challenge on the most basic digital device by creating a fake online persona: botnets, troll farms and online mobs have become ubiquitous from Mexico to Manila. And catching them has become a minor industry across the world.

The Kremlin became famous in 2016 for creating many thousands of deceptive accounts across the world, and in the US in particular, to back its preferred political forces in American elections, usually far-right Republicans.[55] In 2017 one group of Democratic spin doctors then decided to create fake Russian accounts pretending to be fake Americans to accuse a Republican candidate in Alabama of getting Russian support (they later claimed this was an experiment).[56] US far-right groups created scores of fake accounts claiming to represent the Black Lives Matter movement in order to discredit it by planting stories that Black Lives Matter planned to resort to racial violence.[57]

Sometimes, as with Delmer, these fake accounts are created in a good cause. In 2018, when the terrorist group the Islamic State established a torturing, mass-murdering regime in the ruins of Syria and

Iraq, Middle Eastern activists created fake Islamic State accounts in order to confuse the terrorists' plans.[58] After Russia's invasion of Ukraine in 2022, Russian internet researchers claimed that Ukrainians created "quite clever" telegram channels that pretended to be patriotic Russian, while all the time stressing Russian losses on the battlefield.[59] Deception in war is as old as the Trojan horse, and if such operations save lives and help defeat a genocidal aggressor, then, as Leeper put it, "moral indignation does not seem to be called for".

But even if such deceptive operations can achieve precise and short-term goals, they will be found out today much faster than they were in World War II. And the more profound their meaning to their audience, the more confusion and disorientation those audiences will feel when they realise they have been deluded. And this, in turn, only helps political forces that claim they will look after you in a confusing world, that argue no one can be trusted—and that therefore you need a strongman to lead you through the murk. This is the danger of dabbling in disinformation even in a "good cause": it nurtures an environment of endless distrust that benefits authoritarian instincts. If you play that game, take care that the negative side effects don't outweigh the benefits.

However, there is so much more we can learn from *der Chef* than mere deception. Indeed, the Workers' Challenge shows that the Germans were more pioneering, if more inept, practitioners of sock-puppet propaganda than were the British. The Soviets also also created a radio station pretending to be run by German soldiers; the "SA Man Weber" was their attempt to replicate the success of GS1 (without the swearing and pornography).[60]

Delmer's great innovation in countering Nazi propaganda was the truths he was burrowing into through the lies.

His obsession with detail helped him tap into the audience's world, and when he had slipped inside their imagination, he reconnected the logic of cause and effect. Whereas Nazi propaganda blamed everything on caricatures of "global Jews", explaining the world away through conspiracy theories, *der Chef* showed how the troubles of the German people were the result of their own leadership, which they largely were. He helped articulate their hidden resentments and desires in ways that undermined the Nazi hold on people's strongest feelings. He stimulated their curiosity—whereas the Nazis wanted them to give up on truth.

And Delmer was revolutionary in creating a voice that people were interested in listening to: not only "patriotic" but also well connected, daring to say the unsayable, delighting in outrage at sex and corruption. Not someone "worthy" who lectured down at you, but someone repugnant and intriguing. In the summer of 2023, after Russia's invasion of Ukraine faltered like Hitler's had in Russia, the loudest criticism came from Yevgeny Prigozhin, the leader of the war-crime-committing Russian mercenary company Wagner, whose troops fought alongside regular Russian forces. His social media posts, full of rough prison slang, railed at the incompetence of the defence minister and gave details of censored military losses—from a position of ultra-patriotism and even greater warmongering.

When Ukrainian social researchers at the Open Minds Institute polled those who admired Prigozhin, they were surprised to find they were not necessarily the most active supporters of the war, and less avid about going to fight in Ukraine than others.[61] As with *der Chef*, it wasn't his pro-war policies they were necessarily interested in, but what he might reveal. Unlike *der Chef*, Prigozhin had a real political agenda. In June 2023 he led a brief mutiny against the minister of defence. It petered out in a single day. Two months later he was dead—his plane brought down just outside Moscow, Putin's payback for daring to make him look weak.

The example of *der Chef* had shown it was possible to engage German audiences in more subversive ways. But it also showed the vulnerability of deception: you could be found out at any moment. Delmer had his first success—but also his first obstacle.

• • • ▬▬▬ ▬▬▬ ▬▬▬ • • •

AFTER THE AFFAIR WITH Cripps, *der Chef* dialled down the pornography and increased his attacks on a new favourite target: Hans Fritzsche. Delmer stopped doing his own BBC shows in mid-1942 but kept on attacking his rival via *der Chef*. Fritzsche, *der Chef* claimed, had access to special rations that allowed the "patriotic propaganda pisser" to eat to excess. Fritzsche would use his own show to deny *der Chef*'s claims and explain that he was a British operation. *Der Chef* would come straight back at him: "Herr Fritzsche can stand on his head and fart into the microphone with his arse as far as I'm concerned. . . . He can say we are an English or Kyrgyzstan transmitter, because all that doesn't change by a single fart that . . . party bosses receive special rations which have nothing, absolutely nothing, in common with the normal rationing system."[62]

However, the evidence of reception showed that the numbers and enthusiasm for *der Chef* were beginning to fade. Although he would stumble on another year, after the initial shock and novelty wore off, and after his mask had been removed, *der Chef* struggled to maintain the same levels of interest. "While the Chef is thought amusing at first, his coarseness is said to pall," said one evidence of reception that surveyed POWs' listening habits.[63] As 1942 dragged on, Delmer's attention refocused on new ways to subvert Nazi propaganda. His Empire of Tricks was expanding.

• • • ▬▬ ▬▬ ▬▬ • • •

ON FRIDAY, OCTOBER 23, 1942, Peter Wykeman (né Weichmann) boarded a train from Euston Station in the direction of Bletchley Park.[64] He had no idea of his final destination. He was twenty and had just graduated from University College London. All that he knew was that he had made it through a series of strange interviews for his first real job at something he was told was the "Political Intelligence Department" of the Foreign Office. In the first round he'd been called to Bush House in Aldwych to meet a vast man with a huge beard (Delmer) who had tested his knowledge of third-tier Nazi officials and his proficiency in German. Peter's German was fluent: he'd been born in Berlin and, although his Jewish family had moved to Britain when he was eleven, still spoke English with a slight accent. In the second round he was called back to the BBC studios for a microphone test: out of the three candidates he was the only one to make it through. Later he wondered whether Delmer had chosen him because he felt an affinity for the young man: they had gone to the same school; they were both somewhat "too German".

When the war began, Wykeman's German roots made him suspect. He was arrested and then shipped off to an internment camp in

Canada where he chopped giant trees, was eventually released after fifteen months and returned to Britain to finish his degree.

When Wykeman arrived at Bletchley, there was no one to greet him at the platform. Outside the station he cautiously approached a uniformed woman driver, who turned out to have a list of arrivals with his name on it; she then drove him across the countryside and deposited him by a small lodge in the middle of nowhere before riding off again. The lodge was empty, but it had a door to a path that led to a white Palladian villa. Wykeman went in. Here, finally, he met someone he knew: the man who had presided over his voice test at the BBC, the German journalist Hans Berman. He took Wykeman through to the dining room, where a mix of English and Germans were having lunch. The new arrival kept silent and tried to work out where he was from their conversation. But they discussed only gardening and how to raise poultry.

After lunch, the group went down the hill to a red building that looked like it might belong to the headmaster of a village school. "I was taken up to the cramped attics, where people were at work, and given a chair," Wykeman would write in his memoir decades later. "Apart from signing the Official Secrets Act, I spent the next couple of hours or so watching the goings-on with little comprehension." He was at least in the right place: Delmer was here. This was Delmer's new home and HQ, known as the "Rookery". But he had little time for Wykeman. "Delmer's passing remark to me that we were in Norway did not help."

• • • ▬▬ ▬▬ ▬▬ • • •

THE ATTIC IN THE Rookery was the editorial office of Delmer's latest radio venture, "Radio Wehrmachtsender Nord". It purported to be run by soldiers in occupied Norway and was aimed at both soldiers and, more importantly, civilians inside Germany who, Delmer hoped, "want to know what army life and *Stimmung* [morale] is like".[65] As with *der Chef*, the idea was that people's curiosity would be drawn in by this little window onto another world.

Unlike GS1, the Wehrmachtsender sounded like a more regular radio station: a mix of news, music and letters back and forth from the front. Most of the news was true, selected in such a way that it demoralised the enemy. There were multiple speakers: newscasters and DJs and regular soldiers. Delmer's team was expanding.

Max Braun's brother had joined the team—they looked so similar that people would often get them confused. There were also former German Communists Delmer had met during his time reporting on the Spanish Civil War. However, no one in the attic would have referred to anyone by their real name: code names were used for security.

One of the newer arrivals was particularly striking. Sallow, with a monocle rammed in his right eye, he was reading out soldiers' letters in different voices, imitating accents from across the country. This was René Halkett—whom colleagues described as "75 percent genius". His real name was Freiherr von Fritsch, and in Germany he had been an actor, a dancer, a set designer at the avant-garde Bauhaus group and a gliding pioneer. He'd left Germany in 1933, when the Nazis came to power, moved to Ibiza, arrived in England in 1936, and had written a best-selling autobiography, *The Dear Monster*, which showed how German society at every level searched for overbearing authority figures. He also played the lute and was a surrealist artist. His drawings and paintings from his Woburn and later years are full of severed heads attached to mechanical contraptions, women grasping transistors while being nuzzled by deer, the natural and the mechanised amputated and then spliced into each other, any idea of a pure identity undermined: we are fluid, part people and part machines; out of our heads grow stairs, guitars and transmitters; and our backbones are connected by electric wires.

Halkett had immediately grasped Delmer's approach. During his interviews to join the PWE, the artist had been given a pile of BBC German scripts to evaluate. He was scathing in his assessment: "I thought the content of the programmes quite impossible. They wouldn't impress any German."[66] But for all their commonalities, or perhaps because of them, Halkett also disagreed with Delmer's tactics. He disliked the pornography in *der Chef* and thought it would backfire and put listeners off—indeed, some "evidence of reception" did feature a few POWs who found the obscenity and pornography offensive (whether that depressed overall listening figures is another matter). Nor did

Halkett share Delmer's sense of humour. When Halkett enquired about the whereabouts of Voigt, who'd engaged Halkett for his initial PWE interview, Delmer replied: "He was found to be a German agent and hanged." You never knew, thought Halkett, when Delmer was serious or joking. "He liked to bewilder you and put things before you where you couldn't possibly be sure if it was true or not," Halkett would recount to the journalist Ian Fell four decades later in a series of long interviews about his life that were never broadcast.

On October 23, the day Wykeman sat befuddled in the attic, Halkett and the rest of the group would have been preparing the broadcast for the next day. The October 24 show featured a report on how the majority of false fire alarms could be traced to the unwatched children of soldiers' wives. (What were the wives up to? Were they not coping with the burden? Or out having too much fun?) There were reports on pigs being slaughtered because of the lack of pig food, contrasted with details of a lavish party that Göring's daughter held at the La Scala opera theatre in Milan, while ordinary Germans were all waiting for the Führer to announce victory at the battle of Stalingrad. "And now," the presenter announced as he switched to music, "we have a quick German two-step."

Delmer was experimenting with other new stations too. If you were to twiddle the dial of your shortwave transistor to the 48-metre band, you would have come across the "Workers Station", urging "comrades" to rise up against this plutocratic war, seize power and sue for peace. The speaker, who sounded like a factory worker on the shop floor, gave details about injustices in factory pay, explained sabotage techniques and dictated what slogans to stick on factory walls.

The station was a double front. It pretended to be a local workers' station, but it was actually communicating stories that the Polish resistance could use for its newspapers. It was essentially a very elaborately disguised newswire service. Only three people at Woburn knew of this real reason.[67]

On 49.18 metres, you would have stumbled onto a religious programme: "My dear fellow Catholics! I am a German priest and will speak to you daily and pray for you." And there was a lot to pray for, as "Father Elmar" launched into a detailed, accurate litany of sins the

Nazis had committed and then hidden: Hitler's euthanasia programme that killed off German invalids in order to enhance "the master race", the SS groups that mated with unmarried girls in order to breed ideal Aryans, the pillaging of monasteries.

Father Elmar Eisenberger was a real priest—though Austrian, not German.[68] An Austrian patriot, he resented Germany's annexation of Austria in 1938. He moved to Prague, where he worked on a dissertation in religious anthropology studying early prayer rituals in Canada. When his dissertation was returned from the seminary with instructions to include "racial theory", he knew that the Church was caving to the Nazis. A friendly Irish priest helped him move to England, where he was eventually invited to join what he called Delmer's *Propagandatruppe* (the word in German can mean both military "troop" and theatre "troupe"). Delmer's researchers provided the raw facts of Nazi atrocities, and a German priest wrapped the whole thing in religious imagery, equating the Nazis with the great sinners of Bible stories: Hitler was like Herod, slaughtering foreign children physically and German children spiritually; the German people had fallen for the seductions of the Nazi devils, who "with cunning method knew how to convince the German people that they were the most wonderful people in the world and they were called upon to rule over the other so-called inferior races".[69] But redemption was still possible if Catholics repented and resisted Nazi orders.

"Christ the King" was perhaps the closest Delmer ever got to a morally principled station. But it was a pragmatic choice. The Nazis had always worried about the popularity of the Church. More than a third of Catholic priests in Germany were "disciplined", including being imprisoned.[70] A Luftwaffe signalman who deserted to the British told his interrogators: "[The] Catholic priest has many listeners among civilians and servicemen, particularly in Catholic circles."[71]

But Delmer gave a spin to even this more idealistic show. He put out the rumour that the station was secretly sponsored by the Vatican, hinting that the Pope was more opposed to the Nazis than His Holiness's public, conformist posture implied.

With the exception of Christ the King, Delmer was unhappy with these new initiatives. The Workers Station survived just nine months—its editorial philosophy was the opposite of Delmer's. He believed that the Wehrmachtsender Nord was a particular failure. Not only was reception lousy, but increasingly Delmer believed that for a news station to work, it had to be live, rapidly reacting to the day's events as they happened. The Wehrmachtsender Nord was recorded, transmitted a day late, and felt fake as a result.

• • • ▬▬▬ ▬▬▬ ▬▬▬ • • •

ONCE A WEEK, DELMER continued to take trips to London, but no longer to the BBC. Instead, he headed to the ornate, imperious offices of the Admiralty. There, in an office overlooking Horse Guards Parade, he visited the assistant to the director of Naval Intelligence, Ian Fleming. Delmer had got to know Fleming during his reporting days. They had both visited Moscow together in the lead-up to the war. Fleming was already working in intelligence back then (a path that would later lead him to fame as the author of the Bond novels). On the way out of the USSR, Delmer explained to him that they would be searched by the Soviet secret services at the border. Fleming, in a panic, had torn up and eaten all his notes from the trip. They had remained friends ever since. Throughout 1942, Fleming, impressed with *der Chef* and with Wehrmachtsender Nord, had Delmer lecture new Naval Intelligence recruits on his methods of subversion. As Delmer's radio stations grew, it was Fleming and his colleagues in the navy who saw the potential for deeper collaboration.

Frascati's was Delmer's favourite London restaurant during the war: "Its gilded Edwardian cherubs, its plush chairs and elderly waiters held a nostalgic echo of my Paris eating places."[72] It also had the best collection of Champagne and Burgundy anywhere in town. On Christmas Day 1942, Delmer met for lunch with the head of the propaganda unit of Naval Intelligence, Donald MacLachlan. MacLachlan needed help undermining the morale of the German U-boat crews that terrorised British ships in the Atlantic.

Delmer explained how he had tried something similar with the Wehrmachtsender, where he had targeted both soldiers and civilians simultaneously. But he needed a different scale of production: live shows, live bands, live speeches, live guests—a subversive version of the BBC.

MacLachlan said he would make it work.

But as Delmer began rehearsals for the new venture, Goebbels was also reorganising Nazi propaganda—and Delmer would have to revolutionise his own ideas to compete.

CHAPTER 7

STRENGTH THROUGH FEAR

On February 18, 1943, the secretaries at the Reich Propaganda Ministry were startled by an unusual request. Two of them were to accompany Minister Dr Goebbels to the Sportpalast, where he was set to give an important speech. No one knew why—but an order was an order. Most of the more senior employees quickly found work reasons to avoid losing their evening. The responsibility fell to two young secretaries. One was Brunhilde Pomsel. She had joined the Nazi Party late, in 1941, out of what she would later describe in her memoirs as "thoughtlessness": everyone she knew seemed to have joined, after all, and it helped her get a good job. She admired how the Nazis had managed the "re-blossoming of a humiliated people" but had never attended any Nazi rallies.[1]

She liked the "nice people" at the ministry, and she liked the antique furniture. But the mood at work had become less enjoyable recently with the almost nightly RAF bombing raids. The sirens went off at six every evening. There was no more evening cinema, theatre or music. Even Nazi rallies had to be held during the day.

Pomsel would later claim to having had no idea about Nazi atrocities—the people who committed them were too scared to tell others about them. She also never listened to foreign radio stations: it felt too dangerous.[2]

Goebbels was a distant boss, limping up and down the office. The limp made her feel sorry for him, although he compensated for it with an "incredible arrogance". One time she'd heard him shout in the office, but that had been deeply out of character. He was usually a composed gentleman. Her view of Goebbels was about to be transformed entirely.[3]

An SS man picked the secretaries up in an elegant Mercedes, "a lovely start", according to Pomsel. At the Sportpalast they had "very elite" seats close to the speakers' podium, just behind Mrs Goebbels. Pomsel would remember later that the hall was already filled with factory workers when she arrived (in reality, there was a mix of professions). Pomsel guessed they must have been "chosen" to attend.[4] No one volunteered to attend Nazi rallies any more; only loyal party members came. By early 1943, the initial enthusiasm for fascist events was long gone. The war on the Eastern Front was a disaster. In February, after a four-month battle, the Soviet army had won the battle of Stalingrad. German casualties numbered over four hundred thousand.

Hitler's prophecies of swift victory had failed. He was no longer the unassailable Emperor of Space and Time. He was scarcely on the radio. In a radio broadcast later that spring, Goebbels would cast him more like a suffering saint: "Days of uninterrupted work and nights of vigil and worry write their unmistakeable traits into his features . . . the misery and suffering of individuals pile up before him, mountain like, into the misery and suffering of the whole nation."[5]

At the New School in New York, Kris and Speier, the two exiled German academics who were poring over every Nazi propaganda programme, noted that Hitler had gone "from leadership to martyrdom— and martyrs in Nazi Germany speak very little".[6] In Hitler's absence, Goebbels had moved from behind the scenes to centre stage. His persona was very different from Hitler's. Goebbels's radio performances, Kris and Speier summarised, positioned him as "clever, shrewd, complicated. . . . Especially in defeat, the radio listener is given the impression that realism and frankness are the essence of Goebbels's propaganda."[7]

As soon as Goebbels strode onto the dais at the Sportpalast and greeted the hall and the millions of others listening on the radio, he cut straight to his trademark "realism and frankness": "We are not like the ostrich that sticks its head in the sand so as not to see danger. We are brave enough to look danger in the face." Germany was in mortal danger from the onslaught of the Bolshevik "horde" that had triumphed at Stalingrad and was now moving westward.[8]

But the Bolsheviks were only a front for the real threat: "Behind the oncoming Soviet divisions we see the Jewish liquidation commandos, and behind them terror, the spectre of mass starvation and complete anarchy."

Germany had to save European civilisation from the Judeo-Bolshevik threat. What other army could? (The crowd cheered this.) England was penetrated by Jews—those masters of mimicry could imitate Bolsheviks in Communist countries and capitalists in Anglo-Saxon ones (more cheers from the audience). Jewry was everywhere, enveloping and entangling the world: Jews in banking and Jews in the press, Jews in the West and Jews in the East, a contagious infection that brings on a ferment of decomposition, a force demonic, infernal, chaotic—and only noble Germany could see the danger, and only honourable Germany could stop it.

It was time for all Germans to face the danger and prepare for sacrifice together. The home front had to be as disciplined as the soldiers. No more luxury restaurants. No more bars and shows and long vacations. The Führer hadn't had a holiday since the war began! It was time to end any exemptions from conscription. All able men should be at the front. Women would take their places in the factories and fields. It was time for total war (more cheering at this prospect).

"I have invited to today's meeting a cross-section of the German people," Goebbels continued. "In front of me are rows of wounded German soldiers from the Eastern Front, missing legs and arms, with wounded bodies, those who have lost their sight, those who have come with nurses, men in the blush of youth who stand with crutches." The hall exploded into even more cheers at the mention of the armed forces.

"Behind them are party officials, soldiers from the fighting army, doctors, scientists, artists, engineers and architects, teachers, officials and employees from offices. I wish to ask you ten questions that you will answer for the German people throughout the world, but especially for our enemies, who are listening to us on the radio."

The questions that Goebbels asked were posed as responses to claims made by British propaganda, as if the crowd were shouting back at the English across the water. With each answer the shouting in the hall got louder, so Goebbels's voice could barely be heard above the crowd:

> "The English maintain that the German people [have] lost faith in victory. I ask you: Do you believe with the Führer and us in the final total victory of the German people?"
>
> (YES!)
>
> "The English say that the German people are tired of fighting. I ask you: Are you ready to follow the Führer as the phalanx of the homeland, standing behind the fighting army and to wage war with wild determination through all the turns of fate until victory is ours?"
>
> (YES!)
>
> "I ask you: Do you want total war? If necessary, do you want a war more total and radical than anything that we can even imagine today?"[9]

As he went through his questions, the crowd were increasingly on their feet, all heiling frantically as Goebbels asked them whether they still had faith in the Führer. Thousands of voices answered, "Führer command, we follow!" and the flags and standards were raised as the highest expression of the sacred moment.

"Now, people," Goebbels climaxed, "rise up and let the storm break loose!"

Pomsel stood with the rest of the crowd, but she was petrified and could barely move, grabbing her fellow secretary's hand. It seemed to her like an outburst in a mental hospital, as if Goebbels had said, "Now you can all do whatever you want," as if every individual in that crowd had been stung by a wasp and all of a sudden they all let themselves go, shouting and stamping and wishing they could tear their arms out with heiling. She found the noise crushing, unbearable.

An SS man tapped her on the shoulder and told her to clap along. She did. "You couldn't exclude yourself," she explained later. "I think anyone who hadn't cheered along would have been murdered by his neighbours."[10]

• • • ▬▬▬ ▬▬▬ ▬▬▬ • • •

A LITANY OF DECREES, speeches, conferences and publications followed the speech, reinforcing its key theses. Goebbels claimed that the "Yes" shouts by the crowd in the hall amounted to a "plebiscite" approving his total-war policies. Fourteen million copies of "Do You Want Total War?" were distributed to party offices.[11] The speech was repeated constantly on the radio.

In his daily meetings at the ministry, Goebbels was at first delighted at the number of positive calls and letters he received—and pleased how foreign countries had latched on to his slogan about the dangers of Bolshevisation. Here was a cause many countries could get behind. He insisted that the term *Russian* never be used—only *Bolshevik*.[12]

But not everything was going according to Goebbels's plan. For if the Sportpalast speech was the apotheosis of Nazi ideas about crowd psychology, it also showed its limitations. First there were some negative letters sent to the ministry—he dismissed these as having been written by Jews. And then there were the SD reports, which kept on coming back with a drip of sceptical reactions. Hearers in Saxony thought the overblown emotion a "last-ditch appeal".[13] In the north of the country it was written off as "theatrical" and "mere propaganda". The well-to-do were alarmed by the attacks on their bourgeois lifestyle.[14]

Goebbels was getting fed up with the SD's reports: "The authors have been assiduous in gathering all the foul comments they can find into a critical conglomeration. I am making a sharp attack on the SD's methods."[15] The SD, Goebbels convinced himself, was confusing trivial comments with important ones and "turning fleas into elephants".

But the criticism of the speech kept on coming. An editorial in the SS newspaper *Das Schwarze Korps* complained of the overuse of overwrought terms like "fanatical effort", "brazen hearts" and "total war". In this case Goebbels was coming under attack from a newspaper controlled by his rival, Himmler. But other newspapers took up the criticism: "For years our propaganda has revelled in superlatives. Everything for us was most inspiring, fantastic, grandiose, marvellous. The result is these words are worn out. . . . The man in the street has developed an extreme aversion to the exaggerated use of superlatives."[16]

Goebbels had hoped to be made "plenipotentiary for total war" in the aftermath of the speech, but Hitler passed him over for the role. He'd also hoped that his proposals to recruit more men and close bars and restaurants would galvanise the nation. But many of the initiatives proposed in the speech didn't work. Bars and restaurants were closed but then reopened because those working long hours needed somewhere to eat and drink. The supposed masses of men who were shirking conscription were usually either too old or too ill to join the army.

Instead, the war was brought to the home front in another way as British bombers penetrated ever more deeply and regularly, first into the industrial base of the Ruhr valley and then into Düsseldorf and Cologne, lighting up the sky bright red with fires, sending people scuttling into air-raid shelters and listening, like Londoners had in the Blitz, to the approaching drone of bombers and praying that their street wasn't next.

As German cities burned after British air raids, many blamed the Jews, who, they claimed, were exacting revenge for how Germans had victimised them previously. Goebbels encouraged the hatred—which also helped distract from the ever-increasing anger at the Nazi Party. And although his own propaganda for total war was failing, the British and American declaration in early 1943 that Germany had to offer "unconditional surrender" was, Goebbels noted in his diary, "an epoch-making asininity of the first order. I could have not myself have thought of such a compelling slogan for my propaganda."[17] A PWE strategy memo from mid-1943 was aware of the need to "split the German people, not do Goebbels's job and unify them".[18]

As the war came home, Goebbels shifted his philosophy of propaganda: "It is not important that the population should be in a good mood, but that it should preserve its bearing. . . . After the fourth year of war, all men think differently of war than they did at the beginning . . . expressions such as patriotism and enthusiasm are quite out of place. The German people simply does its duty—that is all."[19]

Increasingly, he defined propaganda success less in terms of enthusiasm and more in terms of resolve. He differentiated between *Stimmung* ("mood", which was changeable) and *Haltung* ("bearing").[20] The *Haltung* was being tested to the fullest as the bad news kept coming.

On May 13, Tunis fell. "Make clear to the reader," Goebbels ordered at his daily conference, "that its loss will not be of overall importance for the overall position." In his diary he admitted that the "Reports on Morale in the Reich are nothing to be happy about." The SD concluded that the country was obsessed with two questions: "How long is the war going to go on? How will it end?"[21]

As Kharkiv fell in the East and Italy prepared to surrender, Goebbels raised the stakes to strengthen cohesion. He wrote in the *Reich* newspaper how "every German knows that we can end this war only by victory, we have no other alternative. If we were to miss this victory our whole history would be null and void. If this war is won, then everything will be won. If it should be lost, everything will be lost."[22] He adopted what Kris and Speier refer to as a "strategy of gloom".[23]

At the ministry, Pomsel could see how fear of the approaching Soviet army was augmented: "Whenever there was a report of twenty women raped by the Bolsheviks, the Ministry would ramp the number up to 30." Soviet atrocities were real enough, but it was the Propaganda Ministry's job to blow them up even further.[24]

But along with the fear of the outside threat, inside the country discipline was enforced with even more viciousness. The total number of death sentences in civil courts increased from 1,109 in 1941 to 4,438 in 1943.[25] Pomsel noted how when even famous writers and artists were caught writing private letters criticising Goebbels or Hitler, they were immediately arrested and executed.[26] Denunciations became even more common, with neighbours and colleagues sending each other to the guillotine for black-market trading, breaking laws on racial mixing—and listening to foreign radio broadcasts.[27] There were eleven death sentences for "radio crime" in 1943, including one for merely mentioning to colleagues what they had heard on the BBC.[28]

Victor Klemperer's diaries from early 1943 are defined by fear. The total-war speech "contains a threat to proceed against the Jews, who are guilty of everything, with the most draconian and radical measures". But the speech, Klemperer thought, pressured not only Jews but Aryans too: "The government also threatens and terrorises the 'comrades of the people' . . . whoever resists the necessity of total war will lose his head."[29]

His German landlord explained that "the tyranny, even against Aryans, was unbearable. The question 'what will become of the nation' was now secondary, as everyone was asking himself whether he would survive."[30]

The movies that Goebbels produced were ever more light and rosy: the cinema filled with musical romantic comedies, anything to distract from the relentless air raids and arrests. On the radio, up to half the programmes in 1944 were filled with cheery swing music, more than double the number of political broadcasts. Goebbels permitted tuneful big-band melodies, although free-form jazz was banned. Zarah Leander's tune "I Know One Day a Miracle Will Come" was a hit.[31]

Goebbels's stress on a mix of fear and denial posed new problems for Delmer and British propaganda. The German audience wanted to avoid bad news about the war and to stay alive. Listening to the BBC or to *der Chef*, anything seditious, was ever riskier.

In his novel *Alone in Berlin*, Hans Fallada, writing just one year after the war ended, told the true story of a Berlin working-class couple who spent the war leaving little notes across the city exhorting Germans to resist the Nazis. They knew that many working-class Berliners shared their hatred of the regime. But after risking their lives to leave the postcards everywhere, they were devastated to discover that all the notes were handed in to the Gestapo: people were too scared to show their opposition to the Nazis, and the couple's strategy to inspire resistance failed in the face of this fear.

● ● ● ▬▬▬▬   ▬▬▬▬   ▬▬▬▬ ● ● ●

IF YOU WERE DESIGNING a type of media that felt safe for a scared, increasingly sceptical but patriotic civilian or soldier in the Reich, how should you do it?

For starters, you would want the regime's leaders, ideally Hitler and Goebbels, delivering their speeches on this medium. Even the nosiest neighbour, or the Gestapo, or a superior officer would see nothing suspicious in a station that played live broadcasts of Sportpalast speeches.

And if the station carried announcements of official government statements—who had been made minister for what, who had received state awards and promotions—and even transmitted these official statements earlier than anyone else, then it would give the impression that your station had the highest and most trusted sources in government.

And if you had presenters who sent personal messages of love and support to sailors on U-boats, knew exactly who was on which boat and where they were sailing, then how could this information not come from the Nazi Navy command?

It could feel safe in other ways too: with dance music to keep your spirits up and a female presenter with a voice like the most comforting German glühwein. Of course, it would have to be also on medium wave (MW), not just in the suspicious undergrowth of shortwave, so you could listen to it on your Volksempfänger like any regular Nazi station, the equivalent of broadcasting today alongside the BBC or CBS. And it would feel positively vital for your safety, and the safety of your loved ones, if it could tell you which specific areas and streets and even buildings the British were bombing with their ever-more-frequent air raids.

The "Soldatensender Calais" on medium wave, which was also broadcast as "Radio Atlantik" on shortwave, had all these "safety" features. From 1943 onward, it was being listened to from U-boats under the Atlantic and Messerschmidts in the sky. The SS leader for Munich identified it as one of the three most popular stations in the city.[32]

● ● ● ▬▬▬ ▬▬▬ ▬▬▬ ● ● ●

OVER AT WOBURN, DELMER was no longer working with three men in a billiards room or with half a dozen in an attic. In order to produce the Soldatensender, Delmer now had, according to the rough estimate of one colleague, about a hundred collaborators.[33] We still don't know the precise numbers of those who worked at Woburn. This remains a story where the evidence can come through with occasional clarity, only to be lost again under the jamming of state secrecy.

The site was ringed with a high-wire fence manned by armed guards. At the gate, Sergeant Copperwheat would let you in only if he knew who you were or who you were with: passes weren't enough to get you inside; only personal recognition counted.[34]

Past the fence, the path curved to the right, and you approached a new, specially constructed red-brick modernist building, a set of rectangles with two floors spreading out horizontally and a taller three-storey tower in the centre so that it looked a little like a giant red radio set.

Through the front entrance you passed the telephone switchboard and entered a series of interconnecting rooms with high, opaque windows housing editors, writers, researchers, recording studios, DJ booths, technicians, DJs and any number of visitors: government officials, musicians, and curious American allies. In the middle room at the back sat an unusual apparatus resembling a closet-sized early fax machine, with a telephone connected to transistors and a ticker tape punching out words in columns. This was the Hellschreiber: an essential toy in the box of media magic tricks that enabled Delmer to counterfeit Nazi radio.

Hellschreibers were familiar sights in official Nazi newsrooms: they were the contraption through which the government sent out official statements. A German news agency had left a Hellschreiber behind when it bolted from England at the start of the war, and it had made its way to Woburn. Unlike Delmer's previous efforts, the Soldatensender was broadcast live, and the editorial team could get the messages from the Hellschreiber on air right away, often faster than the more sluggish stations in Germany, especially as the Sender also kept broadcasting during the night.

Peter Wykeman was one of the early newsreaders: "It will not have taken the German authorities long to realise that we were scooping the German Radio, thereby giving the appearance of an official German station or at least of one with instant access to official sources. But to replace the Hellschreiber network with cable distribution would have involved the Germans in prohibitive expenditure."[35]

Broadcasting live also allowed Delmer's team to tune in to any speeches being given on the Nazi radio and replay them on their own wavelength. "The Soldatensender Calais," the presenter would announce, "in common with all other stations in this Reich network, now takes you over to the Sports Palast in Berlin, where you will hear the address of the Führer." As Harold Robbins, the chief technician of the station, switched over the wavelengths, the studios would erupt with laughter and shouts, encouraging one of the presenters to interrupt Goebbels or Hitler with a quick rude comment in one of their pauses. Delmer would calm the crowd down: "One operation at a time my children! We are doing this for cover, cover, cover and nothing else. No dirt this time!"[36]

Max Braun's one-man research operation now had a team of half a dozen. His indexed library of cards with the names and stories of Nazi officials great and small, officers, gauleiters and their corrupt lifestyles had grown so large that it needed several huts around the main building. The navy, the army and the air force, as well as resistance movements, shared intelligence with Delmer's team: the navy told them about the latest U-boat movements; the RAF told them the precise locations of their air raids; the resistance movements provided rumours from the brothels and the bars. The research department could even predict promotions for U-boat crews before they were officially announced. Tom Stevens, an Oxford professor of classics on Braun's team, had worked out how many tons of Allied ships a U-boat commander needed to sink to gain a new decoration. When Navy Intelligence supplied them with Allied losses, they could partner that information with their library of who was on which U-boat and work out who was due to be awarded for his efforts.[37]

The ultimate aim of the news was to draw out what Delmer called "the inequalities of sacrifice" between the "common man" and the privileged party elites. But instead of the angry screeds of *der Chef*, the content about party corruption and privileges was delivered as formal bits of news. The Sender encouraged listeners to feel they could stand up to the Nazis by showing how weak and decrepit the authorities were becoming. The news stressed that as young men were all called up for service, the remaining police were old and feeble; crime was now getting out of control. In sports news the Sender highlighted the defeat of police teams.[38]

The Sender was the soldiers' friend, always looking out for the interests of its listeners. When it reported on the bombings on the home front, the Sender kindly reminded servicemen that they were due comfort leave if their families were affected.

There were special shows for each branch of the German military. Halkett brought his own ingenuity to the Wehrmacht show. When he thought the shows were getting staid, he created the persona of a drunk soldier who barges into the studio with an accordion and interrupts the broadcast. When he wrote and read the news of a whole German division being wiped out, a fellow presenter, a Bavarian pilot named Sepp Opertemeier, came up to him afterwards and complimented him on how moved he had been, that this really was a tragedy for the poor soldiers on the front. "You could tell that really came from the heart," said the Bavarian as Halkett left the studio. Halkett wandered over to Delmer: "You ought to give me a medal, because Sepp took the thing serious. He thought I was really deeply touched by the loss of a German division which was after all . . . well . . . not deeply touching."[39]

The navy show had the most ambitious operation. Ian Fleming and Donald MacLachlan were regular visitors to Woburn. Sometimes they brought concrete missions to fulfill, such as talking up the effectiveness of a new German radar to make German intelligence services think the British were worried about it, when in fact it was useless. Fleming and MacLachlan brought raw intelligence for Delmer's team: which U-boat was sailing where as well as the trivia that made the shows feel so intimate to the listener. It was Naval Intelligence that used its agents in France to find out the scores of U-boat football leagues. Fleming,

whom Frank Lynder describes as "always having a mocking smile playing round his mouth", would compose the odd dirty rhyme:

> There was an old man from Le Havre,
> Who kept a dead whore in a cave.
> Said he "I admit I'm a bit of a shit.
> But think of the money I save."[40]

The Sender was not only live and vastly more varied in content than
der Chef; it also adopted a quite different philosophy about who was
behind it. The ultimate aim of the Sender, unlike with *der Chef*, was
not to convince the listeners the station was something it wasn't. In the
unfinished memoirs he worked on just before his death, Lynder, who
had become the main researcher on the navy programme, claimed that
"at no point did we seek to give the impression that we were based in
the areas occupied by Germany or even in Germany itself. Quite the
contrary—for our naval purposes it was extremely important that the
listeners were quite sure that it was the British navy that was talking to
them!"[41]

This is somewhat of an exaggeration: the station defined itself as
German. But it is true that Delmer understood that many listeners
would work out that the station was likely to be British. The news they
were giving was too keen to point the finger of blame at Nazi officials
to be a true Reichs-Rundfunk station. But the Sender wasn't trying to
pretend it was necessarily Nazi: the listener was welcome to work out it
was British. The aim was not to dupe the listener but to give them a safe
way, both physically and mentally, to escape from Nazi media.[42] Ellic
Howe, the Oxford-educated forger who worked with Delmer, explained
that the Sender "provided the audience with the psychological excuse,
or an alibi, and at the same time ensured the programme was presented
in a manner which did not offend its prejudices".[43]

When Delmer fought for the right to broadcast his stations on MW,
he argued that it would attract "cautious listeners who are afraid to listen to enemy propaganda. They will have the excuse: 'I thought it was a
German broadcast.'"[44]

Wykeman summarised the approach. The Sender would "(i) afford our German customers an excuse if caught listening, (ii) enable them to justify this dubious activity to themselves".[45]

Halkett put the psychological trick as follows: "We went on speaking as if we were Germans, when we said 'we' we meant 'the Germans', but they knew it was British propaganda. Only psychologically if you hear 'we' you think 'we'—even if you know it isn't 'we'."[46]

So here was a radio programme pretending to be Nazi, which understood that its listeners knew that it wasn't, and whose listeners tuned in because they needed the emotional and physical safety of play-acting as if they thought it might be Nazi after all.

But in this sense, can what Delmer was doing with the Sender even be classified chiefly as "disinformation" in the sense of trying to throw the wool over people's eyes? Instead, it is almost the opposite: Delmer was not so much deceiving his audiences as offering them a safe passage towards (if not quite to) reality. Delmer had overcome the risk of a covert station being exposed by not insisting on deceiving the audience in the first place. He made the camouflaged nature of the radio its attraction.

Imagine the process of tuning in to the Sender. If the principle of Goebbels's propaganda, and those like him, was to treat you like passive putty, to attempt to entrance and hypothetically to even hypnotise you, then here was a station that required you to make a series of autonomous, conscious steps when you listened to it. You put on a series of disguises, and in that very process, you were active and self-aware. The contorted mental gymnastics that people went through helped them bend their minds out of the passive mental state that Goebbels wanted.

The music on the Sender played a similar game with the audience. "Vicki, the forces' darling," would open each show with her trademark "This is Vicki with three kisses for you."

She played plenty of jazz banned by the Nazis: Duke Ellington, Count Basie, Glenn Miller. These represented the sort of "cacophonous instrumental squawk", in Goebbels's words, that the Nazis disapproved of yet was popular among young soldiers.[47] But this American music never had any English lyrics. Any songs with words had to be in German, as with the big-band crooners you could also find on the Reich's radio. So someone listening to the radio could always point to the "approved" Nazi tunes while enjoying the banned music too.[48]

In between tunes, Vicki would give anxious wives and mothers news of their loved ones at the front, and worried soldiers were given information about the whereabouts of their families after a heavy air raid, which the Sender knew the location of as soon as it happened, thanks to the RAF. She also indulged in the odd trick:

> I told the good German citizens to put their samples of morn-
> ing urine into small bottles and post them to the Ministry of
> Health in Berlin. The German postal service was clogged for
> weeks. If we wanted to lower the morale of the soldiers, I would
> simply tell a certain battalion that, although it was surrounded
> and possibly trapped, all was not lost, and I would play them a
> cheerful tune.[49]

Delmer compared Vicki to Circe in the *Odyssey*, tempting Nazi sailors and soldiers to grow despondent: "The treacle in her voice would never let you suspect that this Circe had lost half her family in the gas chambers of Auschwitz."[50]

Vicki's real name was Agnes Bernelle. She was twenty and had come to England with her father, Rudolf Bernauer, a Jewish playwright and cabaret impresario who had started his career in the original cabaret of Max Reinhardt. It was Bernauer's idea that Agnes should take on the role of Vicki, and he created her persona, wrote her scripts and later wrote the songs that she would perform herself. The Delmer–Reinhardt connection, which had started all the way back in World War I, was sealed at Woburn.[51]

The "evidence for reception" for Radio Atlantik grew quickly. Interrogations of eighty POWs captured between June and October 1943 showed that a third of them had listened to or heard about Atlantik, although most realised it was foreign. (Regular listening to *der Chef* was now much less common.) Six months later, the number of POWs who said they were listening to the Sender had almost doubled, to

41 percent.[52] This was lower than the 57 percent who tuned in to the BBC, but given how much longer the BBC had been transmitting and its great name recognition, the success of Delmer's show was startling. And although only 1 percent of POWs had heard the BBC being quoted, 9 percent had heard Atlantik. Perhaps this was because it was "safer" to quote a supposedly German station: "Several expressed admiration to the cleverness of its use of cover, some saying that if an officer entered the room during an Atlantik news bulletin listeners were able to prove that they sincerely believed it to be an ordinary German station." The station was also useful: one POW commander of a U-boat said that German submarine flotillas learned of the loss of their boats from "U-boat transmitter Atlantik".[53]

The most spectacular response of all belonged to Vicki. The story doesn't come from the British archive, but from the memoir of one of the first female American OSS agents. Allegedly (for I have located no corroboration for this tale), a German submarine commander whose boat had been lurking off the coast of Scotland had suddenly surfaced and surrendered to the British. When he was interrogated, he said it was Vicki's programme that had made him do so. Vicki had played a special record for him, "Yes Sir, That's My Baby", in German, and she congratulated him on the birth of a son. But this only outraged and demoralised the commander, encouraging him to surrender. "I hadn't been home for more than two years," he told his British interrogators.[54]

● ● ● ▬▬ ▬▬ ▬▬ ● ● ●

DELMER HAD PULLED OFF something unprecedented with the Sender. He had created a media that was both safe for those millions who were not comfortable with taking risks, that let them hang on to their desire for a collective identity, and simultaneously thoroughly subversive. He had created a media the very interaction with which, the way you tuned in to it, stimulated independent thought and even action.

He had created a media that enemy audiences could trust—despite facing the most extreme partisan divides possible: not just across a culture war, but across a real war. How often today we lament that people don't trust journalism any more or that the trust has become politi-cised: people trust the media that represent their social tribe, but see the other side as utterly untrustworthy. Delmer's Sender was literally being broadcast by the British, the side that wanted to kill Germans, yet Germans trusted it. Delmer had shown that trust develops when you are useful to your audience, when they feel that you know their world so intimately it almost stops mattering who you are. Even the deepest and most genuine "partisan" biases can be overcome.

● ● ● ▬▬▬ ▬▬▬ ▬▬▬ ● ● ●

THE NAZI ELITE WERE soon aware of the problem. In an urgent let-ter to his superiors, the SS Obergruppenführer of Munich despaired that since the Sender appeared on medium wave in October 1943, it had become among the three most-listened-to stations in the city and surrounding provinces and had "caused the greatest unrest and confu-sion among the population concerning the situation at the front and at home". Attempts to jam the Sender had backfired spectacularly, block-ing out the Munich Reich's radio instead. Urgent action was needed.[55]

Goebbels took note as well. "The so-called Sodatensender [sic] Cal-ais," he wrote in his diary on November 28, 1943, "which clearly origi-nates in England . . . gave us something to worry about. The station does a very clever job of propaganda, and from what is put on the air, one can gather the English know exactly what they have destroyed in Berlin."[56]

Fritzsche and the Nazi newspapers began a campaign against the Sender, though rarely mentioning it by name. "Official enemy radio stations not only broadcast in foreign languages," complained Fritzsche, "but for hours and minutes every day they hoist down their own flags and as pirates of the ether in flimsy guise try to take in fools." He accused the BBC of feeding "its illegal children, the camouflaged propaganda radios," with fictitious morsels. The English had, Fritzsche explained, adopted the duplicitous methods of the Jews in their propaganda:

The sword somehow looks ridiculous in the hands of the Jew, but the weapon of the coward, poison, suits him very well. . . .

The English have taken over from the Jews not only this absurd notion of the chosen people . . . but also this tendency to warfare with poisoned weapons. They use this method of warfare, which according to our point of view is somehow unclean, in many guises. They use it in the sphere of ether warfare.[57]

The more popular the Sender became, the more the Nazis paid attention to it, and the riskier it became for those who worked there. If one of the German employees' voices was recognised by the Nazis, their families would face retribution back home. "Kurt", a count, swore to a secretary at the PWE that if his wife got into trouble because of his broadcasts, he would kill himself. When another POW who spoke on Atlantik gave an interview to the BBC under his real name about how life was great in England, there was a scandal at the PWE: What if the Nazis connected this voice on the BBC to the one presenting on the Sender? He was sent back to an internment camp immediately.[58]

In October 1943, Frank Lynder travelled to Esher, Surrey, to see his sister:

A weeping wretch opened the door. I gave her my usual kiss. She pulled a letter out of her apron pocket . . . our mother had been transported from the old Czech fortress of Theresienstadt further eastwards, to Auschwitz.

My sister asked me, "Does that mean that Mutti is dead?" Although I shook my head she must have guessed the truth. "Not necessarily," I said. But I knew the truth only too well. Frau Lila had been sent into the gas chambers. My beloved, distinguished mother, who always spent so much time and money on looking elegant and well-groomed, had been stripped naked and murdered with several hundred others in a gas chamber.

By early afternoon, Lynder was "back home" again at Woburn, asking Seckelmann over and over:

"Is it my fault? Is it all my fault? Did they recognise my voice on the radio. Is murdering my old lady the Nazi swines' revenge?"

He tried to persuade me that it had nothing to do with me. Towards the evening Tom Delmer called me into his office. He didn't say much and he didn't mention the subject. But he was very sensitive. I wanted to howl. But even when I was still a very young boy my mother had told me, "Men don't cry!" So I tried not to weep in front of him. Then Tom Delmer said to me, "There is only one form of therapy. Work and more work! And that's what you are going to do, Sergeant. I have a few things lined up for you. In fact, you'll be so busy you won't have a moment to think about Auschwitz."[59]

He wasn't lying. Big things were afoot at Woburn.

• • ▬▬ ▬▬ ▬▬ • •

DELMER HAD STARTED WITH just one experimental radio station and one staff member. By 1943, he had been promoted to Director of Special Operations Against the Enemy and Satellites ("black").[60] ("Black propaganda" was the official term given to the sort of covert communications Delmer was involved with.) Not only was he in charge of all things covert and German, but of all operations in Nazi-allied countries too: his Empire of Tricks stretched from Berlin to Bucharest and Budapest.

"Into new barracks hastily erected in the compound of MB [Milton Bryant] marched intelligence teams, editorial writers, speakers and secretaries from Italy, Hungary, Bulgaria and even Rumania," remembered Delmer. "Our canteen became a tower of Babel, as dark-eyed gypsy beauties from the Balkans flirted with my fair-haired German prisoners over toad-in-the-hole, powdered egg omelettes, spam fritters, soya bean sausages, and other irresistible delicacies from the repertory of war-time cooks."[61]

Delmer didn't speak the new languages under his command, so he could never dominate them editorially as he did the German efforts. But under his stewardship some of the programming became ever more "Delmer-esque".

The Romanian broadcaster delivered handy tips on how to sabotage oil wells: "If you see a valve or a stop-cock in the oil fields just give it a turn as you pass." The Bulgarian "New Europe" pretended to be a German station broadcasting to Bulgarians—but in such a way as to antagonise its Bulgarian listeners. New Europe belittled the Bulgarian army as a mere "police force", told horror stories about the fate of Bulgarian workers in Germany, and generally made Bulgarians resent the Germans ever more. "The simplest and most effective of all black operations," Delmer wrote, "is to spit in a man's soup and cry 'Heil Hitler'."[62]

Delmer's work was ceaseless. As Walmsley recorded,

> From nine until one or two in the morning, discussions on new projects and new themes were only broken by listening to his own station or even to rival ones. I have seen him, sitting on his vast settee, reading through a paragraph of talk, not once or twice but literally dozens of times, muttering crossly to himself as he did so, then sending the wretched composer off to change a few words and repeating the same process with the same talk almost once an hour for three or four hours on end. Stopping in the middle of a sentence, a worried wrinkle would appear on his large brow and, retrieving at least one of his shoes, and giving his braceless trouser a heave, he would stump rapidly out of the room to impart a brilliant idea to one of his writers, probably by that time in bed.[63]

"Delmer," Lynder noted, "often drove his team of co-workers to the brink of breakdown . . . but we made life easier with humour, a lot of mutual stroking, and by playing silly tricks on each other. You could call our little games infantile, but they helped us get through."[64]

"I do not know to this day," wrote Delmer, "whether it was due to a natural mischievousness, or whether it was the psychological effect of the work we were doing. But the members of my team were for ever playing tricks either on each other, or on my guests, or on me."[65]

Max Braun was hoaxed with a fake letter that hinted there was an assassin after him. A visiting US major had dirt thrown at his window to make him think that Woburn was within reach of Hitler's bombs. Halkett was the particular target of many pranks, often from Lynder. As Lynder recalled,

One morning when I came down for breakfast there was a
new man (a priest) sitting at the table with the Corporal [Seck-
elmann] and Halkett. He seemed to be starving, in need of a
good cooked breakfast. But that was the one thing we couldn't
offer that morning. The new man was pale. I asked him if he
was well, and he shook his head, slightly pointing to his chest.
"Ah, the lungs," I said. "Had TB?" He nodded.

I looked at the Corporal. He understood immediately, and
shouted right across the table: "Are you still coughing up gunge,
phlegm and buckets of blood?" No sooner had he spoken, when
Halkett gagged and shot out of his chair like a rocket. The sensitive aesthete and artist fled from the room leaving his cooked
breakfast untouched. We pushed it towards the [new visitor]
and explained, "You have just witnessed, on a small scale, a
successful example of psychological warfare." The priest ate
the lot.[66]

Halkett disliked this whole genre of amusement. Both Lynder's
and Delmer's sense of humour grated on him. He found Delmer's
constant language games puerile: "He might suddenly start during
dinner to talk in a high affected voice in what he hoped was an accent
Midi, or just say 'mimimimimi'." He didn't find Delmer's puns witty:
Delmer would introduce his wife by saying, "This is Isabel, I call her
Horrible."

He was repelled by some of Delmer's stories, which he would tell
at claret-laced dinners culminating with cherry-pit–spitting competi-
tions. There was one story Delmer told about his time in the Spanish
Civil War that Halkett found particularly disturbing. Delmer described
how he saw prisoners being led up a hill: "They were green in the face
and trembling and pushed along by soldiers because they were going
to be shot at the top." The story of men being led to their execution
made Halkett shudder. But then Delmer would exclaim, "And I had no
camera!"[67]

I've often paused on this story, reading out Delmer's voice in different ways, repeating the way that Delmer first sucks you in with the

human pity of men being led to their death, then pauses and complains, like some heartless journalistic diva, that he had "no camera" to capture the moment. Was he being callous? Or was there, like in so much of Delmer, a self-irony, in this case about how reporters feed off tragedy? How journalism warms its hands over the hot blood of war?

$$\bullet \; \bullet \; \bullet \quad \blacksquare\!\!\blacksquare \quad \blacksquare\!\!\blacksquare \quad \blacksquare\!\!\blacksquare \quad \bullet \; \bullet \; \bullet$$

A MORAL AMBIGUITY IMPLICIT in tricks, hoaxes and black humour pervades Delmer's whole propaganda project. The word *trick* turns up continuously in his writing—Hitler's propaganda, he declared, could be defeated only "with a trick". But tricksters have a long history reaching into ancient mythology. And the more I delve into Delmer's work, the more I see him as part of this contradictory tradition.

Trickster gods appear in German and Norse, Native American and Japanese myths and fairy stories, bluffing their way through the cosmos, putting on different masks, causing both life and chaos. Tricksters can do amazing things. The Japanese trickster god steals agriculture from the heavens and brings it to the mortals. But there can be cruelty in their tricks. The Norse trickster god Loki takes advantage of the god Hold's blindness and cons him into throwing a deadly mistletoe at the virtuous god Baldr. And tricksters often get caught up in their own trickery—as Delmer would do after the war.

During World War II, a thousand miles away from Woburn in eastern Nebraska, the anthropologist Paul Radin was studying stories of tricksters among Native Americans. In a previous book, *The Racial Myth*, which I cited in Chapter 2, Radin debunked Nazi claims to racial purity: he argued that all identities are composite and that the most successful ones are open to new influences. The way he describes the trickster, always changing and putting on new guises, sounds like the opposite of static Nazi identity. But he can also bring trouble: "The trickster is at one and the same time creator and destroyer, giver and negator, he who dupes others and who is always duped himself. . . . He knows neither good nor evil yet he is responsible for both. He possesses no values, moral or social . . . yet through his actions all values come into being."[68]

One of the repeating trickster characters in many Native American cultures is Raven, a dark, bird-like figure who also brought light into the world:

At that time the whole world was dark.

The reason for all this blackness has to do with the old man in the house by the river, who had a box, which contained an infinite number of boxes, until finally there was a box so small all it could contain was all the light in the universe.

The old man hid the light because he was afraid to see whether or not his daughter was ugly.

In a ploy to steal the light, Raven shrank himself to become a hemlock needle in a basket of drinking water so that the daughter swallowed him. Raven was reborn from her as a half raven, half human child. The old man accepted him as a grand-son, and Raven began begging that he open the boxes, one after another, each time pleading and crying until the old man yielded.

When the old man finally opened the box containing the light, Raven grabbed it and flew out of the house—causing light to spread throughout the world and revealing that the old man's daughter was as beautiful as the palms of a hemlock tree.[69]

These trickster tales were told on a different continent from the one where Delmer was running his Empire of Tricks at Woburn, but they might almost be describing how the trickster/propagandist used sub-terfuge, deceit, disguise and lies in order to shed light onto the truth.

In 1944 Delmer's trickery was about to be tested to the hilt. The Allied invasion of Nazi Europe, D-Day, code-named Operation Over-lord, was approaching. The Nazis had managed to halt the Allied advance in Italy. "An invasion from the West had to be attempted," wrote Michael Balfour, the PWE official who went on to become a pro-fessor of history. "If it failed, Germany might still be unable to win the war, but would have a good chance to avoid losing it."[70]

Delmer was one of the few people initiated into plans for the inva-sion. The unreliable outsider had been allowed inside because of his ability to imitate the enemy. According to Balfour, "Tom Delmer's virtuoso performance in developing black broadcasting was both inimitable and too successful to be interfered with."[71]

Delmer's D-Day propaganda would show his tricks at their most flamboyant—and their most amoral.

CHAPTER 8

D-DAY AND THE DEATH DRIVE

When I think of the increasingly demoralised but desperate society and soldiers Delmer had to break in the run-up to D-Day, I recall a story that was told to me in the village of Lukashivka, in the Chernihiv region of Ukraine, which had been occupied in the first days of Russia's invasion and liberated a few weeks later.

"This is where we spent twenty-two days living with Russian soldiers—and we got to know them," Iryna Horbonos explained as she took me down into her cellar, the biggest in Lukashivka. After the Russian army had taken the village, five Russian soldiers had requisitioned the cellar to hide from the shelling coming from all sides of the front lines. The house was destroyed, but the cellar was safe. The Russian soldiers allowed Iryna, her husband, Serhiy, and their son, Maxim, to shelter there as well—after all, this was their home.

The soldiers never left their machine guns; they even slept with them. They rarely left the cellar unless called on duty. But after a few days they started to get to know one another.

Alexey was the captain. He was thirty-one and the youngest.

Roman was older, in his forties. His vehicle had ridden over a mine on the way to the village. Half his face was burned, and he was always cursing and rubbing it with ointment.

Ruslan and Yura were in their forties too. They had previously served in Syria, where, from 2015, Russia had bombed hospitals and laid cities to waste in a prequel to its invasion of Ukraine.

Zakir was the fifth. He was small, an ethnic Tatar, always jabbering and singing Tatar tunes and getting on everyone's nerves. When the artillery would start, he would be the first to scamper into the cellar. The others would tease him. They were from Siberia.

At first, the Horbonoses were too scared to talk to the soldiers. Then, slowly, as they sat in the dark, they began to talk about neutral subjects: food and Ukrainian recipes. The Russians explained they were a team of military mechanics. They fixed tanks. They also took them apart. When there was a break in the shelling, they would disassemble the destroyed Russian vehicles and smelt down the plates that had complex wiring to retrieve gold. One plate would get them 15,000 roubles, a couple of hundred dollars, back home.

Alexey, the captain, spoke fervently in the ready-made sound bites of Kremlin propaganda. He told the Horbonoses that he was there to rescue them, that he wasn't fighting them but America, that this wasn't a war but a "special operation". They would all live happily under Putin together.

Iryna pushed back: Rescue them from whom? She didn't need rescuing. There were no American soldiers or bases here. She didn't want to live under Putin.

The other soldiers were less fervent than their captain.

Ruslan and Yura retreated into their cynicism: they didn't trust the propaganda from any side, not their own or others. They had served previously in Syria. This was just a job for them.

Roman was as fervently anti-Putin as his captain was pro-Putin. He openly cursed Putin as he rubbed ointment onto his burned face. Putin was a donkey. Roman claimed that he never voted for Putin's party in the elections.

The soldiers claimed they were impelled by financial commitments: they had taken on loans, mortgages and medical bills for their families, and they needed the army to pay them off. Some of them were just a few months away from clearing their debts, and then they could quit.

In the first days, Alexey was buoyant with imminent conquest. He would rush into the cellar: "Kyiv is surrounded! Chernihiv is about to fall." Then he would take out a map and ask Serhiy where Kyiv was. He was surprised to hear it was hundreds of kilometres away.

As the weeks went by, and Kyiv and Chernihiv didn't fall, Alexey's mood soured. Russian losses were heavy.

When the five soldiers would go for a drink and a smoke outside, they would invite Serhiy with them. They diluted a little raw alcohol with water, and rolled tobacco with newspaper.

"What are you doing here?" he would ask. "What's the point of this war?"

"We didn't come here to fight," they answered. "We came for a victory march in Kyiv."

The shelling meant that the whole of the Horbonoses' house, a home they'd been building for thirty years, was destroyed. Their lives were reduced to rubble. The library had been the last to go: it burned for two whole days.

When Iryna couldn't take it any more, she would begin to cry and scream at the soldiers in the darkness of the cellar: "We had everything! What are you doing here?"

The soldiers first sat there in the dark. "Would it be so much better if we just came here as your guests?" they asked the Horbonoses.

"You've come here to kill me and destroy my home," Serhiy told them, "and we are meant to be friends? We can only be enemies."

The day they left, the Russian soldiers grabbed everything they could from the village. The tanks were piled high with mattresses and pink suitcases, the armoured vehicles stuffed full of bedsheets, toys and washing machines.

Beneath the veneer of propaganda slogans, the soldiers from the cellar were self-interested men. They showed no remorse about the war crimes their army was committing; there were no arguments about "democracy" to appeal to in them. But maybe that didn't matter. Not right now. What mattered was to make sure they lost.

After the retreat from Chernihiv, the soldiers' unit was transferred to the east of Ukraine, to Donbas, into the meat grinder where Russian soldiers were being sent by their commanders to be killed en masse.

Though the real figures were hidden, some fifty thousand Russian soldiers were calculated to have died in Ukraine in the first year of the war.[1] Russia sent waves of experienced soldiers alongside even larger numbers of mobilised kids, conscripts from poor families who couldn't avoid the draft or went to war in the hope that they could rape and loot, and convicts recruited from jail and sent into battle, stumbling, seemingly on narcotics, into gunfire. Mounds of corpses were left to stagnate on the fields of the front lines. Tens of thousands were sent to their deaths for a few pointless kilometres.

"Your son did not die in vain," President Putin told the mother of a soldier killed in Ukraine, speaking to a long table of specially selected mothers of dead soldiers, many sitting in the black headscarves of mourning, many of them members of pro-government organisations. "Some people die of vodka, and their lives go unnoticed. But your son really lived and achieved his goal," argued the president. The mothers nodded obediently for the cameras.[2]

As the death count in Ukraine rose, the Kremlin tried to glorify the sacrifice. "Life is highly overrated," intoned one of Russia's top political talk show hosts, Vladimir Soloviev, dressed as always in all black like a sorcerer. The war had given Russians "non-material dreams" and "lofty goals".[3]

Would the sort of soldiers who were in the basement in Lukashivka also nod and accept the "lofty goals"? Or would their inner Schweine-hund be sniffing desperately for a way out?

● ● ● ━━━ ━━━ ━━━ ● ● ●

As the war worsened for the Nazis, Joseph Goebbels was also try-ing to make sacrifice more attractive. In mid-1943 he commissioned a colour film on the siege of the German town of Kolberg, on the

Baltic, by Napoleon's armies in 1806. Goebbels gave the film a budget of 8.5 million Reichsmarks, twice the budget of most Nazi films. He hired 4,000 sailors and 187,000 soldiers to act in the battle scenes, when the real front desperately needed them. The film was to be a hymn to death. Goebbels wrote the speeches extolling sacrifice himself: "Death is entwined with victory," says the mayor of Kolberg. "The greatest achievements are always borne in pain."[4]

Nazi propaganda claimed that it celebrated death for a higher cause, the construction of the thousand-year Reich. As the prospects for the glorious future faded, the accent became ever more on glorious death as an end in itself.

Picking apart the attraction of heroic death was one of Delmer's foci in the preparation for D-Day. His main job was to "soften up" German troops in the run-up to the invasion, to develop the desire to defect, desert, and generally make them less willing to sacrifice themselves for Hitler's cause. He needed to bring out the Schweinehund like never before.

● ● ● ▬▬▬ ▬▬▬ ▬▬▬ ● ● ●

As D-Day APPROACHED, GERMAN soldiers, sailors and airmen who liked to smoke self-rolled cigarettes would have felt themselves most fortunate to pick up a free pack of Efka cigarette papers, with their familiar drawings of palm trees and pyramids, that someone had left behind on a café table or on the seat on a train, or to discover a pack they had completely forgotten about buried deep in the pockets of their greatcoats.[5] But when they opened them, instead of the expected fifty cigarette papers, they found ten tightly folded sheets of thin paper. On opening these sheets, the members of the Wehrmacht found excerpts from a manual titled *Krankheit rettet* (*Illness Saves*), authored by a certain "Dr Wohltat" (Dr Do Good). Flicking through them, they would glimpse an introductory letter from the good doctor, followed by instructions and delicate drawings of various plants—just printing these intricate drawings on such thin and tightly folded paper was already a feat in itself. Someone had clearly taken great care in the

production of whatever *Krankheit rettet* was. And what did this para-
doxical title mean? How can illness save?

The man behind Dr Do Good was Professor John T. MacCurdy of
Corpus Christi College, Cambridge. MacCurdy dressed in a long black
coat with a lion's-head clasp, which he rarely took off. Delmer called
him "MB's very own Witch Doctor. A wise one-eyed Canadian."[6] He
would visit Delmer and his team weekly at Woburn, guiding one of the
PWE's most sustained projects to undermine Goebbels's propaganda
of glorious death and to encourage German soldiers to abandon their
missions.

A psychiatrist who had been an early, if sceptical, part of the psy-
choanalytical movement, MacCurdy taught courses like "Dreams and
the Unconscious" and "Theory and Practice of Psychoanalysis" at Cambridge. Since World War I he had researched the mental states of soldiers. He advanced the view that there were two principal wishes
involved in what he labelled "war neuroses": "the wish for death and the
wish for a wound. . . . Those who suffer from anxiety states have wished
for death during the period of strain and fatigue preceding the final
collapse . . . or for some disabling illness."[7]

Some soldiers yearned for death to relieve the stress of war in an
honourable way or to rid themselves of the burden of responsibility of
commanding fellow soldiers; others wished to save themselves with an
injury that would get them sent home from the front. At Woburn, the
challenge for MacCurdy was to stimulate the desire to abscond from
the fighting and downplay the desire to sacrifice yourself for a greater
cause. But that meant working out what could make death attractive in
the first place.

Ideas about the attraction of death were being debated among psychoanalysts at the time. "There is an age-old conviction," explains Josh
Cohen, "important to religious, national, and other affiliations that
to believe in an entity means readiness to die for it, as though it only
becomes real at the moment you're ready to sacrifice yourself to it. It
endows death with meaning, and to the true believer, it gives assur-
ance you'll be remembered. It is a death you choose, that endows the
choice with agency. Freud suggested more than once that you could

love being in an army or a religion with the same force and energy as loving another individual."[8]

In Delmer's memoirs, curiously, he associates such feelings with Ukrainians: indeed, it is only when he sees Ukrainians ready to die for their nation that he starts to realise that Ukraine is a "real" country. In 1939 he was reporting from western Ukraine as it was seized by Nazi-backed Hungarians, when he saw a group of Ukrainian partisans who had been captured: "A gang of prisoners were marched down the main street carrying a heavy log on their shoulders. For the first time I really believed there was such a thing as the Ukraine. Seconds later I saw them shot, all six of them, one after the other. They went down in a shrieking, sobbing, kicking tangle, still chained to the log."[9] In the 1930s, as in the 2020s, Ukrainians were seen as emblematic of people dying so that their cause might live.

"But there's another way psychoanalysts at the time looked at death in war," says Cohen. "Not death for a greater cause, but death for the sake of death, and murder for the sake of murder."[10] After having witnessed the self-destructive horrors of World War I, Freud concluded that "thanatos", the death drive, was as powerful as the "love drive" of "eros". In *Beyond the Pleasure Principle* he related thanatos to a desire to dissolve oneself back into a state before all the responsibility and burden of being oneself: "An urge inherent in organic life to restore an earlier state of things which the living entity has been obliged to abandon . . . the expression of the inertia inherent in organic life."[11]

"But as this drive was self-destructive," Cohen explained, "Freud believed it bumped up against a desire to live and was then turned outward into aggression: we kill others so as not to kill ourselves. It bred a condition where passivity was interspersed with spurts of aggression."[12]

MacCurdy had been early in spotting how the focus on death for the sake of death was becoming an ever greater part of Nazi propaganda. In an analysis of a Hitler speech from April 1942, MacCurdy observed that Hitler had lost the belief that he could enter a state of "shamanic" ecstasy and transmit "truth". Instead of leading the nation on a journey to glory, Hitler now dwelt on his death as a sacrifice in the struggle against the ultimate evil: Jewry. "The notion of a great military victory had passed into the background while he poses more as a martyr, the speech ending on the theme of his death." Hitler was embracing "the dying god myth".[13]

In the debates MacCurdy was steeped in, death propaganda offered two attractions: the "positive" seduction of dying for a greater cause; and the darker desire to surrender your will to live and just dissolve into nothingness. Any plan to undermine the allure of the Nazis' appeal to sacrifice had, first of all, to position itself as part of a positive collective mission, had to be somehow a part of your duty to your fellow Germans; second, it had to restore your sense of being able to act and overcome the desire to just sink into passive acceptance of your demise. A PWE strategy document put the challenge bluntly: "A lust for self immolation is not infrequent among Germans. While it may lead to a willingness to fight on to a Nibelungen end it should not be impossible to divert this urge to an acceptance of surrender as a great self-sacrificing and honourable act of patriotism."[14]

This was the trick *Illness Saves* tried to put into practice. In the manual German soldiers pulled out of the EFKA packets, Dr Wohltat explained the dangers of "war strain" that came with years of service, how fatigue built up quietly over the years and was so subtle that doctors could miss it, but it could cause a breakdown at any moment. The doctors' lack of knowledge about "war strain" was clearly a disaster in waiting for the safety of a military unit during an operation. Indeed, this oversight in medical science meant it was the soldiers' patriotic duty to fake illness and get sent home or to a hospital from the front.[15]

MacCurdy insisted that "the malingerer must give the physician the impression that here is a patriotic citizen, dedicated to his duty, who has the misfortune to be ill despite himself". And he must never try to name or define his disease, for that was up to the doctor to do: "One single symptom which the doctor has discovered by his own questions, is worth ten the patient has volunteered."[16]

The rest of the manual was filled with examples of how to give yourself serious symptoms—without causing lasting damage.

For a throat infection, for example, apply silver nitrate on the tonsils and swallow a small amount of gunpowder.[17] Faking TB was harder but effective because there was so much of it about a doctor could easily be convinced you had it. If you were working at a munitions factory, obtain a few drops of dinitrophenol, which is used in the manufacture of explosives. A tiny amount taken every day will cause high temperature and fever. Then tell the doctor you also have blood in your mucus. He will test it for bacilli. To create counterfeit TB bacilli, avoid washing for a few days and allow some "cheese" to form beneath your foreskin. Then mix this "cheese" with your mucus and a little blood you draw from out of your finger—and swallow the mixture.[18]

For violent diarrhoea, munch on the dried seeds from the corn cockle flower, which grows wild in cornfields.[19] To make sure you could find this and other useful plants, there was a whole appendix of beautifully drawn flora that caused various rashes, lesions, burns and blisters on the skin. Isabel Delmer drew all the illustrations: "I had to make drawings so accurate there could be no mistake about the plant."[20]

Dr Do Good was always spurring you towards action, towards being a sort of theatrical actor on the stage of deception, nudging you away from passively accepting death.

For the manual to be credible, it had to actually work. And that meant someone at Woburn had to test all the formulas. For such tasks, Delmer inevitably turned to one man: "Halkett will see to it" had become a commonplace order. "I tried out everything in that book—it was sometimes painful," Halkett would recall. He didn't detail whether he tried the formula for faking TB but was certainly upset that Delmer's memoirs didn't credit him properly for his work.[21]

For Delmer, these "malingering manuals" had a double purpose: to help soldiers get out from the front lines but also to force German military medics to trust their patients less as they learned about the existence of the manuals. This distrust, in turn, meant that real patients would suffer, and this could increase the enmity between medics and soldiers. Almost everything that Delmer did had a double, often triple, purpose.

The malingering manual would be so successful that the Germans made a copy, translated it—and then directed it across British lines. The concept had, Delmer admitted, boomeranged.[22]

• • • ▬▬ ▬▬ ▬▬ • • •

No one handled death as deftly as Father Elmar. In a broadcast from February 28, 1944, Lent, he contrasted how the Nazis and the church treat the subject of sacrifice. While Christianity offered personal immortality and salvation, the Nazis peddled dying for the "eternal life of the German people". You sacrificed yourself so that "Germany can live forever". But the Germany the Nazis were creating was a misery, where life itself had no value, where they would "kill anyone who does not suit them, let them die through cold or starvation". The Nazis had "shaken the Christian belief in Judgement Day and life after death", promised to build heaven on earth, but instead had merely built a hell. And because the Nazis "made the lives of their subjects so miserable, many prefer not existing at all to living painfully". This has caused a "rising suicide curve in the German Reich". Suicide was the logical end point of the Nazi "religion". Christ, concluded the broadcast, offered the "redemption and the eternal life of the soul".[23]

Delmer's exploitation of the Germans' feelings about death could be less elevated—though pursued a similar agenda.

As D-Day approached, the grieving relatives of German soldiers started to receive letters on the letterheads of the hospitals their sons had died in. The letters claimed to be from a fellow patient who had witnessed the last, often painful hours of the deceased. They wrote movingly to the distraught parents about how they saw their beloved child pass away, how nobly their dead child had struggled, and then, almost as an afterthought, mentioned a precious ring or crucifix that the recently deceased had given the Nazi official at the hospital to send on to their relatives. Delmer was behind these letters, forged by Ellic Howe, and he calculated that the parents would be upset at this extra information: they had not received these precious mementos. What had happened to the rings and crucifixes? A little while later the Sender would be full of stories about the "corpse robbers", corrupt Nazi officials who took away the valuable souvenirs that dead soldiers had intended for their loved ones. The Sender's presenters would solemnly read out names of those who had been thus burgled—the same names as mentioned in the letters. Instead of granting a glorious death and eternal glory, the Nazis were robbing people of their lives, their futures, their treasures.[24]

Other letters accused the Nazis of even more terrible treatment of
their own soldiers:

> Dear Frau Muller,
> They told you that your son Heinz died from jaundice. That
> was not the case. We were in the same Company and he was
> a fine Chap. They had to amputate his leg and afterwards gave
> him a lethal injection. This often happens to war cripples.[25]

The Nazis, these letters insinuated, would rather kill those who were
unable to fight than look after them.

When Delmer asked Halkett to read one of these stories on the
Sender, the artist was affronted: "Please don't give me that sort of script
again. It's dirty."

But Delmer's tricks were only getting dirtier.

Some parents could never accept that their sons had been killed in
action. They were convinced, or rather wanted to convince themselves,
that their sons had actually been captured by the Allies, and they kept
on writing to the British and American governments, asking if they
held their sons as POWs. And even after the Allies explained that there
was no trace of their children, some parents still couldn't accept they
were really dead. And so they kept on writing, as if their children were
still alive. "Immensely moving they were," remembered Delmer, "these
letters written by the old mother of the dead man or the father. They
gave him the family news just as though he was still alive. 'Dear Martin. Your sister Erna is married to Fritz Klausen. They were married on
his last leave. And she now has a delightful little boy. She named him
Martin after you. Think of it, dear Martin, you are an uncle now . . . do
let us hear from you soon, dear boy. We think of you all the time.'"

These "dead letters" made Delmer feel what he called "weepy", but
he nevertheless took full advantage of them, "for here was a ready made
opportunity to push our desertion campaign".

Soon enough these parents were receiving mysterious letters,
posted from inside Germany: "Dear Frau. . . . Please make no inquiries
about the whereabouts of Martin. He is safe and well in a neutral country with a good job. . . . When this terrible war Hitler caused is ended,

he will either return to you or send for you. He asks me to send his best greetings to you and Erna. . . . Please tell no one about this letter."[26]

Delmer's "calculation was that no parents would be able to resist the temptation of passing the good news of their son's salvation to at least one close friend. And thus the news of the successful desertion of German soldiers to neutral countries would spread, and more and more Germans, I hoped, would be encouraged to follow their example."

It was, Delmer admitted, "the only one of our many operations against the Germans of which I feel a little ashamed when I think of it today". So he tried to make up for it in his own weird way. The deceived parents received hampers of food from neutral countries, supposedly sent from their resurrected children, that showed how good life was beyond the Reich:

> Some of the grateful parents became our best propagandists. One old baronial Lord of the Manor in Pomerania was so moved . . . he placed it on a table in front of his house and made the whole of the village march past the parcel to inspect what his dear son Siegismund-Sizzo had sent his old father "from over there". . . . I felt sorrier than ever for the wives and parents and sisters in whom we were stimulating these false hopes. But this time they were at least getting something out of it. Something to eat.[27]

Delmer's "dead letters" and food hampers from hell were being delivered by a network of underground agents throughout Europe.

> As though to symbolise the TOP secrecy of my work for OVER-LORD I had been assigned an office on the top-most floor of my department's new headquarters in Bush House . . . here in this eyrie, high up over London, I now received our hush-hush callers—Poles, Danes, Frenchmen, Hollanders.

Delmer's guests were members of resistance groups working covertly inside German-controlled territory, who had come to be briefed for D-Day. Beyond delivering the letters, Delmer had more requests of them. When they killed a German, they should make it look like it was done by a German resistance movement. In the absence of a genuine anti-Nazi struggle, Delmer wanted to simulate one and confuse the Gestapo and SS. The stories of Nazis murdered by mysterious German resistance movements would then be reinforced on the Sender.[28]

A dismal death was coming for them too—and from their own brethren.

●　●　●　▬▬▬　▬▬▬　▬▬▬　●　●　●

IF THESE "DEAD LETTERS" made Delmer feel ashamed, *Nachrichten für die Truppen*, his largest D-Day project, was "of all the enterprises I launched during the war . . . the one of which I am the proudest".[29] Bruce Lockhart called it the PWE's "most ambitious achievement in the war".[30]

Nachrichten was a daily newspaper. A team of twenty-five American and British editors and journalists worked on it in a barrack rapidly constructed by Milton Bryant (MB). Production started at 11:00 p.m., when the editors took the latest Sender broadcasts, adapted them for text, added photos and maps and included specially written columns. Halkett was in charge of the German copy. Isabel worked on the layout, photos and illustrations. At 3:00 a.m. a female dispatch rider would motorcycle the proofs to Delmer's rooms and wake him. The telephone in the editing suite would soon ring with Delmer shouting changes, which were then fixed before the copy was sent to be printed, guillotined and packed into laminated-wax, sixty-inch packages. At 6:00 p.m., US Army trucks picked up the copies and drove the newspapers to Cheddington, home to the US Leaflet Bombers. At a height of a thousand feet a fuse burned the container, and the printed materials fluttered down, nine thousand leaflets to a bomb, over an area of just one square mile, so by night-time hundreds of thousands of copies of *Nachrichten* were over enemy lines, ready to be read by German soldiers in the morning, often earlier than the Nazi newspapers. This was one of the most dangerous news runs in history.[31]

In French fields and roadsides, German soldiers picked up the newspaper that had just dropped from the sky. They knew perfectly well it wasn't German. Unlike the Sender, it used neutral language: German troops were not "ours" but were defined by their army and squadron number. The *Nachrichten* took no sides, just matter-of-factly reinforced how the German army was losing, implying that the leadership had lost its way and it was time to think about self-preservation, not self-sacrifice. It calmly informed the reader that the Americans were supplying the Russians with new armour-piercing bombs, that the police in occupied France were so impotent they were unable to locate murderers on the loose, that the number of German soldiers deserting to neutral territories was growing and that some were even sending food parcels back home.[32]

With D-Day nearing, the tenor of the radio shows rose. On Christ the King, Father Elmar railed against the arrest of Catholic Austrian cardinals by the Vienna SS, urging his listeners to tear out of their hearts "the poison of National-Socialism which makes blind and insensible against injustice and misery". He no longer disguised his desire for Austrian independence: "We Austrians long for the day when we can live again as free citizens in a free land."[33]

On Short Wave 30.7, there was something new. The programme opened with "SSKGY, the SS Battle Group York". And then came the presenter: an SS man who was sick of Himmler and of the party, and was leading a rebel SS cell in Poland. The presenter was Hans Zech-Nenntwich, who had served in the SS in Poland, where he had supplied arms to the Polish resistance, which in turn helped him escape to England. That part of the story was corroborated. The rest was uncertain: Zech-Nenntwich claimed he was part of an internal SS resistance cell. Delmer had no idea if it was true. Halkett thought the story nonsense. But Zech-Nenntwich was useful for all the latest SS gossip and the latest SS slang.

Over on the Sender, Vicki's concerts were becoming ever more elaborate: "We began to manufacture whole troop concerts. Pretending that our songs and sketches were performed by soldiers and nurses at the front, we acted and sang them ourselves in the most endearing and amateurish way. One of our soldiers even managed to fall into the drum with a resounding crash on his way up onto the stage."[34]

In the weeks leading up to D-Day, the news on the Sender was giving ever more details about petrol and supply shortages for the army, about how all the best kit was being given to the Eastern Front, and about how General Rommel was coming up with a clearly absurd and desperate plan to attack England with gliders. The news was rife with examples of almost casual desertion, sabotage and insubordination.[35]

In Dresden, Victor Klemperer heard more rumours about demoralisation in the army, along with grumblings of revolt:

> Over Whitsun the Windes visited their navy twins in Swinemünde. Frau Winde said: "It" would start in the navy, as in 1918. Unpopular officers had been thrashed. Emergency slaughtering of livestock was now being carried out on a large scale, food for the winter was no longer assured, the government was staking everything it had.[36]

Rising in the morning of June 6, Halkett came out on the lawn behind the house and heard an enormous noise. Looking up, as far as he could see, covering the whole horizon, were aeroplanes flying in one direction. One of the planes let forth a burst of gunfire, and a lot of tracer bullets came down. It was a gunner trying out his machine gun. The invasion had started.[37]

For listeners across Europe, the Sender was the first radio to break the story of the landings, reporting on them at 4:50 a.m. while Goebbels's radio still slumbered: "The enemy is landing with force from the air and from the sea. The Atlantic Wall is penetrated in several places."

The leaflet bombers were already delivering the latest *Nachrichten*. A million copies had been printed specially for D-Day.[38] "Armour penetrates deep into the interior," went the headline; "there are reports of bitter fighting with parachute commandoes in Normandy and the Mouth of the Seine."

The mention of the "Mouth of the Seine" was a piece of deception, helping the Allies distract from the Normandy focus of the invasion. The other article on the front page of the *Nachrichten* was about an impending Soviet offensive, which casually mentioned that the head of the German general staff was currently visiting the Eastern Front: the soldier on the Western Front was meant to infer that the East was Berlin's priority and he was being abandoned to the Allied onslaught.[39]

The mood at Woburn, Delmer felt, was a little subdued. As the German POWs and émigré newsreaders gathered for programmes the week of D-Day, Delmer thought he could detect that despite their desire for Hitler's Germany to perish, despite the risks of Nazi retribution against them and their families, there was also among them

> a secret, often subconscious sympathy and sadness with which these men now watched their countrymen across the channel being bludgeoned into extinction. . . . Not for nothing had we immersed ourselves so completely in the life and surroundings of our Wehrmacht listeners. We were able to feel those cannonades as though they were coming down on our own heads, and the talks which my speakers now put out reflected this. They had in them an undertone of personal tragedy which made these ephemeral pieces of psychological warfare as moving for me to listen to as if they had been the greatest literature.[40]

The first D-Day broadcasts spoke of how:

> the will to sacrifice on the part of our men and our navy was extraordinary. One torpedo flotilla against large destroyer groups. Of course one can't expect success from such proportions. You get the feeling that if our men shoot down one enemy bomber, there are many more coming right behind. In the area between Le Havre and Cherbourg the enemy has landed, they were able to land tanks and armed cars, it will be pretty difficult for our infantry to cope with all this.[41]

To Delmer's ears, Halkett's speech was the best of the lot. He delivered it in the staccato rhythm of a Prussian officer, as 1.5 million leaflets fluttered down onto German troops urging surrender:[42]

This is a report, an epitaph, a warning. It is a warning to all of those who may be lying in an outpost somewhere on the beaches, or are stationed somewhere up on a hill, or on the coast. And as they lie there they may get the order, "Hold on, the reinforcements are on their way to you."

The reinforcements will not come. They cannot come because nothing is being done about sending reinforcements, because all these men have been written off—written off as dead and lost.

Here is the warning story which the few survivors of the 716th Infantry Division have brought back with them. On Tuesday came the first attack on the coast. The division got the order "hold on, reinforcements are on the way." By Thursday for all practical purposes the division was surrounded and overrun. In its rear were the enemy parachutists. In front lay the enemy battlecruisers firing at them, hacking their concrete dugouts to shreds. Overhead in the sky, a thick curtain of enemy aircraft. They drop a never ending barrage of bombs and explode what is left of the minefields. Far and wide not so much as a single German fighter. But an order did get through at last from the Command: "Hold Out. Hold out to the last round of ammunition."

Halkett paused for a moment for the senselessness of the order to sink in. Then he went on:

There they lay in their smashed and slit up dugouts, naked, without cover. Grenadiers with pistols and machine guns and anti-tank guns. Guns which they were never to get a chance to fire.

After another pause,

That was literally all that was done for the 716th Infantry Division. Left behind to be overrun and rubbed out were 4,000 men, 4,000 comrades left in the trap, defenceless, deserted, without cover or help. In front of them on the water lay the enemy battleships. Those enemy battleships had fun with a little target practice against our fortification and our boys. That was the end of a division. The end of comrades who held out and waited for reinforcements or relief. Who did not know they had been written off—written off from the very beginning.[43]

Delmer thought that it was a "brilliant performance" and that behind it was genuine "misery and bitterness" in Halkett's voice.[44] Part of it, Delmer judged, may have been conscious acting. But most of it, he thought, was genuinely felt—the resentment and sorrow of an officer seeing his fellow countrymen laying down their lives for a regime of criminals and cranks.

In the interviews about his life recorded decades later, Halkett never quite confirmed or denied whether he had any genuine feelings during his speech or whether he had been purely "putting it on", as with the earlier talk that his co-host Sepp had fallen for. But he resented how Delmer had reduced him to something of a caricature: a Prussian officer with German sympathies, "an actor owned by the character he performed".[45] One can understand Halkett's frustration at being made a mere character in someone else's story. He was an artist. He'd acted on the stage professionally. He was one of the creative forces at Woburn: co-author of the malingerers' handbook, co-editor and lead writer of *Nachrichten*, always innovating on the radio shows. He was an author, not someone else's sketch. And who was Delmer to define when he was genuine and when he was acting? Who was Delmer to define what reality was, what the truth was, in the first place?[46]

CHAPTER 9

VALKYRIE

At 8:10 p.m. on July 20, 1944, the ribbon of the Hellschreiber printed out a piece of news so stunning that Dr Hans Berman, the newsreader on duty at the time, had to call Delmer at dinner right away: "It has happened. The Army has risen against the Party. They have tried to murder Hitler."

Delmer thought this was one more of his Propagandatruppe's tricks. It was too good to be true. A revolt of the army against the party was all that he had been working for.[1]

Berman put the phone receiver to the speakers in MB, which was playing the official Nazi radio news reporting on the assassination attempt. Only the bare facts were known. A bomb had been planted to kill Hitler, but it had failed. The same evening, Fritzsche was already blaming the failed plot on "enemy work".[2]

At 12:59 a.m., on July 21, Hitler broadcast a speech—proof that he was alive. Bruce Lockhart thought he sounded "shaken".[3] The assassination attempt, Hitler claimed, had been the work of "an extremely small clique of ambitious, unscrupulous and at the same time foolish and criminally stupid officers". He named a renegade officer, Colonel von Stauffenberg, as their ringleader: he had already been arrested and executed. Hitler claimed that the coup had nothing to do with the armed forces in general.[4] At midday Fritzsche again stressed how small the conspiracy had been: "Two figures left over from the past, together with a quarter of a dozen collaborators."[5]

Reading the Hitler speech reprinted in a newspaper, Victor Klemperer noted a contradiction: the Führer also ordered that no one follow the orders of the "usurpers" and made Himmler, head of the SS, in charge of the Replacement Army, which was based inside Germany proper. Maybe this "clique" of usurpers wasn't so small after all? How big was this rebellion?[6]

Delmer's aim was to make the conspiracy sound as widespread as possible. The Sender labelled it a "peace putsch" led by a widespread network of people in the highest echelons in the army who knew that the war was lost and wanted to save Germany. The Sender demanded that the war be stopped and for the first time attacked Hitler himself. "The British, the Americans and the Russians are the last people to want to rid us of the Führer," read Halkett, his customary monocle jammed into his left eye. "On the contrary, the enemy can wish for nothing better than to have us led by a man who has never learned the soldier's trade, who relies on mystic inspiration, who in his conceit and ignorance interferes in everything and everywhere. Why, a fellow like that is for the allies . . . an ally!"[7]

Delmer hoped to exacerbate the split between the German army and the party. In its first reports, the BBC played along and stated that "in Germany, a civil war has broken out".[8] In Dresden, Klemperer heard through the other inhabitants of the special house set aside for Jews about the BBC announcement: "English broadcast: There was 'civil war' in Germany. Joke from Professor Winde (his own?): All Germany was standing in mourning at Hitler's empty coffin."[9] He heard other rumours, too: five thousand officers had been shot, numerous workers arrested. The story about workers seemed consequential to Klemperer: Was the rebellion spreading?[10]

Anthony Eden, the foreign minister, ordered the BBC to be more circumspect—he wanted more proof of the size of the conspiracy before committing to such rhetoric. The PWE's analysts would eventually

decide that "there is no civilian political opposition capable of supporting, let alone initiating, a revolution. . . . This rising is effectively suppressed; it is unlikely that any similar rising will be possible for some
time."[11] The conspirators had hoped to create so much chaos by killing
Hitler that it would give the sense they were more numerous, and this
perception would allow the plotters to seize control. They had planned
for the bomb to go off during a meeting scheduled to take place in a
bunker, which would have multiplied the blast. When the meeting (and
the bomb) was moved to a cabin, the plot failed.

Delmer still thought it a missed opportunity. The BBC, Delmer
rued in his memoirs, was "stopped from saying anything to encourage the rebels, they were specifically ordered to announce that His
Majesty's Government was not prepared to absolve the army from its
responsibility for the war or to differentiate Germans and Germans. All
were responsible. The only terms on which Germany could have peace
were—as before—unconditional capitulation."[12]

The botched assassination had the opposite effect from what the
conspirators and Delmer hoped: it united the army and the party. On
July 26, Klemperer recorded how a soldier on the street lifted his arm
as if to give a regular army salute—and then suddenly contorted it into
a "Heil Hitler". Soldiers had never given the Hitler salute before. The
order had come from the army's High Command, so desperate were
they to exhibit loyalty.

The language of the army, Klemperer noticed two days later, was
intermingling with the party's: "For the first time the word 'fanatically'
is in a military bulletin! After the introduction of the German greeting,
this word has now been taken into the official language of the army!"[13]
"Fanatical" had been one of the negative terms given a positive spin by
the Nazis, an insult they had remodelled as something to aspire to. It
had never been used by the army—until now.

On July 26 Goebbels gave a long radio address on the failed assassination attempt. That morning Hitler had finally granted him his wish
and made him plenipotentiary of total war. He was riding high again.

Goebbels put himself at the centre of the story to suppress the coup.
He talked slowly, deliberately, with a restrained, purring passion about
how he had gathered loyal soldiers at his house on the first day. How he

organised the loyal troops to hold Berlin from the few units that had followed the orders of the "usurpers".

The plot itself, Goebbels explained, his voice now rising, was of foreign origin. The explosives had been English. Hadn't Allied media always talked up splits between the army and the party, priming Germans for just such an assassination attempt? Clearly, they were to blame.

Goebbels described in indulgent detail Hitler's miraculous escape from the attempted murder, as if he worshipped every piece of furniture and pose of every person in this near religious happening. The Führer had been standing up in the long cabin at the Wolf's Lair field headquarters in East Prussia, dictating his military plans over war maps, pointing the way forward. His generals surrounded him, seated along the long table, all enraptured with attention. When the bomb went off, the table with war maps had protected the Führer.

The miracle, Goebbels went on, had restored his sense that history had meaning, that Hitler had been sent to Germany with a mission that he would now clearly fulfil, despite all the trials and tribulations of the war.[14]

"People's comrades connect directly mystical, religious notions with the figure of the Führer," wrote the SD in the immediate aftermath of the assassination attempt.[15] Since the Allied success at D-Day, their reports had made depressing reading for Goebbels. Now there was a unity of outrage at the attempted assassination. For many Germans the act seemed downright sacrilegious. In different streets in different cities, women burst out in apparently spontaneous tears of gratitude, calling out thanks to God for saving the Führer's life. Around 350,000 (according to the SD) came out on the streets of Vienna to express their loyalty, love and relief, and 50,000 in the smaller city of Freiburg. When the SS opened letters home from soldiers, these too displayed renewed fealty to the Führer—and fury at von Stauffenberg's conspirators. The Allies' research showed that among German POWs in France, belief in Hitler rose from 57 percent to 68 percent in the month after the failed assassination.[16]

On the surface at least, the people were displaying a renewed adoration of their leader. What dissent there was had to be muted: an unpatriotic letter could have you sentenced to death. You had to keep your real thoughts disguised. In Berchtesgaden the SD recorded how in the darkness of an air-raid shelter, a woman's voice was heard saying, "If only they'd gotten to him."[17]

"I am in fact very depressed," wrote Klemperer. "They [the Nazis] still have the press and the power and all that goes with it, contrary to every natural law they have once again maintained their invulnerability. In terms of propaganda they have drawn something rousing, a mood of victory out of a most serious defeat, millions will once more believe in final victory."[18]

On August 6 *Das Reich* ran an article by Goebbels on the new spirit: "The one good aspect to 20 July was that it brought each of us to attention. Suddenly the nation stood before an abyss and peered into its terrifying depth. If 20 July has any larger meaning it is this: It brought each one of us back to the essence of our struggle for existence."[19]

Now the nation could be reunited in a common purpose. Goebbels mobilised an extra million soldiers; theatres and orchestras were closed down, and actors and musicians were called up; the maximum age of mobilisation was raised. A home guard, the *Volkssturm*, recruited men from six to sixty to defend every last street and square: every part of life was being militarised. On the Volksempfänger the Reich's radio prepared the people with one last propaganda push: temporary loss of territory didn't matter, for it could always be retaken; all that mattered was the spirit of no capitulation; Germany's lethal new weapons, the V1 bombs, were sweeping down on Britain; it is only the final spurt that counts in the race.[20]

Delmer's desire to use the assassination attempt to finally split the army and party failed. But he would soon realise that he had played an important part in influencing the assassination attempt in other ways.

Delmer considered most of the coup plotters to be opportunists who had waited for Hitler to start losing the war before they acted. He made an exception for Otto John, who had been involved in the plot together with his brother. A senior manager at the state Lufthansa airline, John had been cooperating with the British since 1942 and escaped from Berlin to Madrid and from there to Britain in the weeks after the failed assassination. He would become a vital figure in Delmer's inner editorial circle in the final year of the war, living in Delmer's house and spilling the latest gossip about the Nazi elites. He was, Delmer became convinced, one of the few examples of Germans who were genuinely motivated by a "deep Christian conviction . . . to expiate their nation's crimes".[21]

The conspirators had, John explained, taken Delmer very seriously: "I learned that our broadcasts had indeed been heard by the conspirators." All high-level officers of course knew that the Sender was British but saw in it a message that Delmer claims to have planted on purpose, that a revolt against Hitler would lead to a peace deal with the Allies. "Such a separate peace was of course out of the question," admitted Delmer:

> I am sorry the generals ended their lives on Hitler's meat hooks. But I cannot say I have any compunction about having raised false hopes in them. For these men and their caste were the original patrons and sponsors of Hitler's movement. They were the profiteers of his Reich. And they only rose against him when it was clear that he and his war of conquest were doomed.[22]

But the case of the failed assassination coup forces a question that has been stalking this story: To what extent, and how exactly, did Delmer's tricks help win the war? The example of the botched coup showed how, on the one hand, the Sender had managed to influence the behaviour of a specific group of people and helped bolster an action that, if it had worked, would have severely undermined the Nazis. However, the larger aim of splitting the army and the party had failed. German soldiers would keep fighting and dying, street by street, until the Soviet army took Berlin. Is this not a sign that Goebbels actually won the propaganda war? There's even a renowned book from the 1970s about Nazi propaganda that is simply called *The War That Hitler Won*.

Sir Michael Balfour, the PWE official who would later write a history of the role of propaganda in World War II, was brutal in his final assessment of all propaganda efforts (from the BBC to Delmer): "British propaganda to Germany must . . . be said to have failed" because of the imposition of "unconditional surrender".[23] It didn't matter how clever the PWE could be, for the Allies demanded total military victory as the only strategy. Germans simply had no choice but to fight to the last street. Historians to this day debate this argument. Some argue that other factors were more important: a desire not to repeat the capitulation of World War I, the theoretically pragmatic hope that fighting on would force the Allies into milder peace terms, and on the Eastern Front, fear of Soviet atrocities that kept Germans fighting.[24]

When asked about his impact, Delmer tended to avoid answering head-on. Propaganda was a mere aid to military and political success; it could work no miracles. Moreover "our task as I saw it was to corrode and erode with a steady drip of subversive news and 'evidence' the iron system of control in which Hitler's police state had locked the body and soul of the German people . . . helping to hasten the collapse of Hitler's military and social apparatus".[25] And although many Germans did fight until the end, there was corrosion of their will.

German soldiers on the Western Front, the target of Delmer's media, did desert and surrender in droves, unlike those on the Eastern Front. They did so for many reasons—not least because they had good reason to think the Allies would respect the rights of POWs while the Soviets did not, but the Sender and *Nachrichten* could have helped. Delmer tells an anecdote about how when the 9th US Infantry Division approached the fort in front of Cherbourg, they appealed to General von Schlieben to surrender. The general called out over the ramparts: "I cannot surrender, my orders are to fight to the last man and cartridge. It would be different if you could prove to me that our position is hopeless." He asked the Americans to fire a new phosphorus super-weapon that the Sender had been spreading rumours about, claiming it could cut through concrete. If the Americans could show they had it, he would have to surrender. The super-weapon didn't exist: it was a Sender story talking up the Allied threat. So the Americans fired a plain shell into the air. Von Schlieben raised a white flag. If he had ever suspected the concrete-busting weapon existed, which is unlikely in the first place, he must have known it was a fib when he saw the simple shell fired. Both sides were pretending that a Sender rumour was true in order to give the Germans an honourable way to surrender. The story is not confirmed, but it shows again how propaganda for

Delmer was about giving people the excuse to do what they secretly desired anyway.[26]

On the home front, the energy that came after the assassination attempt soon faded. SD reports for the end of August 1944 stated that few people believed in victory. By September, the Stuttgart branch of the SD recorded people regularly making negative comments about Hitler himself: "The Führer was sent to us by God—in order to ruin Germany."[27] When Goebbels wrote an article in December praising the Führer as possessing a sixth sense that allowed him to see hidden truths, readers criticised Goebbels for making Hitler into a demigod; that trick was wearing very thin. Passive fatalism was taking over: "The majority of the population take refuge in resignation, and say as they shrug their shoulders 'everything is the same to me'."[28]

But how can one measure Delmer's influence on something as ineffable as "corrosion"? One would need to measure Germans' attitudes and behaviours before and after they had been exposed to Delmer's media, then somehow filter out other factors like military, diplomatic and political decisions that might affect them, control the attitudinal and behavioural changes in this group against another that wasn't exposed to the Woburn content and measure the difference. Delmer had no such opportunities.

But perhaps we can ask another question. Did Delmer have the right idea of how to engage his audiences? The effectiveness of propaganda, or counter-propaganda, indeed of any communication, depends on how well you understand your audience. By 1945, there was some research that could define this.

Since the middle of the war, Henry Dicks, a psychiatrist working for Military Intelligence, had been exploring the mindsets of German soldiers. Dicks spoke fluent German: his mother was Baltic–German, and he had spent his childhood in Estonia before his parents immigrated to Britain. He conducted and reviewed more than six hundred interviews with POWs and concluded that "the psychology of Nazis, as disclosed by detailed individual investigation of large numbers of them and subsequent statistical validation, fails to show gross mental disorder. It is characterised by an unconscious over-emphasis of paternal authority, evasion of responsibility by blaming scape-goats, over-valuation of masculinity, and depreciation of feminine and tender influences."

Dicks argued that Nazi supporters had overbearing, often abusive and frequently absent father figures, with the child simultaneously humiliated by them and yearning for acceptance.[29] The ensuing weak sense of individual agency led to a search for strong leaders and identification with an all-encompassing, abstract nation/family. Deifying impossibly perfect mother figures, and then attacking any woman who failed to live up to that, was common. Irrational spurts of aggression were a way to deal with the sense of inadequacy. Dicks saw the Nazi insistence on a "Lebensraum", the vast territories in Ukraine and Eastern Europe that the Nazis claimed as theirs, partly as a compensation for this cycle of frustrated recognition and humiliation: a geopolitical demand born not merely out of "rational self interest" but out of irrational "secondary narcissism".

"If primary narcissism is structural and necessary," explains Josh Cohen, "and is basically our investment in our own self-preservation, secondary narcissism involves specific character traits and habits—vanity, self-inflation, superiority, all of course masking an underlying fear of one's own inadequacy."[30]

Since Dicks's time, other researchers have cast doubt on the consistent connection between family dynamics and fascist tendencies: you can worship abusive strongmen without having a similar father, and having authoritarian parents can lead you to become highly liberal. But the way that propaganda narratives reflect personal psychological preferences and needs is now commonly accepted.[31]

"The relationships between earlier and later stages of life are too complex, and subject to too many variables, to be easily predictable," says Cohen. "But by now we can see that propaganda exploits vulnerabilities and anxieties that can originate in childhood and persist throughout our lives."[32]

Dicks would have had a field day with contemporary Russian propaganda, which seethes with the language of unhappy families. It's easy to hear Dicks's analysis when Russian propaganda both deifies Kyiv as the "mother of all Russian cities" and then accuses Ukraine of being a treacherous whore that deserves rape. You can hear it in the worshipping of political father figures like Putin or Stalin, with their "strong hand" that both protects and punishes. Dicks's interpretation of Nazi desires for a

"Lebensraum" maps onto how the Kremlin claims that Russia, already the world's largest country, deserves territory far beyond its gargantuan reach. This sense of fluid borders ranges from Russian far-right fantasies about a Eurasian empire that stretches from the Indian Ocean to the Atlantic, to the more common notion of a vague "Russo-sphere", which sometimes means anywhere where people happen to speak Russian. The Kremlin's diplomatic demand for a Russian "sphere of influence" denotes less something hard and defined, which can be hammered out with other "great powers" in some grand new geopolitical deal based on rational self-interest, but a sphere that also swells with suppressed resentment and what Dicks described as "secondary narcissism".

And just as scholars define different types of Russian audience today—ranging from "active supporters" to the larger groups of "passive supporters", "loyal neutrals" and the "apathetic"—so Dicks could segment Germans. Although some Germans were a psychologically ideal fit for Nazi propaganda, not all were. He calculated that 10 percent of German soldiers were "fanatical" Nazis and a further 25 percent were "believers with reservations". As the war neared its end, Dicks was most worried about this 25 percent: their Nazism was mixed with a more general admiration of German militarism, and they could easily blend in as good patriots in the Germany of the future without changing their underlying authoritarian predilections.

The largest group of German soldiers was the 40 percent of "unpolitical men." They were largely indifferent to the type of regime as long as it gave them "order and security". "Passive anti-Nazis" made up 15 percent; 10 percent were active anti-Nazis.[33]

In "Some Principles of Psychological Warfare Policy", Dicks suggested how to use his analysis and undermine the German war effort. Although some soldiers loved how the army allowed them to give up the burden of personal decision-making, others were upset at the constant "starvation of private interests, the injury to self-esteem" that can "lead to a re-activation of private needs".[34] Indeed, the more pressure the army applied to break people, the more individualistic they could become in contrast. Even the ones who yearned for a "strong hand" simultaneously resented it.

But "playing up that latent rebel" needed to be done carefully, with "sympathetic, insightful emphasis of the soldier's grouses" while stressing how "yes-men" and "party smart-Alecs" were being promoted in the system. The soldier needed to be reminded of the real emotional bonds he shared with his loved ones and relatives, which were stronger than connections to an abstract "Volk".[35]

This is very much what Delmer had been doing (and much else besides). *Der Chef* had dived into the resentments and grievances that Germans felt, redirected them against the Nazis and made his audiences see how artificial the Nazi identity and the Parteikommune were. For people already inclined towards overbearing, charismatic strongmen, trying to force them straight into listening to the opposite type of personality would be difficult. *Der Chef* was an ersatz strongman, but one who was filthier and funnier than Nazi leaders and who permitted you to release your Schweinehund. "Delmer gets tantalizingly close to Goebbels's methods," concludes Cohen, "in order to undermine them completely."[36]

The Sender had given Germans a "safe" environment in which they could quietly rebel, cleave away from the homogenous mass into . . . well, into what, exactly? Into the sort of persons who are free enough to think for themselves, look at evidence, act independently.

How ultimately, utterly different Delmer's theory of communication was from that of the Nazis! They thought that people were easily malleable, passive, manipulable objects to be shaped into anything the propagandists required. Goebbels had declared that people were "mostly just a gramophone record playing back public opinion". We are just animals in the propagandist's circus: "Nothing is easier than leading the people on a leash. I just [hold] up a dazzling campaign poster and they jump through it."[37]

Delmer's propaganda, or anti-propaganda, perceived people as potentially active, curious, their minds in movement. His media wasn't trying to "brainwash" them but to stimulate them into curiosity, thought, individuality. Even the complex game that they were playing when tuning in to the Sender, this triple masquerade where they knew what they were listening to wasn't really German, and knew that the British who made the programmes knew they knew, was already a way to move away from the "hypnosis" of the crowd, to break the patterns of repetitive, unthinking behaviour that the Nazis were trying to instil.

Dicks references the term *Schweinehund* in his analysis, with no reference to Delmer. Hitler's fear of people's secret Schweinehund was the idea that Delmer hung all his approach around. Delmer usually referred to it as something negative, the opposite of "idealism". But Dicks uses the term differently: below the surface of Germans' "desire for coercion" by a higher authority, many "German soldiers are rebellious and 'Schweinehund'".[38] But what, after all, is so "bad" about rebelling against the desire to be ruled by a genocidal dictator? We are talking about Hitler's Schweinehund here, the pigdog that Hitler fears, an opposite to Nazi political psychology. A Schweinehund that rebels against Nazism is a beautiful animal—or at least not a repulsive one.

Is this, then, Delmer's most curious trick of all? To disguise a sort of idealism under a cynical pose, thus smuggling the good into the empire of the bad? Is he, after all, a Goody Goody and not a Baddy Baddy?

But can you ever smuggle in the good under the guise of the bad without contaminating it?

After the war, Delmer would try to be an open Goody Goody and create a type of media that would never let fascism reappear—but his Baddy Baddy would catch up with him.

CHAPTER 10

HOW DEAD IS HITLER?

It was always Delmer's joy to find a story he had himself invented being retold as fact by a POW," remembered the novelist Muriel Spark, who had joined Delmer's propaganda troupe in 1944. She was twenty-six and not yet a writer. As "duty secretary", she sat in the office at MB adjacent to Delmer. Scanning an English newspaper just after D-Day, she found "a Delmer-invented story reported as news". The newspaper related how the Allies found so many Italians among the Axis forces' POWs, they needed to hire Italian translators to interrogate them. This news would demoralise Germans, who had been

> conditioned by their own home-distributed propaganda to despise Italian fighters. . . . To fight on the same side as Italians would be decidedly depressing to the German troops. . . . Of course the story was false. I had seen and heard it invented by Sefton Delmer at his desk in the little newsroom where I occupied the other desk. He had tried it out on me as there was nobody more important around.[1]

In the final months of the war, Delmer's operation was reaching new heights of subversive creative destruction.

The technique of hacking Nazi propaganda had reached technical perfection. When René Halkett got hold of a Goebbels radio speech in advance, he also saw a chance to sabotage it. He had learned the cadences of Goebbels's speeches and where the propaganda minister would leave little pauses and gaps. When the Sender broadcast the Goebbels speech, Halkett would interject: "I got enough pauses to put in all kinds of things, beginning with hackneyed things like 'says you', but also jump in with 'no, that's a lie'," and then correct the number of dead Germans that Goebbels had claimed in a battle to a higher number.[2]

Delmer's team had even learned to create ersatz Nazi programmes that imitated them perfectly, then hack into Nazi airwaves when they went off air during air raids and "continue" them. A POW who had worked as a trainee on German radio and a German actress at Woburn played the Nazi presenters, rehearsing for days to get their voices just right, while the Woburn technicians added foil to the studios in order to replicate the metallic timbre of the Reich's radio.

The RAF gave Delmer the precise time of their raid on Cologne, at which point the local branch of the Reich's radio would come off air, leaving the bandwidth open. At the precise moment the Nazi station came off air, Delmer's troupe hacked into their wavelength and broadcast their own content. The imitation was so perfect that Delmer, listening in, first thought the hacking operation had failed: he couldn't notice the difference between his own presenters and the Nazis'. But though the style was the same, the message was different, designed to cause chaos in the German retreat: in the name of the Gauleiter of Cologne, local Nazi leaders were to put all women and children in columns and, taking no more than fifteen kilograms of their belongings, march them out of the town and across the Rhine, preferably on bicycles.[3]

Inside Germany, the confusion was growing with every air raid.

• • • ▬▬ ▬▬ ▬▬ • • •

ON THE NIGHT OF FEBRUARY 13, 1945, in Dresden, Victor Klemperer had just been informed by a friend that all remaining Jews in the city were about to be murdered when the air-raid siren went off. The British and American air forces were on their way. "If only they would smash everything up," one of the inhabitants remarked. "They" would.

"We very soon heard the ever deeper and louder humming of approaching squadrons, the light went out, an explosion nearby," Klemperer recorded in his diary, in a series of broken sentences that seem too hot for the pen to dwell on them. "Pause in which we caught our breath, we knelt head down between the chairs, in some groups there was whimpering and weeping—approaching aircraft once again, deadly danger once again, explosion once again. I do not know how often it was repeated. Suddenly the cellar window on the back wall opposite the entrance burst open, and outside it was bright as day."[4]

It was actually night outside; the brightness came from the flames: "Fires were blazing at Pirnaischer Platz, on Marschallstrasse, and somewhere on or over the Elbe. The ground was covered with broken glass. A terrible strong wind was blowing. Natural or a firestorm?"[5]

The bombings paused—then started again:

I ran across the yard to our Jews' cellar. The door was wide open. A group of people cowered whimpering to the right of the door. An explosion at the window close to me. Something hard and glowing hot struck the right side of my face. I put my hand up, it was covered in blood, I felt for my eye, it was still there. Bangs, as light as day, explosions. I had no thoughts, I was not even afraid, I was simply tremendously exhausted, I think I was expecting the end.

As soon as they seemed to end, the bombings resumed. They went on for two days. The boundaries between Aryan and Jewish spaces broke down; everywhere was equally on fire; you could run anywhere; no one policed the racial lines:

I saw only flames everywhere, heard the noise of the fire and the storm, felt terribly exhausted inside. A group of people were clambering up through the public gardens to the Buhl Terrace. Then I was standing at the top in the storm wind and the showers of sparks. To right and left buildings were ablaze. Whenever the showers of sparks became too much for me on one side, I dodged to the other. Within a wider radius nothing but fires. Standing out like a torch on this side of the Elbe, the tall building at Pirnaischer Platz, glowing white; as bright as day on the other side, the roof of the Finance Ministry. The storm again and again tore at my blanket, hurt my head. It had begun to rain, the ground was soft and wet.[6]

In the tumult Klemperer had lost sight of his wife. She too was looking for him: "Once, as she was searching, she had wanted to light a cigarette and had had no matches; something was glowing on the ground, she wanted to use it—it was a burning corpse."[7] Klemperer found her the next day, sitting by the river on a suitcase, wearing her fur coat.

In the following days, "there was a dreadful smell of corpses, the authorities estimated 200,000 dead".[8] The 200,000 figure was a lie from Goebbels's propaganda: an extra zero was added to stoke outrage and make the mass murder sound even more heinous.[9] The real figure was closer to 25,000. Anyone tuning into Delmer's Sender would have heard the more accurate figure for the numbers killed, followed by a lament for the devastation of the city, how the defences were so useless, only twelve enemy bombers out of a total of sixteen hundred had been shot down, how nothing seems to be able to "stop the fanatics from crying 'hold out to the last' while all the beauty of Germany is irretrievably destroyed". The Sender then reported how the government was insisting that "Ours is the Fuhrer, Ours is the Victory" be stamped on all letters and postcards.[10] On the ground the Klemperers found "there was a weak supply of water, no gas, there were no newspapers, instead a leaflet from the Freiheitskampf which threatens shooting for 'everything', narrow alleyways had been cleared through the rubble, one sees slips of paper put up: 'I am safe.' 'I am looking for—'"

The Klemperers saw a chance to reinvent themselves. Eva cut the yellow star off Victor's coat with a pocketknife. From now on they travelled as the "Kleinpeters", an Aryan couple who had lost their documents.

If the Allies' aim had been to destroy Germans' morale, Klemperer found that initially at least the firebombing backfired. At an air base where refugees were sheltering, he heard an indignant woman express a common attitude: "They are trying to use terror to force us to capitulate. They have made a mistake!"

But when the Führer came on the radio, not everyone was overjoyed. "I've heard enough Führer speeches!" another woman exclaimed.[11]

The "Kleinpeters" encountered a Reich adrift: many Volksgenosse were now homeless, destitute. Some told stories that the army was collapsing, others that the lines of defence were holding firm.

On March 1, on a mild spring afternoon, a family he had stopped with invited him in to listen to the 7:00 p.m. radio broadcast. Klemperer does not name the station, but it appears to be one of the newer radio stations the Allies set up after D-Day, calling for revolution in Germany:

> Over and above the roaring rise and fall of interference, interrupted by individual scraps of words and melody from various countries, we could clearly hear the speech of a network addressed to the German forces, which compared the Party programme with the actual conditions and achievements, then again the accusatory speech of a prisoner of war in England, calling for the pointless war to be brought to an end and the criminal regime, which had murdered "millions of Jews, Poles, etc.," to be brought down.

Klemperer took a dim view regarding such direct exhortations: "Listening to these speeches I had a sense of their utter futility. Millions have been listening to them for many months and don't lift a finger."[12] Delmer would have agreed. On March 1 the Sender was as ever avoiding lecturing Germans, and instead giving damning detail about the progress of the war. Much of it was, according to the PWE archives, true (the "true" sections are underlined in the archives): reports on the surrender of German garrisons in Mönchengladbach; on an enemy offensive that had left supply routes in southwest Germany immobilised; about a Munich chemist, Dr Trumpp, who justified why officials in high party positions should get special allocations of tobacco and cigarettes while others went without. The invented part of the programme concerned a supposed

Nazi propaganda campaign exhorting workers to continue operating in fuel factories despite air raids: a trick to make the Nazis look bad by claiming they were spreading a policy harmful to Germans.[13]

Klemperer also found the focus on dispiriting detail to be most effective in the radio broadcasts he listened to—allowing the listeners to work out the damning conclusion for themselves:

> Then we heard, sometimes drowned out by the noise of inter-ference: News from the Front. The English say that in the last 24 hours they have advanced 10 miles near Cologne, there had been heavy air raids on Berlin again. And then suddenly Goebbels's speech was there after all, the crudest antithesis to the earlier accusations, and I drew hope precisely from that. Goebbels spoke differently from usual. He largely dispensed with rhetorical tone and structure and instead let the individ-ual words fall very slowly with a strong, even emphasis, like hammer blows, with a pause between every blow. And the con-tent was utter despair. The language of sport even now: We are like the marathon runner. He has put more than twenty miles behind him, he has another six miles to go. He is covered in sweat, he has a stitch, the sun is blazing, his strength is giving out, again and again he is tempted to give up. Only the great-est willpower keeps him going, drives him on, perhaps he will collapse unconscious at the winning post, but he must reach it! . . . How often has a dying man overcome death through his sheer will to live! . . . We are strained to the utmost, the terror attacks have become almost unbearable—but we must stay the course. We shall "coldly and calmly put a rope round the neck" of anyone who tries to sabotage us. And now the old tune: His-tory would lose its meaning if we were not victorious over the hordes "from central Asia". Then, as practical consolation: Our enemies were "just as tired as we were". And as future prospect: We had to "economise and improvise" and "reconquer" Ger-man territories as soon as possible.

All in all: This "marathon runner" speech was totally despairing, and in conjunction with the English report, that the pace of the advance on Cologne had quickened, it gave me at least a little spark of hope that the next few days could perhaps after all see a change.[14]

However, Klemperer still worried that his Jewish identity might become apparent, and he considered his chances of survival at only 50 percent.

In Berlin, Goebbels's propaganda machine was creaking, spluttering, buckling. In farthest west Germany, where the Americans and British were breaking through, the Allies had both air superiority and superiority over the airwaves: it was almost impossible to receive German broadcasts. An SD report in the last days of February had conceded that locals were putting their hope in Allied promises that they would be treated well. As reports came in of occupying Americans behaving "much better than German troops", the SD wrote that civilians were putting out white flags, burning party memberships and refusing to support retreating German troops. On March 3 Cologne fell, welcoming in the occupiers with "white kerchiefs and Rhein wine".[15]

Nazi leaflets tried to besmirch the image of the American occupiers, claiming that the nicer Yanks would be followed by nasty Jews who would "act ruthlessly against the population". But when nothing of the sort happened, these messages were ignored. In March a Propaganda Division report related the mood in a Hamburg bar: "No gas, no light, no electricity, no heating. Only beer, which no one wants to drink in the cold. One worker remarked: 'I wish the English would come and put an end to it.'"[16]

Goebbels's last line of propaganda defence was to promote fear of Soviet atrocities, which the Red Army provided ample evidence for. On March 8, Goebbels travelled to areas recently retaken from the Soviets. In Görlitz he made a public speech—his last. Nazi newspapers were now so short of paper they were just four pages long, and had only enough space to print a description of the talk and some short quotations. The newsreels showed a longer version:

We will enter this offensive as if we were entering a religious service. And when you take up your weapons and climb into your tanks, you will have before your eyes your murdered children and raped women, and a cry of revenge will rise up before which our enemies will turn pale. As the Führer overcame the crises of the past, so will he overcome this crisis. He is firmly convinced of this. The day before yesterday he told me he was sure we could overcome this crisis and begin our new offensives.[17]

But the Führer himself was refusing to speak publicly, however hard Goebbels begged him to. "The Führer now has a fear of the microphone that's incomprehensible to me," the minister for propaganda admitted in his diary.[18]

Goebbels's reliance on people's fear of Soviet atrocities to inspire resistance in the East was having the opposite effect on the Western Front—wouldn't surrender to the Allies be preferable to occupation by the Soviets?

On March 13 the Propaganda Ministry itself was hit. "The whole lovely building on the Wilhelmstrasse was totally destroyed by a bomb," Goebbels wrote. "It is 12 years to the day—13 March—since I entered this Ministry as Minister. It is the worst conceivable omen for the next twelve years."[19]

At the end of March, the SD reported that the "Volk no longer has any confidence in the leadership. It is sharply critical of the Party, of certain leaders, and of propaganda."[20] Another report for March 31 compared Nazi propaganda to a band on a sinking ship merrily continuing to play.[21]

Klemperer, who continued to take notes on propaganda, would still come across people who clung to the vestiges of the great delusion:

On Monday, 9th April, we were joined [at breakfast at a hotel] by an interesting young couple. The man, a minor civil servant, was on his way to Berlin, to claim his overdue salary. . . .

It was amusing to observe how isolated and crumbling scraps of NLI [Nazi language], which had been dutifully learned by heart, still floated around like islands in the man's disillusioned and embittered head. "The Führer had said, 'Nothing was impossible,'" and then: "We were Europe's rampart against Bolshevism."

We let the couple go on talking and took a friendly leave of them.[22]

On April 13, Vienna fell. The US Army advanced into Nuremberg, the Soviets into Berlin. On April 14, *Das Reich* ran a Goebbels article in which he turned to the theme of suicide. In "Committing One's Own Life", he wrote that in the case of defeat, "how could anyone imagine wanting to continue to live in such a situation?"[23]

• • • ▬▬ ▬▬ ▬▬ • • •

ON THE MORNING OF April 14, Delmer stood in front of the mirror in his bathroom with a razor in his hand. Ever since he had started at Woburn, he had grown a great bushy beard that hid much of his face. Many who met him for the first time remarked on it; the beard had defined his wartime look. Lynder described it as a "black unruly pirate's beard". Delmer's pirate days were now over. Now that the Allies occupied much of Germany, there was no need to disguise the broadcasts any more. They could speak openly. The estimated audience for the BBC German broadcasts was now between ten and fifteen million a day—up from one million in 1941.[24]

The British government had a different job for Delmer: create a new media system in Germany. It was a chance to ensure that Germany didn't repeat the same cycle as after the previous war: that authoritarian habits, and the propaganda that helped feed them, didn't return. "That would be a mission," thought Delmer, "to which I could readily dedicate my life." His days of subterfuge were over. But "as my razor shaved the soap ridden whiskers from my face . . . there, staring at me, was the pallid flabby-mouthed face of a crook. Was this, I asked myself, what four years of 'black' had done to Sefton Delmer?"[25]

He gathered his whole team in the canteen at MB: the whole Propagandatruppe of POWs, scholars, singers, priests, politicians, cabaret stars and spies. It was meant to be an emotional, solemn moment: "But my team had never been brought up to be solemn and emotional."

Frank Lynder was first to change the mood—shouting out "Der Bart ist Ab! Der Krieg ist Aus!" (The beard is off! The war is over!) Everyone laughed and took up the cry.

When they calmed down, Delmer gave his goodbye speech. He urged the troupe to avoid talking publicly about their exploits. Their story had to stay secret. Delmer recalled how the exposure of British propaganda in World War I was then used by Nazi propaganda to claim, falsely, that the German loss had been brought about by mere "tricks and lies" and not by military defeat, and how this "fostered the illusion of illusion-hungry Germans" that their defeat in 1918 had been the result of some grand deception and that they could and should take vengeance with another war. "The defeat of Hitler," Delmer insisted, "is the work of the fighting services. Our role has been purely subsidiary. . . . If we start boasting of the clever things we did, who knows what the result of that will be. So mum's the word. Einverstanden?"[26]

• • • ▬▬ ▬▬ ▬▬ • • •

ON MAY 5, 1945, Klemperer, still wandering the German countryside, recorded a fresh rumour in his diary:

> Woman, from north Berlin, told us she had "heard from a sergeant, that Fritzsche, as prisoner of the Russians, had announced on the wireless: Hitler and Goebbels had shot themselves, the Russians were helping the Berliners to put out the fires, the war was completely over." But it was impossible to find out anything reliable, we have been without electricity for one week. The latest rumour—someone is always "said" to have heard such a thing on some wireless somewhere.[27]

In this case the rumour was true. On April 30, Hitler had shot himself. On May 1, Goebbels and his wife had killed themselves after poisoning their six children.

While Klemperer wondered what Soviet occupation had in store for his part of eastern Germany, a shaven, uniformed Sefton Delmer was driving through the bombed-out autobahn into the western port of Hamburg. Acres of the city he had once thought the most comfortable in Germany had been burned out by the RAF's "tornado of fire":

"wherever any shelter was left, however rudimentary and precarious, however insalubrious, there lived Hamburgers, ragged, wretched and hungry".

Throughout the country, the rubble was being slowly cleared by hand. Many of those enlisted into this arm-aching work were former Nazi Party members, forced into it as a sort of penance by local groups. In Duisburg, for example, posters announced that party members were ordered to "clear away street obstacles. If you fail to appear, freed political prisoners will make sure that you do."[28] A rough reckoning with the past seemed to be emerging from the rubble.

Delmer's team was placed in a row of houses opposite the radio station. The houses were crammed with families, several of them in one apartment with one tiny kitchen. To Delmer's horror these families were promptly evicted by the British administration to make room for the "No 10 German News Service-Deutscher Pressedienst".[29]

Delmer's ambition was nothing less than a "journalistic revolution in Germany. I wanted to set up a new media of mass communication which would . . . show the German press and radio how to free themselves from defects which in my opinion had helped to plunge a gullible German public into two world wars."[30]

Newspapers in the Weimar Republic, or at least the sort of newspapers that claimed to value truth and evidence-based argument, had been too "turgid" and aloof from people. They had been helpless in the face of vicious political partisanship that simmered near civil war; they could do nothing to defend the immature institutions of democracy; they left a disoriented population open to "unscrupulous leaders". Meanwhile, local newspapers had been too small to stand up to the powerful, even before the arrival of the Nazis, and "grovelled before authority in venal servility".

Other Weimar newspapers had been full of vicious slander, picking on people through "trial by newspaper". Innocent citizens, officials and often minorities—more often than not Jewish—were frequently accused of heinous and illegal acts with no basis in fact. Hitler, an avid reader of crime reports, had then set the "logical crown on this prejudicial practice".[31] He had built on the existing slanderous, character-assassinating, dehumanising media practices of the Weimar

Republic and then used them as a weapon to cudgel opponents, critics, dissidents and whole races.

Delmer's aim was to first create a newswire that would "provide Germany's newspapers and radio stations with a news service following British techniques of crisp, objective and accurate reporting and showing the respect of the rights of the citizen that I so missed in German reporting of the past". He would then create a model newspaper as a new standard setter for others in Germany. He also planned to work with the new German judiciary so that it guaranteed people's rights in the face of unsubstantiated media attacks.[32]

The concept was approved by the British government, and Delmer set about importing his finest team from Woburn for the job. Immigration records from the time suggest that Lynder and Halkett were both invited to join, although Delmer doesn't name them.

But not everyone trusted Delmer. Internal British government correspondence notes that the American Office of War Information was not convinced that "he has left off his Black Operations with his beard".[33] Michael Balfour worried what might happen if it came out that "our chief agent in teaching the Germans the virtues of objective news was the man who had shown such a brilliant ability to pervert it in his black transmissions during the war".[34]

On September 5, 1945, a scoop in the Swiss newspaper *Die Tat* revealed the secret of Delmer's war work. The article described him as "the most powerful man in British propaganda for Germany", tasked with creating a pro-democracy German media that could compete with the Soviet propaganda that was streaming across the airwaves. Although the article in many ways paid respect to Delmer as an "excellent journalist" and a "connoisseur of Germany", it went on to list the "pornographic stories" of *der Chef* and Delmer's pre-war closeness to the Nazi elites. It stressed his wartime stations' lack of ideology and scruples, contrasted with the more moral and politically engaged Sender der europäischen Revolution. It asked whether he would be the right man to lead the media competition of democracy against dictatorship. Would the new Labour government, which had beaten Churchill at the last UK election, put up with this sort of man?[35]

Delmer had no doubt who was behind the leak to *Die Tat*: "At the back of the agitation was the same group of 'European Revolutionaries' who in their petty jealousy at the success of Gustav Siegfried Eins station had already, once before the war, attempted to trip me up." With "sublime contempt for the Official Secrets Act", they had briefed the journalist at *Die Tat* and, Delmer claims, were now warning the new British government that "Sefton Delmer, the unscrupulous Tsar of the Black, was up to no good in Germany".[36]

Whether this controversy played the decisive role or not, Delmer's grand schemes were scrapped, and he was offered the much more truncated position of just running the newswire. He quit. So did Leonard Ingrams and Robert Bruce Lockhart. Perhaps none of them would have flourished under the new government anyway. However, the new government did award Delmer an OBE (Order of the British Empire) in 1946, much earlier than many of his more senior colleagues. His achievements had not gone unnoticed.

Delmer returned to the *Express*, which reinstalled him as its star world-roving international reporter. They explained his wartime absence to their readers: "Exactly what the task was cannot be disclosed. But it can be said he brought to the secret department for which he worked a remarkable experience of European affairs and a particular close understanding of the mind of the enemy."[37]

The next year he was back reporting in Germany to cover the Nuremberg tribunal, the trials meant to hold senior Nazis to account. Among the accused was his old radio rival Hans Fritzsche. The prosecution accused him of "deliberately falsifying news to arouse in the German People those passions which led them to the commission of atrocities". He had "created in the German people the requisite psychological and political conditions for aggressive war".[38]

In his defence, Fritzsche argued that during the war he had no idea about the extent of Nazi war crimes and the fate of the Jews in occupied territories. Goebbels had assured him that stories about the gassing of Jews was Russian propaganda, and he had believed the minister. He had never pushed "noisy" anti-Semitism himself, had been only "moderately" anti-Semitic, merely wanting Jews to leave political and economic life. He had never used terms like "master race". He had believed the official line about Hitler's invasion of the USSR being "preventative". He reaffirmed his belief in "the absolute cleanliness and honesty of the German conduct of the war. I still believe today that murder and violence . . . only clung like a foreign body, a boil, to the morally sound body of the German people and their armed forces."[39]

He was found not guilty, the tribunal deciding that his "position and official duties were not sufficiently important . . . to infer that he took part in originating or formulating propaganda campaigns" and that his radio talks "did not urge persecution or extermination of Jews".[40]

As soon as Fritzsche heard that Delmer was in the building, he strode across to him with an outstretched hand: "Are you really Sefton Delmer? I always dreamt of shaking your hand. How often, listening to your responses to my talks, did I wonder what a pleasure it would be to meet you." Fritzsche grabbed Delmer's hand and began to shake it vigorously. "Sefton Delmer, you were a fair opponent. I hope you can say the same thing." Taken aback, Delmer could only grin awkwardly. An American reporter took a press photo of the two. The next day German newspaper columnists were appalled: How could Delmer have shaken hands with a representative of the murderous regime? "If this was all just a boxing match," complained the Berlin Telegraf, "with a 'shake-hands' at the end. Then we regret ever having risked our safety listening to the BBC!" Delmer felt that he had been played by his old rival: "It was game, set and match for Fritzsche."[41]

Fritzsche's victories did not last long: in 1947 a German court charged him as an "intellectual creator" (Urheber) of the Nazi regime. This court had more radio transcripts of Fritzsche's broadcasts and cited how he had accused Jews of starting the war and needing to pay for it, how he had called on Germans to fight even as Berlin was falling, and how he had reported on a listener who wrote to him criticising the regime and who had then been executed.[42] It deemed him "Gruppe I—Hauptschuldige"—that is, the first group of Nazi criminals, comprising those most guilty—and sentenced him to nine years of forced labour.[43] Evidence that hadn't been available at the Nuremberg tribunal later convinced the Nuremberg prosecutor Alexander

Hardy that Fritzsche's work as chief of the German Press Division "was far more important than the task of venting his golden voice. . . . [The press directives that were later discovered] brought the lie to Fritzsche's denials . . . of knowledge of such crimes as the extermination of the Jews and atrocities in concentration camps. He not only knew of them but played an important part in bringing them about."[44]

Before they parted, Fritzsche told Delmer what the Nazi leadership in the Führer's headquarters had thought about his programmes. The information on the Sender was so accurate, Fritzsche explained, that they began to believe there must be a traitor among them. Several arrests were made, but the traitor was never found.[45]

It was the sort of success that Delmer would soon start to regret.

• • • ▬▬▬ ▬▬▬ ▬▬▬ • • •

AFTER THE WAR, KLEMPERER was living under Soviet occupation: Dresden was now part of Communist East Germany. Klemperer had regained his university seat but was seeing disturbing parallels between Soviet and Nazi propaganda. The Communist "class consciousness", which defined certain classes such as peasants or bourgeoisie as worthy of destruction, was, he believed, similar to race consciousness under the previous regime. "Revolting", if, in his opinion, not "quite as poisonous". Klemperer loathed the Communist regime's jargon and political values, with its celebrations of authoritarian-sounding "leadership", which it tried to instil into small children: "This is purest Nazism, in *even* worse German!"[46]

On Delmer's visits back to West Germany in the late 1940s and early 1950s, he was appalled in a different way: "Only four years after Germany's defeat and the suicide of Hitler," he wrote in the *Express* in September 1949, "only three years after the Nuremberg trials, in a Germany which is still in ruins, the Nazis are once again coming out into the open. And they are once more coming out on top."[47]

The Americans, Delmer lamented, with the British following them, had abandoned attempts to "denazify" the country and were "seeking as allies against the Russians those very social strata in Germany" whom they had sworn to eliminate. "What gave me particular concern was that to justify this reversal of policy—which entailed the restoration to power of the forces that had ruled Germany for the first forty-five years of the century—both the Americans and our new German allies were proclaiming as historical fact our black propaganda legend that the German Officers' Corps and the German generals had been in opposition to the Führer and his party."[48] The legend of "good" German soldiers who defied or were at least ideologically opposed to the Nazis, a legend Delmer had done so much to ferment, was now being claimed as having been a reality, and it was enabling former senior Nazi officers to ascend to the commanding heights of the West German government, security services and industry.

In the late 1940s and early 1950s, amnesty laws forgave former Nazis their crimes as long as they weren't guilty of homicide or if they could just prove that they were ordered to commit their offences.[49] Fritzsche was "amnestied" in 1950. SS men were able to claim state pensions, and an author of the racist Nuremberg laws that had stripped Jews of rights in 1934 became head of the Chancellery. Delmer broke the story of how Nazi general Ernest Gehlen had worked with the CIA to recruit a network of hundreds of former Nazis to spy in Eastern Europe: "Gehlen and his Nazis are coming," wrote Delmer in the *Daily Express*, complaining of their "monstrous underground power in Germany".[50]

"Even the SS were being rehabilitated now," confessed a guilt-ridden Delmer in his memoirs. "I examined the propaganda claiming to justify the rehabilitation of the SS, and I found it was in closest conformity with the line put out by our SS Resistance Radio. The fighting units of the SS, it argued, were an elite corps of honourable soldiers who had nothing in common with Himmler's gas chamber attendants wearing the same uniforms. Forgotten were the massacres of the Poles and Ukrainians. That black boomerang I had feared had indeed returned to hit me full in the face."[51]

While the fake past was becoming real in post-war West Germany, the real past was being avoided. When US officials showed Germans documentary films about the concentration camps, many viewers simply looked away or else spent the whole time staring firmly at the floor. Returning to Germany, the philosopher Hannah Arendt found the "most striking outward symptom of a deep-rooted, stubborn and sometimes brutal refusal to face up to what actually happened and come to terms with it".[52] When she told people she was Jewish, they did everything to avoid talking about anti-Semitic atrocities: "no sign of sympathy such as 'What happened to your family'—but a deluge of stories about how Germans have suffered".[53] Arendt argued that "such an escape from reality is also an escape from responsibility. In this the Germans are not alone; all the peoples of Western Europe have developed the habit of blaming their misfortunes on some force out of their reach." Arendt tied the lack of responsibility to the Nazis' relativist attitude to truth: if you thought facts and truth were all "subjective", then everyone could choose their own reality and avoid responsibility:

> In all fields there is a kind of gentlemen's agreement by which everyone has a right to his ignorance under the pretext that everyone has a right to his opinion. . . . The average German honestly believes this free-for-all, this nihilistic relativity about facts, to be the essence of democracy. In fact, of course, it is a legacy of the Nazi regime.

Arendt thought the very ease with which Germans had surrendered Nazi ideology without any serious debate about its precepts was itself part of Nazism: "What one is up against is not indoctrination but the incapacity or unwillingness to distinguish altogether between fact and opinion."[54]

Delmer also noted how Germans didn't want to confront the horrors that had been wrought "in their name". As well, he thought that the Nuremberg trials could have been broadcast better: the radio broadcasts had been delivered in a flat way, and by a presenter with an Austrian accent that would have sounded grating to many Germans.[55] Delmer began to regret he hadn't stuck to his guns and tried to create a new type of media. He worried that the old tendencies—militarism, centralisation of power and slanderous ad hominem attacks—were making a return. He wrote incessantly about the return of Nazi elites to power, so incessantly that one wonders if he was also powered by a desire to make up for the consequences of his own lies and distortions: "How

Dead Is Hitler?" he asked in the *Express* in 1954, bringing his concerns together about the return of Nazi-era "militarists and industrialists", whose democratic values were a sham and who "regret nothing of the past but their defeat and the mistakes in strategy and leadership which caused it".[56]

In *The Hothouse on the East River*, Muriel Sparks's novel that draws on her time with Delmer and the PWE, former practitioners of deceptive propaganda at Woburn spend their later years in New York surrounded by the ghosts and guilt of their past work. They hallucinate and see in the streets former Nazi POWs who once worked on the radios and whom they have wronged. The lies they have created take on lives of their own until the borders between past and present melt away, communication between people breaks down, and the main character's shadow even points the wrong way. At the end of the book all the characters, dead and alive, indeed you can no longer tell who is dead or alive, unite in one great dream-scene cabaret act in the East Village.

CHAPTER 11

HOW TO WIN AN INFORMATION WAR

As she lay dying in a North London hospital in 2010, my grandmother started to hallucinate scenes from her Ukrainian childhood. All around the ward she saw starving children, skeletal, collapsing in the long, white, strip-lit corridors and lying, leaning, barely breathing by the hospital beds. At first my mother and I couldn't understand what she was referring to. What children? There were only old people in the ward.

Then we realised that Galina Ivanovna was surrounded by suppressed memories from her childhood. She was back in the wide, high streets of her home town of Kharkiv. She was back in 1932 and 1933, the height of Stalin's man-made famine meant to break the resistance of the Ukrainian peasantry to his rule. His victims were staggering from the countryside into the city in search of food, their dead bodies scattered across the dusty roads and pavement.

In July 2022, I was back in Kharkiv, and there were also dead bodies on the streets. A ruler in Moscow wanted to break Ukrainians again. The city was hot to the touch from a sadistic sun, and people and buildings shook from the frequent rolling breakers of artillery fire. The Russians had failed to take the city in the spring, so now they were launching sudden waves of missiles in order to terrorise the population. Several attacks per week managed to penetrate the air defences. The day I arrived, Russian artillery hit two residential buildings in the centre, nineteenth-century mini-mansions full of flats, killing five and injuring many others. On local news I watched the clip of a man whose wife was killed as they went out shopping. He knelt on the street by the bloodied body bag that contained her corpse, wept, ripped it open and began to kiss the dismembered limbs. His son tried to tear him away. A few days later the Russians hit a hospital for the hearing impaired. Twenty-one died.

When I passed through the empty, destroyed, working-class area of Saltivka, there were craters where there had been playgrounds, apartment blocks with the front walls blown off like the faces of soldiers in those photos you see from World War I, their cheeks torn away so that you see the gaping mouths and teeth through the side. In Izyum I saw an apartment block split in half from bombings. The insides of apartments were open to the world. A wardrobe full of clothes—trousers and shirts still on their clothing hangers—swayed in the sky, as if waiting for an angel to fly down, pull out a hanger and put on a suit.

The artillery attacks forced the people of Kharkiv to shelter in their basements. When I arrived, there were still dozens of people living under the children's theatre, legs sticking out from bunk beds beneath the suspended, paused-in-movement limbs of large marionettes hanging from the walls. During the height of the bombardment earlier in the year, when the rockets rained like a hellish hail all day and all night, about fifteen thousand people had lived in the subway stations. Children had classes there. There were concerts and soup kitchens on the platforms. Some people became so paralysed by fear that they refused to emerge for months. Months later you could still see people frozen at the bottoms of the escalators, paused in silent panic, unable to ride up because of the memory of those months.

The scenes of thousands of citizens hiding in the Kharkiv metro had been beamed across the world, and the recognition for many was immediate: we are back in the Blitz; history has returned; the borders of past and present and future were not as solid as some had thought.

Cellars have become one of the recurring symbols of the invasion. Across the country, Ukrainians retreated to cellars for safety, seeking shelter from indiscriminate bombardment, ears attuned to measuring the proximity of each missile blast, bodies reverberating with every tremor. Over fifteen hundred resistance fighters and civilians hid in the labyrinthine passages and halls underneath the vast, four-square-mile factory complex of Azovstal in Mariupol as the Russians obliterated the city above them.[1] There were the cellars I'd come across in Yahidne, the village where 350 villagers had been imprisoned. The cellar where the Horbonoses confronted the Russian soldiers. There are the cellars where Russian troops interrogate, torture, tie up and rape, where captives are given electroshocks with wires from wind-up field telephones, have gas masks wrapped around their faces and have flashlights shined in their eyes during interrogation.

In Kharkiv I stayed in the cellar of a colleague, the journalist Nataliya Kurdiokova. She had been working with me on the project to record Russian atrocities in the war—and then to try to communicate them to the outside world. After an artillery strike knocked out the toilet of her apartment, she moved underground. It's a comfortable cellar that she was already using as an office before the war. There's a broadcast studio, bean bags, bright lighting, a kitchen and a bedroom. Here she beams out the truth of the atrocities as they happen. Their veracity is then immediately undermined by Russian propaganda that claims the crimes never happened or were somehow justified because they actually hit military objectives. For too many across the world, and especially inside Russia, such blatant lies can be welcomed. And for the rest, the atrocities can start to seem like nothing out of the ordinary, abhorrent but no longer outrageous.

Nataliya recalled how much she used to enjoy climbing up on her roof to gaze out over the city and beyond: "They want to take away our sense of the horizon. Of the sky."

Climbing up high always inspires a sense of possibilities. The barrages of Russian artillery were making such ascents impossible. Russia was not only forcing Ukrainians physically into cellars; it was trying to do so mentally as well: to rob Ukrainians of their sense of a future, of horizons, and drag them back to the totalitarian past.

Delmer had been worried that Germany wouldn't be able to overcome its history. Eventually it did, for the most part. In the 1960s and 1970s a generation of young Germans finally rebelled. There were bloody protests on Germany's streets opposing the inclusion of former Nazis in leading positions in government and business. School programmes explored Germany's fixation with authoritarianism. German and European films revealed the fascist relationship to sadomasochism. In *Salò* the Italian director Pier Paolo Pasolini set the work of the Marquis de Sade in the last days of Mussolini-occupied northern Italy (which was known as the Republic of Salò). Powerful politicians engage in mass sadomasochistic orgies with teenage boys and girls, literally devouring shit, before erupting into atrocities, mass murder and torture.[2] When I lived in Germany as a teenager in the 1990s, there was a whole channel dedicated to footage of concentration camps and the other parts of Nazi history. The self-exploration is never quite enough—but it's a lot more than what exists elsewhere.

In Russia there has been no similar systemic attempt to deal with the Russian and Soviet past, let alone the present. The way the Kremlin repeatedly colonises, ethnically cleanses, deports, starves and murders other nations is left locked up in the cellar of the Russian public mind. There is no longer a museum dedicated to the tens of millions of Soviet citizens killed in Stalin's gulags, let alone a willingness to confront Russia's colonial crimes.

Instead of the crimes being recognised and atoned for, they return in the latest remake of Russian imperialism. Russia's current invasion replays Soviet-style mass executions, deportations, mass destruction of cities, show trials and totalitarian propaganda. Just as in many centuries past, Russia destroys Ukrainian-language schoolbooks and arrests and "disappears" those who stand up too vociferously for Ukrainian language and letters. It's as if Russia wants to lock Ukraine into its cellar of horrors and force it to replay the past in a fantasy where the mass murders, war crimes, crimes against humanity and intent to commit genocide are all very real. Unable to overcome the past, Russia drags others into its blood-stained re-enactment.

Travelling farther along front-line Ukraine, you feel the barriers between past and future start to become more porous. You come across trench warfare right out of World War I. You come across liberated villages where the Russians had put in place a system of rule and a system of propaganda that was cut and pasted from the propaganda model current in Delmer's time. In Vovchansk they set fire to Ukrainian school books and burned them behind the meat-packing factory; in Kherson they sent the children for "re-education" to summer camps to teach them how to love Russia; in Izyum they set up a radio station that blasted propaganda about the "historical unity" of Russia and Ukraine from loudspeakers in the central square. They opened up the long-closed cellars of old Soviet police stations, tortured anyone whom they felt wasn't obedient and tossed the dead into mass graves.

But it is also a journey into the future of propaganda. The Russian soldiers film themselves casually shooting captured Ukrainian POWs in order to sow fear, and they post the videos on social media. They film themselves murdering their own soldiers with a sledgehammer—punishment for having been captured by the Ukrainians. They also post videos complaining to their commanders of poor weapons and poor rations.

Ukraine is full of advertisers and hackers, activists and journalists—who after the start of invasion formed their own improvised civic political warfare executives. They buy ads on Russian porn sites and bootleg movie portals, then target them with videos about Russian war crimes, the economic problems their government has caused them and advice to soldiers on how to surrender. They hack into Russian TV channels and play clips of messages from President Zelensky. They quickly found that "moral" content didn't take off. What was more successful were issues that touched on Russians' immediate self-interests, the Russian pigdog. To give one small example: When Ukrainian activists tried mass telephone calls to Russians, they found that some 80 percent would hang up during the first twenty seconds if the calls were about the devastation caused by the war, but only 30 percent hung up when the call focused on their personal interests, such as a special tax they had to pay to support Russia's newly occupied lands. When the call was about help to Russian veterans, 43 percent hung up, but only 25 percent hung up when the call was about travel limitations caused by the war.[3]

As in World War II, such information efforts can be only as effective as the military operation. As I write this in the summer of 2023, the

Russian invasion of Ukraine is ongoing. Perhaps by the time you are reading this, Ukraine will have won the war, and the full story of these campaigns can be told then. Perhaps when you are reading this, we will be in some version of a new cold war against an authoritarian Russia and its other authoritarian friends, where propaganda and counter-propaganda will be even more important. Or perhaps something drastic, seemingly democratic, will have changed in Russia. But how deep will that change be? Delmer and Arendt worried that post-war Germans wanted to see themselves as passive victims of the Nazis. But that passivity was itself a product of Nazi propaganda, with its desire to wipe out your sense of agency. The same problem might beset Russia. Only by taking responsibility do you overcome propaganda that encourages apathy and passivity.

But the lure of the nastier types of propaganda is always with us. Delmer and his contemporaries were always pushing us to see how it can arise anywhere, exploiting needs and desires that lie within many, if not all, of us. Propagandists across the world and across the ages play on the same emotional notes like well-worn scales. They manipulate the desire to belong; provide a sense of false community to those left feeling deracinated by rapid change; help project our worst feelings about ourselves onto others; allow you to feel special, even superior, and foster the sense that you are surrounded by enemies that want to take something from you, something that's yours and only yours and only you deserve. They play into the yearning for a figure to protect you; tap into, or even produce, humiliation—and then the aggression that makes up for it. At their most effective they can construct whole alternative realities, conspiratorial worlds where you have no responsibility. And many people can be eager to play along with this.

And just as the patterns in propaganda repeat, so do our ways of failing to deal with them.

Delmer was always frustrated at how the media that claim to represent "democratic values" simply preach to the converted. He wanted us to break out of our bubbles, to appeal to the groups vulnerable to the propaganda that plays into the desire to submit to strongmen. He would likely be even more frustrated now, when social media and cable television have created the incentive to talk only to one's own ersatz digital community.

In summer 2023, there is a media scandal in America. News Corp, the owner of Fox News, has been forced to pay $784 million for spreading conspiracy theories stating that the 2020 US election was "stolen" by the company that ran the vote-counting machines in some states. This, the network claimed, rigged the results in favour of the candidate from the Democratic Party, a conspiracy theory that about a third of Americans, and the majority of Republican voters, believe. During the trial it transpired that the network's presenters and senior management all knew that they were telling lies, but continued telling them because these were the stories their audience desired.[4]

Even if Fox stops transmitting this particular lie, the fear is that new networks will pop up to feed similar conspiracies to audiences that want an escape from reality, like those Arendt once described, who desire a remedy for loneliness no less than Ellul's lonely crowds. How does a system that relies on trust in common processes such as elections thrive, or even survive, when so many deny their validity? We need a way to reach these audiences, or at least some of them, for democracy to function. For that we need to understand their motivations. Is claiming the election was "rigged" a case of misinterpreting facts, or about showing off your loyalty to a political identity? Is it a badge of belonging? If so, how can one start to unpick those bonds?

What is at stake is whether we can create a communication environment where democracy can function, or whether other systems are more efficient in the new information era. We are repeating the challenge of a hundred years ago, when after the new propaganda of World War I many thought that people in modern society couldn't cope with the information abundance that had been produced by new technology, that people were too easily manipulated, too keen to be manipulated, to trust them with any power. The argument then, as now, is that any hope for a public square where citizens could meet, debate and decide their future is a delusion. That, at best, a caste of enlightened experts should guide society, or indeed that a successful society needed centralised, dictatorial control.

Similar arguments are being made today.

The one hundredth birthday party of the "great, glorious and correct" Chinese Communist Party in 2021 was celebrated with an all-singing, all-dancing, light-show extravaganza in Beijing's National Stadium. A cast of thousands played scenes from the party's founding to the present, with relentless torrents of actors rushing from different angles across the vast stage, coalescing first into an arrow, then into a star, the physical embodiment of common will. A huge screen showed videos of President Xi Jinping giving speeches. Every clip of the president was greeted with high-pitched squeals from the audience.

The political message behind the aesthetics was familiar: our system achieves success when the masses are directed by a few superior leaders in the party. But there was an update. At the climax of the birthday performance, instead of celebrating some Soviet-style five-year plan, a great neon blue "5G" hovered above the stage, celebrating next-generation digital technology, while hologram 1s and 0s drizzled down. The show's host, holding a red book, celebrated how China will lead the world in the online era, an era when centralised control will triumph as it amasses ever more online data about people. Give up your online privacy, allow the Chinese Communist Party to know more about you, and it will use that knowledge to deliver you the optimal education system; the finest health programme; the most appropriate job; the safest, sleekest city; and the ideal entertainment. You will be delivered the ideally tailored reality if you will submit. Liberal democracy is a mess, the message goes; "checks and balances" just cause chaos; the "marketplace of ideas" is inefficient; this time, centralised control will win.

When you cross Beijing, you see how the skyline is dominated by the giant gleaming ouroboros of China's international state "news" corporation, just one element of its vast $10 billion international information infrastructure that is intent on shaping the world to its aims.[5]

Digitally enhanced, new versions of the old propaganda are emanating from dictatorships and from inside democracies. We know how they operate: their mix of disinformation spewing from troll farms, TV channels blaring paranoid conspiracies, digitally targeted "alternative" facts and leaders legitimising cruelty and dehumanising victims. And today you don't even need a leader around whom to form a crowd. An online algorithm does that: encouraging people to follow one another, prioritising their most extreme feelings, egging one another on more effectively and at much larger scale than at the Sportpalast.[6]

Can those who fancy themselves as "saving democracy" compete? How can we engage those people inside dictatorships like Russia, or those inside democracies, who have become apathetic to the truth, who embrace the propaganda of bullies and dictators? What can we learn from the tricks, innovations and mistakes of Sefton Delmer?

As Delmer showed, we can gain even the most sceptical audiences' attention if we understand their motivations. His audiences knew that the British, their mortal enemy, were behind the Sender. Yet they tuned in to Delmer's media nonetheless, intrigued by how well it understood their world. The Sender spoke their slang, provided advice that was useful to them and told the jokes out loud that they whispered behind closed doors. It spilled the dirty secrets of their bosses, related the exhaustion of the factory worker, detailed the symptoms of soldiers' diseases. It broke the news of whether their loved ones had lived or died. Delmer evoked a community of family, friends, fellow soldiers and co-religionists stronger than Goebbel's Volk. And it worked.

So if propaganda is the remedy for loneliness, we need to provide a better cure.

But Delmer was not rosy-eyed about what people can long for in their leaders. As a result he was often accused of having a cynical view of human nature, and of lacking idealism. But this also meant he could experiment in the bloody operating theatre of our darkest desires.

Delmer recognised that people get satisfaction from propaganda. Often the viler it is, the more effective. The nastiest leaders gain followers by offering a way for you to feel powerful through them and in humiliating others. *Der Chef* likewise tapped into Germans' resentment and debasement, breaking the Nazi's monopoly over expressing their strongest, most secret feelings. He used the same language of hate, superiority and sadism the Nazis used. But then he turned the propaganda back on them. He poured the vitriol on so thick it started to overflow with its own paranoia, spouting so much viciousness it broke its banks, so that it started to carry "into the ridiculous".

Through showing how easily you could use the Nazis' own propaganda against them, and magnifying its distortions, Delmer was reminding Germans how fabricated Nazi propaganda was, and this undermined the foundations of its power. Delmer saw how propaganda gave people a sense of identity in a confusing and unstable world. The Nazis wanted you to fully inhabit the vile roles they offered: as SS men, Aryans, Volksgenosse and many others. By constantly shining a spotlight on how these roles were actually acts, Delmer was showing you could choose not to play them, or you could transform them.

Delmer was always welcoming you into games where you could take back control and define yourself. The Sender involved you in a masquerade where you knew the British were behind the station, and the British knew you knew, but everyone kept up the role play because it helped reveal censored truths. You were no longer passive, submitting to the power of propaganda, one small limb in a mass, coordinated show—instead you had agency once more.

Delmer constantly focused on empowering people to take action that was good for them and bad for the Nazis. Provoking runs on clothing and rations, or giving you a manual for how to feign sickness and get sent home from the front, was important not just for their immediate impact on the German war effort, but broke the habit of following the Nazis' diktat.

Through these four processes—creating media communities stronger than the propagandists'; breaking the propagandists' monopoly on expressing the darkest feelings; making people aware of how Nazi social roles were a ghoulish cabaret you could discard; and provoking people to behave more independently—Delmer created a distance between the German people and the Nazi propaganda. And once that distance had been opened up, he could start to communicate with them in a new way.

Delmer's aim, however, was never to replace one hate-filled political cult with a different one. The listener was not meant to worship der Chef like Hitler and morph with some hypnotised mass. Delmer always believed that people were never fully entranced by propaganda. He thought there was always another person inside us all—grounded in reality—and ready to break free of the propagandists if there was enough reason to do so. It's our job to find that reason. This process can start with the most basic self-interest and survival.

So much of contemporary propaganda is designed to make you feel overwhelmed by the amount of confusing content out there, undermine the difference between truth and lies, and through this confusion find relief by placing your faith in a leader who reduces the world into crass conspiracies. This is why fact-checks rarely work when they directly challenge a political identity. What we need to do is give people the motivation to care about truth again.

Delmer only had radio and print to play with. We have so many more ways to engage people: online town halls and social media channels; interactive websites; streaming platforms; messaging groups; pop-up ads that lead you on an online trail; and the chance to broadcast movies, dramas, lectures and audio into even the most closed societies. We have many more ways of analysing audiences, their motivations and their reactions than Delmer did. Dictators and authoritarian propagandists use these tools all the time—and we should compete. What we don't always have, however, is Delmer's wit, his ability to descend into the origins of propaganda's power and then subvert it.

Some of Delmer's best insights came from recognising his own susceptibility to propaganda. In his memoirs he describes his own childhood, when, as a British boy in Berlin, he surrendered to German war-fever in World War I, repeating the patriotic words that took him over, so that their exaltation became his and he was swallowed up by propaganda. He felt so impelled to imitate others that he was about to hang out a British flag to celebrate German victories. As he rushed to hang it from the window, his mother's hand shot out and pulled him back, and with a start he realised how ridiculous his actions were.

I keep thinking about this jolt, this moment when you suddenly step outside the performance you didn't even realise you were putting on. The struggle against propaganda starts with this jolt into awareness. Delmer may never have preached lectures about democracy, but so many of his games, disguises, deceptions and misdirections were designed to pull you free.

CHAPTER 12

ORDINARY ORDINARY

Note PFPP 16823 in Sefton Delmer's MI5 file, dated October 4, 1954, relays an enquiry from Number 10 Downing Street: "The Prime Minister had received a report that Sefton Delmer had Communist sympathies, probably clandestine ones. He instructed that SIS and the security services should jointly make discreet inquiries on this matter."[1] Sefton Delmer's loyalty and identity were again under suspicion.

His articles in the *Express* about the return of Nazis into German positions of power coincided with the line that Soviet propaganda was taking on West Germany, that it was a hotbed of secret Nazis and the inheritor of the Nazi Reich. Suspicion of Delmer only increased when Otto John—one of his collaborators at Woburn who had gone on to become head of the West German Bundesamt für Verfassungsschutz, a national security agency—suddenly disappeared and then reappeared in East Germany, saying that he was disenchanted with West Germany's weak stance on "former" Nazis. John then returned to West Berlin and claimed that he had been kidnapped and forced to speak by the East German secret police but had managed to escape. The West German courts disagreed and sentenced John to four years in solitary confinement as a traitor. Delmer always stuck by his old Woburn colleague.[2]

The secret services concluded that although "we had a good deal of information about Delmer, we see no reason to suspect him of Communist sympathies". Nevertheless, MI5 suggested setting up a "telephone check on Delmer" just in case. Delmer continued working as a roving international reporter throughout the 1950s.

When Delmer reported on East Germany in 1954, he was damning. He described a court system where people were found guilty with no serious trial. He compared East German youth groups to the Hitler Jugend. He accused the school system of continuing Nazi traditions. The school shirts had changed from brown to blue, but the way children had to salute teachers, the quasi-military behaviour and the ideological indoctrination were all too similar to Nazi Germany.[3]

He was the main character in many of his articles, going on round-the-world adventures but always coming back to his rural English idyll at the Valley Farm, describing himself tending his chickens after some far-flung journey, writing himself into the English landscape. By this time he was no longer married to Isabel. She had left Woburn months before the victory, exhausted and sick of Delmer's relentless schedule. Her biographer, Carol Jacobi, references a love affair with a colleague at Woburn, a member of the "rumours" department named John Rayner, though Isabel insisted she had no plans to live with him. She retained warm feelings for Sefton: "This did not mean I forgot the richness and fascination, gaiety of our life together. . . . There was my gratitude for the way he looked after me and taught me many things."[4] In his memoir, Delmer briefly mentions Isabel leaving Woburn, and that this was the start of the end of their marriage. In 1948 he married Zoë Ursula Black, whom he met when she worked with Leonard Ingrams during the war, and they had two children, Felix and Caroline Selina.

In 1959, in his fifty-fifth year, Delmer retired from the *Express* after an "issue" with his expenses: his gourmet lifestyle was no longer tolerated. "I can only think clearly in a five-star hotel," Delmer had told his employers as he left. "If I'd known the job was temporary, I wouldn't have taken it." He had been at the paper for thirty years.[5]

The next year he visited a cinema in Frankfurt and was affronted in another way. The film he watched told the heroic story of brave

Wehrmacht soldiers who had fought a secret war against the Nazis. One of these "courageous" officers fled to England and was recruited by the leader of a secret propaganda organisation: "A potbellied fellow. He is a terrible cynic. As he talks to the German hero—who is of course an idealist—the British boss contemptuously twirls a huge globe. He explains to the hero some of the dirty things he will have to do now that he is irrevocably committed as a traitor." This nasty mastermind directs a radio station called "Soldatensender Calais" (also the title of the movie) and works together with the "good" Wehrmacht to under-mine the Gestapo.[6]

Delmer already felt responsible for how he had helped create the image of the "good" German soldier. Now he was accused of collab-orating with the phantoms he himself produced.

His memoirs gave him the chance to respond and tell the truth about his lies. The two volumes came out in 1961 and 1962: *Trail Sin-ister* and *Black Boomerang* in English, *The Germans and I* in German. *The Times* wrote that "Mr Delmer is the sort of foreign correspondent more often seen in the cinema than in real life." The *Guardian* said that "he must be one of the most dashing and romantic figures outside fiction". Richard Crossman reviewed the memoirs in the *New States-man*. Always a believer in the more idealistic propaganda efforts, he described Delmer's work as "nihilistic in purpose and solely destructive in effect", though he conceded that by the end of the war the number of Delmer's readers and listeners "had become a serious rival to the Nazi radio and press, and may well have outstripped the German service of the BBC".[7]

The German edition of the memoirs climbed to number seven on the best-seller lists. In the immediate post-war years the West German press had accused Delmer of being a determined *Deutschlandhasser* (German hater) for seeing Nazism returning. By the time the memoirs came out, that criticism of Delmer had grown milder as Germans began to analyse the truth about the continued presence of senior Nazis in their system. Delmer's worries that the worst of the past would return also softened with time as he saw a new generation of Germans confront the Nazi legacy.[8]

In East Germany the memoirs became, according to the mem-oirs of Stasi agents, "a sort of bible" in the department responsible for spreading East German disinformation against the West: another case of Delmer's work "boomeranging".[9] No doubt, Delmer was also read avidly at the Information Research Department, the IRD, the British Foreign Office unit that organised covert propaganda in the Cold War and that hired some people from Woburn.[10]

His former colleagues at Woburn went their separate ways, though often in journalism, creative writing and the more experimental arts. Peter Seckelmann worked with the IRD in Berlin; his secret service file describes him as "talent spotting" among German groups. In 1955 he became the editor of the weekly *Weltwoche* newspaper in Zurich and later wrote historical novels set in ancient Greece. Frank Lynder became a reporter with the Springer newspapers in Germany, Britain and Denmark. Before he passed away, Frank told his daughter, Libby, how the meticulous records he kept at Woburn of prominent German Nazis were later useful in tracking down renegade Nazis across the world, including Adolf Eichmann, one of the main organisers of the Holocaust.[11] Donald MacLachlan became editor of the *Sunday Telegraph*. Ian Fleming wrote spy novels, and Robert Bruce Lockhart wrote memoirs about his career after having been a spy. Peter Wykeman received another degree, this time at the same Oxford college as Delmer, and then worked for British Steel and the EU. Leonard Ingrams returned to business, and his son, Richard Ingrams, founded the satirical political magazine *Private Eye*. Agnes Bernelle recorded seven albums of cabaret songs and surreal theatrical pop. Her 1985 album *Father Is Lying Dead on the Ironing Board* was voted the strangest LP of the year by *New Musical Express*.

Isabel went on to become an important painter in her own right. Her paintings often focused on human figures, dancers and animals, which seemed almost plucked from the air, as if she was pulling the human back into a coherent shape again after it had dissolved into the ether. At the time of her death, in 1992, she was still largely seen as the muse of great male artists. Her work finally got recognition in 2021 with a retrospective at the Tate Gallery and a biography, *Out of the Cage*, soon after.

Father Elmar quit his priesthood when he returned to Austria, and he focused on his anthropological research. He didn't publicise his PWE exploits at home in Styria. Many likely wouldn't have approved of his "treachery": a known Nazi war criminal was president of Austria until 1992. Elmar finally told his story to the historians Siegfried Beer and Wolfgang Mutschich, who discovered him by accident in the mid-1980s. On their initiative Eisenberger was finally posthumously honoured by the Austrian government for his contribution to the liberation of Austria in 1995.[12]

Of the fictional figures from Woburn, perhaps *der Chef* deserves his own obituary. According to Delmer's memoirs, he had *der Chef* killed off in November 1943, with a spectacular scene where the Gestapo discovered him and shot him mid-broadcast. However, this grand finale was played twice by the transmission team, who spoke no German, giving the game away that the scene was staged. That, anyway, is the version in Delmer's memoirs. Lee Richards suggests otherwise; he says, "The monitoring transcript for der Chef's final broadcast, which is backed-up by the Milton Bryant log-book, shows that the transmission contained just a coded message consisting of a sequence of numbers in five digit groups."[13]

Halkett remained in radio. His fortnightly *Brief Aus Cornwall* (Letter from Cornwall) on the BBC German Service blended old stories from his coastal village of Camelford, bringing the English closer to Germans to help break down the resentment and stereotypes propaganda can exploit.

He also continued with his surrealist paintings and poems. Three years before Halkett's death in 1983, the musician David Jay of the experimental gothic rock group Bauhaus set two of Halkett's poems to wailing ambient soundwaves. One of these poems, "Armour", delves into the tensions between identity and disguise that permeated so much of the work at Woburn.

At the start of the track a "distressed" Halkett first laments how the metal armour he wears to protect himself from the world is eating away his naked flesh. He has "no more protection left against my armour". So he throws it off and tries to use disguise for survival instead:

> *Play the fool, the hero,*
> *Play the lover, the monk, the peasant . . .*
> *Let hero play the fool and fool the hero . . .*
> *Lover play them all . . .*
> *Endless permutations of disguise.*

But at the end of the poem the metal armour is still there; you never seem quite able to lose it, and the very armour that is meant to protect you starts to eat away your skin and leaves "your secret core disclosed".[14]

However much we reinvent ourselves, Halkett seems to be lamenting, we are always brought back to the defensive identities we put on to shield ourselves, but which in turn consume us and reveal our vulnerabilities.

Perhaps something similar happened to Delmer.

Throughout the 1960s and early 1970s Delmer wrote two more non-fiction books about wartime espionage and Weimar Germany, and he was a frequent guest on media in the UK and Germany. But as the years went on, he seemed ever more at odds with the age.

During interviews he continued to defend the political role of the British empire, arguing that some rulers of decolonised countries were corrupt, that it was wrong to surrender responsibility for the people there and that Britain and America were allowing the Soviets to dominate in Africa. In one 1966 radio programme, the interviewer pressed him about whether this meant he was against the "liquidation of the colonial Empire", whether he believed countries should not have become independent of Britain. Delmer conceded that, essentially, yes, that's what he meant.[15]

In his memoirs, Delmer subverts any solid notion of what "you" are, always showing how any role you play in life quickly tips into the ridiculous. And in his descriptions of himself, he always turns around and laughs at the image he has created: he plays the heroic war reporter—and then subverts this picture of himself. He plays a Nazi—but only to laugh and show the flimsiness of fascism. Could someone so self-aware really have got stuck inside a single act—that of a nostalgic imperialist?

As Delmer admitted in his memoirs, he had always been plagued by the sense he was not seen as quite British enough. Even into middle age he suffered nightmares about it, always returning to his experiences as a child with a strange German accent at a London school in 1917, desperate to prove that he was truly British. In the 1960s he was still doubling down on that old version of imperial Britishness that he had struggled to fit in with as a child. So much about him revolved around the need to simultaneously belong—and yet also express his uniqueness. And even in this final role he never comes across as taking himself altogether seriously. In a television interview from the 1960s we see him dressed in the cravat and tweeds of an Edwardian gent, strolling around the Valley Farm, with its low, white farmhouse untouched by modernity, the windows slanting from time. The German accent is quite gone, and he speaks in the upper-class manner of the late Queen of England, where the vowels are tucked in like a neat, tight shirt. "I expect you will want to talk to me about Hitler," he tells the interviewer, sounding most serious at first. "Well, there's one firm rule I make about Hitler," Delmer continues, suddenly breaking into a more mischievous tone, "we must have a drink in our hands when we're talking about HIM"—and mixes a handsome cocktail.[16]

Sefton Delmer died on September 5, 1979. In his obituary the *Express* described him as "a friendly Flagstaff who knew Hitler well—and Hitler lived long enough to regret the association". The *Guardian* wrote that he had been "a sort of guru, a prophet. That was the role he loved to play and was perfectly cast."[17]

But when it came to his propaganda work, what was that role?

In the introduction to his memoirs is the passage I've invoked throughout this book:

> *"I come out of all this as rather a prig, I fear," I said to my wife, when I had read through the manuscript of this book for the umpteenth time.*
>
> *"What is a prig, daddy?" inquired my daughter Caroline Selina, aged eight.*
>
> *"Oh, a goody goody sort of chap," said I.*
>
> *"You're not a goody goody," says Caroline Selina.*
>
> *"No, I'm a baddy baddy."*
>
> *"You're not," says Carolina Selina.*

But it also has these last lines.

> *"Well, what am I then?"*
> *"You're ordinary ordinary."*[18]

"Ordinary ordinary" perhaps seems strange given how extraordinary his life actually was. But Delmer's insights and innovations stemmed from his ability to see how "ordinary ordinary" he was too, in the sense that he was vulnerable to propaganda for the same reasons we all are—through the need to fit in and conform. He understood his own need to feel ordinary—and how dangerous that could be. Propaganda at its most malign exploits this need, impels a type of belonging where you give up the capacity to differentiate between good and bad. At its most extreme it makes mass murder ordinary, ordinary.

Delmer knew it would be hard to rouse people from this mix of apathy and mass identity through direct lectures on morality. Instead, he pioneered something different. He created grotesque characters like *der Chef*, who gave a "patriotic" mask under which you could call out the Nazis for their evils. He roused the inner pigdog, involving people in a game where they could start feeling and thinking independently, while never being disloyal to their group. He welcomed you into a cabaret where you could find roles that gave you a chance to act yourself.

Throughout the writing of this book I've been trying to work out if Delmer is a "baddy baddy" or a "goody goody"—but "ordinary ordinary" is where the real drama is. To win an information war you need to understand how propaganda exploits this ordinariness—and then outplay it.

ACKNOWLEDGEMENTS

A huge thanks for advice and read-throughs to Nick Cull, Henk de Berg, Monica Garnsey, Josh Appignanesi, Devorah Baum, Jon Day, Liana and Igor Pomerantsev, Josh Cohen, David Schneider, Linda Kinstler, Michael Mirny, Oleksandra Sllavinskaya, Natalya Gonchar, Igor Romanov, Thomas Rid and, as ever, Paul Copeland. Aunt Sasha has given unstinting support. Daniel Pick has been highly helpful on Henry Dicks and MacCurdy. My colleagues at the Reckoning Project are an endless inspiration. I would also like to acknowledge those members of the PWE whose stories I didn't have the scope to tell but whose writings I learned much from, among them the Foreign Office's Clifton Child, Oxford's C. E. Stevens, the BBC journalist Charles Roetter and the historian Raymond Klibansky.

This book is by a journalist and would have been impossible without the work of historians. Lee Richards has collected, organised and digitised the PWE archives and put together superb books on the output of Delmer and his colleagues. Karen Bayer's biography of Delmer is a wonder of detail—I hope it appears in English as well as German.

I have learned so much from the famous classics of World War II and Nazi scholarship: the works of Ian Kershaw, Richard Evans, David Welch and Peter Fritzsche, among many others. The endnotes show how I have relied on them. It has also been a joy discovering some out-of-print books that I hope can be republished, given our current interest in propaganda: Ernst Kris and Hans Speier's *German Radio Propaganda* is required reading; Michael Balfour's *Propaganda in War, 1939–1945* is a grand guide. A special mention is necessary to those who have already researched the story of the PWE in academic works, including Will Studdert's "Music Goes to War" (PhD thesis, University of Kent, 2014) and Pauline Elkes, "The Political Warfare Executive: A Re-evaluation Based on the Intelligence Work of the German Section" (PhD thesis, University of Sheffield, 1996).

I have been extremely fortunate to have been granted access to unpublished memoirs and interviews with those who worked at Woburn:

Siegfried Beer and Wolfgang Mutschich kindly shared their record-ings of Elmar Eisenberger.

Peter Wykeman's children, Gina Watson and Nick Wykeman, kindly provided access to Peter Wykeham's (né Weichmann's) memoirs.

Frank Lynder's daughter, Libby Ainley, kindly allowed me to quote her father's memoir.

Ian Fell's recordings with René Halkett were revelatory, and I look forward to seeing Ian establish an accessible Halkett Archive in collab-oration with Ursula Klimmer, Halkett's picture curator and German translator of *The Dear Monster/Der Liebe Unhold*.

In Ian's words:

As was the case with many of his friends, René and I spent many a nicotine-aired hour together in Camelford, me trying to capture as much as possible of his life on the hundreds of hours of tapes that have ultimately accumulated.

After Delmer, Halkett had worked for America at the Nürnberg trials; had scheduled films for the "re-education" of occupied Germany; and took high-level responsibility for man-aging delivery of humanistic lectures in Britain's POW camps.

In the years since his death, his works have become ever more collectable and appreciated. So, for instance, in 2006, the Oberhessischen Museum, Gießen, held an exciting retrospec-tive exhibition of his work. Another artifact-rich exhibition reflected his work at the Falmouth Art Centre in Spring 2019. Other exhibitions are on the cards for future years.

René had recorded some of his powerful poems—*Nothing* and *Armour*—on the hissing cassette recorder which sat in the aforesaid nicotine cloud in Camelford. David Jay took these raw recordings and produced in July 1980 a notable "pop" record from it of poetry and (for want of a better word) rock. It proved a cult success.

Know then that nothing lasts for ever
And nothing will remain when I have written
These words on nothing written will remain
For nothing lasts forever...

His remarkable creativity—his "nothing that lasts for ever"—remains our privileged inheritance. A considerable collection of his papers, books, and recordings, a proto-archive of his lives, for which we are still exploring the best way of sharing what might be Halkett's own tribute to the wartime valour of our friends, the "enemy aliens."

—Ian [Sefton] Fell, September 2023

NOTES

PREFACE: THE REAL LIVES OF SEFTON DELMER

1. Sefton Delmer, *Trail Sinister: An Autobiography* (London: Secker & Warburg, 1961), 40.

2. Richard J. Evans, *The Third Reich in Power, 1933–1939* (New York: Penguin, 2009), Kindle edition, 120. See also Helmut Heiber, ed., *Goebbels-Reden*, 2 vols., (Düsseldorf, 1971–1972), vol. 1, *1932–1939*, 131–41 (Berlin, Grosser Saal der Philharmonie—Eröffnung der Reichskulturkammer, November 15, 1933), and 82–107 (Berlin, Haus des Rundfunks—Ansprache an die Intendanten und Direktoren der Rundfunkgesellschaften, March 25, 1933), at 82, 88, 131–134.

3. Heinz Boberach, ed., *Meldungen aus Dem Reich, 1939–45: Die Geheimen Lageberichte des Sicherheitsdienstes der SS* (Munich: Hermann Luchterhand Verlag GmbH, 1965), ix–xii.

4. Boberach, *Meldungen aus Dem Reich, 1939–45*, 2563.

5. "Audio presentation to George VI and Queen Elizabeth at Woburn Abbey, Beds, 11/1941", Imperial War Museum, IWM Sound 5217, www.iwm.org.uk /collections/item/object/80005174.

6. Erich Kästner, *Das Blaue Buch: Geheimes Kriegstagebuch, 1941–1945* (Zurich: Atrium Verlag, 2018), 96.

7. Sefton Delmer, *Black Boomerang* (London: Secker & Warburg, 1962), 75.

8. See *Woburn at War*, documentary by Anglia TV, 1987, directed by Graham Creelman.

9. See, for example, Kirill Rogov, "Having It Both Ways: Russians Both Support and Oppose War", *Russian File* (blog), Kennan Institute, Wilson Center, March 17, 2023, www.wilsoncenter.org/blog-post/having-it-both-ways-russians-both-support -and-oppose-war.

10. Daria Subkova, "Russians Tired of Propagandists: Solovyov and Skabeyeva 'Dropped' from Top 10 Programs on TV", *Ukrainian News*, November 19, 2022, https://ukranews.com/en/news/896154-russians-tired-of-propagandists-solovyov -and-skabeyeva-dropped-from-top-10-programs-on-tv; Alexey Kovalev, "Russia's Ukraine Propaganda Has Turned Fully Genocidal", *Foreign Policy*, April 9, 2022,

https://foreignpolicy.com/2022/04/09/russia-putin-propaganda-ukraine-war
-crimes-atrocities/.

CHAPTER 1. PROPAGANDA IS THE REMEDY FOR LONELINESS

1. Oddly, Delmer never names his mother and sister in his memoirs, as if he doesn't want to distract from his propaganda parables with too much personal detail. Sefton Delmer, *Trail Sinister: An Autobiography* (London: Secker & Warburg, 1961).

2. See Delmer, *Trail Sinister*, 22.

3. Delmer, 22.

4. Delmer, 23.

5. Delmer, 25.

6. Adolf Hitler, *Mein Kampf*, trans. James Murphy, https://greatwar.nl/books
/meinkampf/meinkampf.pdf, 141.

7. "Famous Hitler Photograph Declared a Fake", *Sydney Morning Herald*, October 20, 2010, www.smh.com.au/world/famous-hitler-photograph-declared-a-fake
-20101019-16sfv.html.

8. Delmer, *Trail Sinister*, 29.

9. Delmer, 22.

10. Delmer, 19.

11. For background on imperial Germany's innovations and shortcomings in propaganda, see David Welch, *Germany and Propaganda in World War 1: Pacifism, Mobilization and Total War* (London: Bloomsbury, 2014), Kindle edition. For example, "The German government had, in fact, from an early stage in the war—certainly earlier than the Allies—developed a sophisticated notion of propaganda and its reception by different publics, and had established a national network of monitoring stations to provide feedback on the 'pulse of the people.' It is the contention of this book that the moral collapse of Germany was due less to the failure to disseminate propaganda than to the inability of the military authorities and the Kaiser to reinforce this propaganda by responding positively to public opinion thus forging an effective link between the leadership and the people" (1).

12. For this and more on the mood and media in Berlin, see Jeffrey Verhey, *The Spirit of 1914: Militarism, Myth and Mobilization in Germany* (Cambridge: Cambridge University Press, 2000). News quotations come from *Berliner MorgenPost*, August 4, 1914; *Der Tag*, August 9, 1914; and *Tagliche Rundschau*, August 2, 1914.

13. Peter Fritzsche, *Germans into Nazis* (Cambridge, MA: Harvard University Press, 1998), 38–40.

14. Fritzsche, *Germans into Nazis*, 58; Verhey, *Spirit of 1914*, 2.

15. Delmer, *Trail Sinister*, 30.

16. Delmer, 25–26.

17. Daniel Cérézuelle, "Jacques Ellul's Social and Political Commitments", trans. Lisa Richmond, International Jacques Ellul Society, https://ellul.org/life/social
-commitments; Jacques Ellul and Patrick Troude-Chastenet, *Jacques Ellul on*

Politics, Technology, and Christianity: Conversations with Patrick Troude-Chastenet (Eugene, OR: Wipf and Stock, 2005), 63.

18. Jacques Ellul, *Propaganda: The Formation of Men's Attitudes* (New York: Vintage, 1964), 148.

19. See, for example, Fergus Peace, "How to Tackle Populism: Rebuild Rural Civic Life", *Apolitical*, November 2, 2018, https://apolitical.co/solution-articles/en/how-to-tackle-populism-rebuild-rural-civic-life; Louisa Slavkova, Dobrena Petrova, Leonie Sichtermann, and Mila Moshelova, "From 'Civic Deserts' to Civic Cohesion: How Exploring Europe's Peripheries Can Inspire Ways of Improving Civic Life", Mapping Civic Deserts, February 2022, https://mappingcivicdeserts.com/from-civic-deserts-to-civic-cohesion.

20. See Peter Pomerantsev, *This Is Not Propaganda: Adventures in the War Against Reality* (New York: PublicAffairs, 2019), 171.

21. See, for example, Peter Jelavich, *Berlin Cabaret* (Cambridge, MA: Harvard University Press, 1993), Chapter 3.

22. Martin Esslin, "Max Reinhardt: 'High Priest of Theatricality,'" *Drama Review* 21, no. 2 (June 1977): 3–24, esp. 7.

23. Delmer, *Trail Sinister*, 45.

24. Delmer, 23.

25. Delmer, 38.

26. Delmer, 42.

27. Delmer, 43.

28. "Berlin Today. An Australian's Record. The Return to Liberty", *The Times* (London), June 5, 1917, 7.

29. "Berlin Today. An Australian's Record. The Return to Liberty".

30. Delmer, *Trail Sinister*, 51.

31. Frederick Delmer's June 1917 series in the *Times* was then republished in one essay as "Berlin After Three Years of War, Observations of a University Professor", *Current History* 6, no. 3 (1917): 508–511. https://online.ucpress.edu/currenthistory/article/6_Part-2/3/508/192525/Berlin-After-Three-Years-of-War Observations-of-a.

32. Delmer, *Trail Sinister*, 55.

33. "Journalism in the First World War", November 3, 2014, https://studylib.net/doc/9879455/new-version-journalism-in-ww1.

34. Welch, *Germany and Propaganda in World War 1*.

35. Delmer, *Trail Sinister*, 55.

36. Delmer, 54.

37. Delmer, 56.

38. Delmer, 37.

39. Delmer, 57.

40. Delmer, 15.

CHAPTER 2. THE NAZI CIRCUS

1. Sefton Delmer, "Piston Shots and Screams", *Daily Express*, May 1, 1929.

2. Sefton Delmer, *Trail Sinister: An Autobiography* (London: Secker and Warburg, 1961), 75.

3. Richard J. Evans, *The Coming of the Third Reich* (New York: Penguin, 2005), Kindle edition, 185–186.

4. Delmer, *Trail Sinister*, 75.

5. Delmer, 77.

6. "Rekord der Revue: Neun Berliner Theater wollen Revue spielen!", in *Berliner Tageblatt*, July 7, 1926; Ernst Bloch, "Berlin, Funktionen im Hohlraum", 212, and "Revueform in der Philosophic" (1928), 368–369, both reprinted in Bloch, *Frhschaft dieser Zeit* (Frankfurt am Main: Surhkamp Verlag, 1962); Siegfried Kracauer, "Kult der Zerstreuung" (1926), in *Das Ornament der Masse: Essays* (Frankfurt am Main: Surhkamp Verlag, 1977), 314–315.

7. "Noble German Greeting Received in Silence", *Daily Express*, August 1, 1930, 3.

8. "Be English", *Daily Express*, August 26, 1931, 3.

9. Delmer, *Trail Sinister*, 77.

10. Delmer, 102.

11. Delmer, 103.

12. Paul Radin, *The Racial Myth* (New York: Whittlesey House, 1934), 135–136.

13. Svyatoslav Khomenko and Natalia Zotova, "'School Mistake': Russian and Ukrainian Historians Analyze Putin's Article on the Unity of Peoples", *BBC News*, July 13, 2021, www.bbc.com/russian/news-57807736.

14. Ernst Röhm, *The Memoirs of Ernst Röhm* (Barnsley, UK: Frontline, 2012), Kindle edition, 379.

15. Eleanor Hancock, "'Only the Real, the True, the Masculine Held Its Value': Ernst Röhm, Masculinity, and Male Homosexuality", *Journal of the History of Sexuality* 8, no. 4 (1998): 616–641, www.jstor.org/stable/3840412.

16. Delmer, *Trail Sinister*, 108–109.

17. Delmer, 109–110.

18. Delmer, 111.

19. Delmer, 114–115.

20. Sefton Delmer, "Herr Hitler Talks to the Daily Express", *Daily Express*, May 4, 1931, 1.

21. Sefton Delmer, "Hitler Flings His Challenge to the World", *Daily Express*, December 5, 1931, 11.

22. Delmer, *Trail Sinister*, 121.

23. Peter Longerich, *Goebbels* (New York: Random House, 2015), Kindle edition, 170.

24. See Viktor Reimann, *Joseph Goebbels, the Man Who Created Hitler* (London: Sphere, 1979), 157–158.

25. Goebbels, diary note, Kaiserhof, March 2. Quoted in Reimann, *Joseph Goebbels*, 158.

26. Quoted in Longerich, *Goebbels*, 172.

27. Gustave Le Bon, *The Crowd: A Study of the Popular Mind* (Overland Park, KS: Neeland Media), Kindle edition, 48.

28. Rudolf Semler, *The Man Next to Hitler* (London: Westhouse, 1947).

29. Adolf Hitler, *Mein Kampf*, trans. James Murphy, https://greatwar.nl/books/meinkampf/meinkampf.pdf, 392.

30. Sigmund Freud, "Group Psychology and the Analysis of the Ego", www.sigmundfreud.net/group-psychology-and-the-analysis-of-the-ego.jsp.

31. Interviews with Josh Cohen by author 2020–2023, by email and in person.

32. Sefton Delmer, "Hitler Air Tour", *Daily Express*, April 5, 1932, 9.

33. Sefton Delmer, "Hitler and the Crown Prince", *Daily Express*, April 6, 1932, 1.

34. Quoted in Karen Bayer, *"How Dead Is Hitler?" Der Britische Starreporter Sefton Delmer und Die Deutschen* (Mainz am Rhine: Phillip von Zabern, 2008), 51.

35. Delmer, *Trail Sinister*, 155–157.

36. Sefton Delmer, "The Soul of Hitler", *Daily Express*, 1939, Sefton Delmer Archive, https://web.archive.org/web/20210223052146/https://www.psywar.org/delmer/2013/1001.

37. Roger Money-Kyrle, "The Psychology of Propaganda", in *The Collected Papers of Roger Money-Kyrle* (Perthshire, Scotland: Clunie, 1978).

38. Henk de Berg, *Trump and Hitler: A Comparative Study in Lying* (London: Palgrave Macmillan, 2024).

39. Shaun Walker, "Putin Approves Legal Change that Decriminalises Some Domestic Violence", *Guardian*, February 7, 2017, www.theguardian.com/world/2017/feb/07/putin-approves-change-to-law-decriminalising-domestic-violence.

40. "National Opinion Poll: Most Russians Want a 'Strong Hand'," *Читайте больше на*, February 25, 2020, www.politonline.ru/comments/22895029.html.

41. Shane Harris, Karen DeYoung, Isabelle Khurshudyan, Ashley Parker and Liz Sly, "Road to War: U.S. Struggled to Convince Allies, and Zelensky, of Risk of Invasion", *Washington Post*, August 16, 2022, www.washingtonpost.com/national-security/interactive/2022/ukraine-road-to-war.

42. "State Paternalism", press release of research by Levada Centre, February 25, 2020, www.levada.ru/2020/02/25/gosudarstvennyj-paternalizm.

43. Chris Jewers, "Putin Is Accused of Making a Rape Joke About Ukraine by Calling the Country His 'Beauty' amid Invasion Fears", *Daily Mail*, February 6, 2022, www.dailymail.co.uk/news/article-10490623/Putin-accused-making-rape-joke-Ukraine-calling-country-beauty.html.

44. Jürgen Falter, Thomas Lindenberger and Siegfried Schumann, *Wahlen und Abstimmungen in der Weimarer Republik. Materialien zum Wahlverhalten, 1919–1933/Elections and Votes in the Weimar Republic: Voting Behavior, 1919–1933* (Statistische Arbeitsbücher: Beck, 1986). In the second ballot, Hitler had won two million new votes, Larry E. Jones points out in his book *Hitler Versus Hindenburg:*

The 1932 Presidential Elections and the End of the Weimar Republic (Cambridge: Cambridge University Press, 2015), and it was not just a result of the speeches; the pamphlets, posters and the whole activity of the campaign made Hitler a person the voters knew (Chapter 9).

45. Quoted in Reimann, *Joseph Goebbels*, 160.

46. Delmer, *Trail Sinister*, 149.

47. Delmer, "Soul of Hitler".

48. Sefton Delmer, "Goose Step in Berlin", *Daily Express*, January 31, 1933, 2.

49. Quoted in Evans, *Coming of the Third Reich*, 788.

50. Delmer, *Trail Sinister*, 178.

51. Delmer, 152.

52. Sefton Delmer, "Whirlwind Election Tour by Airplane", *Daily Express*, February 25, 1933, 3.

53. Delmer, *Trail Sinister*, 116.

54. Delmer, 182.

55. Sefton Delmer, "Germany's 21 Day Chancellor", *Daily Express*, February 22, 1933, 10.

56. Delmer, *Trail Sinister*, 183-184.

57. Delmer, "Whirlwind Election Tour", 3.

58. "Rumbold to the Foreign Office, April 7, 1933", The National Archives, London (hereafter TNA) TNA FO 371/16722, pp. 30–38, quoted in Bayer, "*How Dead Is Hitler?*", 59.

59. Delmer, *Trail Sinister*, 143.

60. "Phipps to the Foreign Office, June 2, 1934", TNA FO 371/17716, quoted in Bayer, "*How Dead Is Hitler?*", 66.

61. Delmer, *Trail Sinister*, 238.

62. Delmer, *Trail Sinister*, 241–243.

63. Carol Jacobi, *Out of the Cage: The Art of Isabel Rawsthorne* (London: Thames & Hudson, 2021), 27, 62, 98.

64. Jacobi, *Out of the Cage*, 49, 62.

65. Jacobi, 70–115.

66. Jacobi, 63; Delmer, *Trail Sinister*, 243.

67. Bayer, "*How Dead Is Hitler?*", 87–88; "10 Years Ago I Walked Out on Hitler", *Daily Express*, April 20, 1939, 12. In his memoirs, Delmer would admit he had made himself "the echo" of his newspaper, though he never felt comfortable with the narrative. Sefton Delmer, *Die Deutschen und Ich* (Hamburg: Nannen-Verlag, 1962), 368.

68. Letter from Lord Marley to Otto Katz, July 5, 1934, National Archive, London, TNA KV 2/2586.

69. Robert Bruce Lockhart, *Diaries*, vol. 1, *1915–1938* (London: Macmillan, 1973), 253.

CHAPTER 3. NOT RELIABLE

1. William L. Shirer, *Berlin Diary* (New York: RosettaBooks, 2011), Kindle edition, 452.

2. "My Last Appeal to Great Britain. A Great Empire Will Be Destroyed", by Adolf Hitler, Chancellor of Germany, Speech Made to the Reichstag, July 19, 1940, *Vital Speeches of the Day*, vol. 6, 617–625, www.ibiblio.org/pha/policy/1940/1940-07-19b.html.

3. Shirer, *Berlin Diary*, 454.

4. Shirer, 453.

5. Michael Balfour, *Propaganda in War, 1939–1945* (London: Routledge, 1979), 196.

6. Willi A. Boelcke, ed., *The Secret Conferences of Dr Goebbels* (New York: Dutton, 1970), 67.

7. Sefton Delmer, *Black Boomerang* (London: Secker & Warburg, 1962), 17.

8. Shirer, *Berlin Diary*, 453.

9. Boelcke, *Secret Conferences*, 68.

10. Quoted in Karen Bayer, *"How Dead Is Hitler?" Der Britische Starreporter Sefton Delmer und Die Deutschen* (Mainz am Rhine: Phillip von Zabern, 2008), 106.

11. "Duff Cooper Defends Delmer's Broadcast on Hitler's Speech", *Daily Express*, October 16, 1940, 5.

12. Lord Halifax, "We Remain Unmoved by Threats", radio address, July 22, 1940, London, *Vital Speeches of the Day*, vol. 6, 625–626, www.ibiblio.org/pha/policy/1940/1940-07-22a.html.

13. Balfour, *Propaganda in War*, 196.

14. Boelcke, *Secret Conferences*, 69.

15. Delmer, *Trail Sinister* (London: Secker & Warburg, 1961), 328–331.

16. Richard J. Evans, *The Coming of the Third Reich* (New York: Penguin, 2005), Kindle edition, 140.

17. Delmer, *Trail Sinister*, 377.

18. Delmer, *Black Boomerang*, 21.

19. John Baker White, *The Big Lie* (New York: Thomas Cromwell, 1955), Chapter 1.

20. PWE German Region Committee, Agenda of Sub-Committee, July 17, 1940, TNA FO 898/180.

21. Bayer, *"How Dead Is Hitler?"*, 108. Voigt's description is in the 222nd meeting of the Planning and Broadcasting Committee, August 3, 1940, TNA FO 898/8.

22. Capitalisation emphasis in original. Delmer, *Black Boomerang*, 14.

23. Delmer, 15.

24. Delmer, 31.

25. Balfour, *Propaganda in War*, 167.

26. Delmer, 39–41.

27. Jade McGlynn, *Russia's War* (Cambridge, UK: Polity, 2023), 12.

28. Figures quoted by Dr Jade McGlynn, personal online interview with author, August 6, 2023.

29. Denis Volkov and Stepan Gonacharov, "Russian Media Landscape", Levada Centre press release, August 22, 2017, www.levada.ru/2017/08/22/16440.

30. Brianna Richardson, "Axios|Momentive Poll: January 6th Revisited", Curiosity at Work, January 3, 2022, surveymonkey.com/curiosity/axios-january-6-revisited.

31. Laura Hazard Owen, "Republicans and Democrats Live in 'Nearly Inverse News Media Environments', Pew Finds", *Nieman Lab*, January 24, 2020, www.niemanlab.org/2020/01/republicans-and-democrats-live-in-nearly-inverse-news-media-environments-pew-finds/; Mark Jurkowitz, Amy Mitchell, Elisa Shearer and Mason Walker, "Democrats Report Much Higher Levels of Trust in a Number of News Sources than Republicans", Pew Research Center, January 24, 2020, www.pewresearch.org/journalism/2020/01/24/democrats-report-much-higher-levels-of-trust-in-a-number-of-news-sources-than-republicans/.

32. Daniel Kreiss, "The Media Are About Identity, Not Information", https://danielkreiss.files.wordpress.com/2019/10/kreiss_mediaidentity.pdf.

33. Jeremy A. Crang and Paul Addison, *Listening to Britain: Home Intelligence Reports on Britain's Finest Hour, May–September 1940* (New York: Random House, 2011), 421–424.

34. Winston Churchill, "Every Man to His Post, 1940", America's National Churchill Museum, September 11, 1940, www.nationalchurchillmuseum.org/every-man-to-his-post.html.

35. Crang and Addison, *Listening to Britain*, 421–424.

36. BBC Monitoring, Workers' Challenge, 213 Metres, 1417 kcs, 2010 hours, Monitor F. W. Watts, BBC Written Archives Centre.

37. Martin Docherty, "Black Propaganda by Radio: The German Concordia Broadcasts to Britain, 1940–1941", *Historical Journal of Film, Radio and Television* 14, no. 2 (1994): 173, 176.

38. Adrian Weale, *Renegades: Hitler's Englishmen* (London: Lume, 2021), Kindle edition, 59–60. See also Horst J. P. Bergmeier and Rainer E. Lotz, *Hitler's Airwaves: The Inside Story of Nazi Broadcasting and Propaganda Swing* (New Haven, CT: Yale University Press, 1997), Chapter 7; and Docherty, "Black Propaganda by Radio", 167–197.

39. BBC Monitoring. Radio Caledonia. September 10, 1940, 9:20 p.m., Monitor, Biggs, P2, BBC Written Archives Centre.

40. Docherty, "Black Propaganda by Radio".

41. Boelcke, *Secret Conferences*, 68.

42. Balfour, *Propaganda in War*, 142.

43. Paul Laity, "Uneasy Listening", *London Review of Books* 26, no. 13 (2004), www.lrb.co.uk/the-paper/v26/n13/paul-laity/uneasy-listening.

44. Balfour, *Propaganda in War*, 140.

45. Balfour, 139–140; Docherty, "Black Propaganda by Radio", 179.

46. Docherty, "Black Propaganda by Radio", 172.

47. Docherty, "Black Propaganda by Radio", 182–184.

48. "Broadcasting to Foreigners: Lack of Colour and the Human Touch", *Daily Telegraph*, September 30, 1939, Broadcasting Press Cuttings, BBC Written Archives Centre, P 381/1; "How to Win the War of the Wavelengths", *Daily Express*, October 10, 1939; Vike Martina Plock, *The BBC German Service During the Second World War: Broadcasting to the Enemy* (Cham: Palgrave Macmillan, 2021).

49. Bernhard Wittek, *Der britische Ätherkrieg gegen das Dritte Reich: Die deutschsprachigen Kriegssendungen der British Broadcasting Company* (Münster: Verlag C. J. Fahle, 1962), 187; Edward Tangye Lean, *Voices in the Darkness: The Story of the European Radio War* (London: Secker & Warburg, 1943), 52; Plock, *BBC German Service During the Second World War*.

50. Balfour, *Propaganda in War*, 169.

51. Delmer, *Black Boomerang*, 26.

52. Report on Otten by E.3, dated January 10, 1942, TNA KV 2/2586-39a.

53. From report by Blimp re Mrs Dalison, dated June 30, 1942, TNA KV 2/2586-41a.

54. Internal memorandum from E.1.a/USA, Mr Ramsbotham to E.2.a., dated July 21, 1942, TNA KV 2/2586-43a.

55. Information given by Mr Powell, Friday, December 20, 1918, TNA KV 2/2586-2.

56. Delmer, *Black Boomerang*, 24.

57. Delmer, 24; Carol Jacobi, *Out of the Cage: The Art of Isabel Rawsthorne* (London: Thames & Hudson, 2021), 136.

58. With reference to the case of Sefton Delmer, dated February 10, 1941, TNA KV 2/2586.

59. Delmer, *Black Boomerang*, 26–29.

60. Jacobi, *Out of the Cage*, 137.

61. Len Barcousky, "Eyewitness 1940: Leaving London's Blitz Wasn't Easy for Reporter", *Pittsburgh Post-Gazette*, November 8, 2015, www.post-gazette.com/news/nation/2015/11/08/Eyewitness-1940-Leaving-London-s-Blitz-wasn-t-easy-for-reporter/stories/201511080114.

62. Nicholas Kinsey, "Commercial Flights During WW2", https://nicholaskinsey.com/15-commercial-flights-during-ww2.

63. Dusko Popov, *Spy/Counterspy: The Autobiography of Dusko Popov* (New York: Grosset & Dunlap, 1974).

64. Delmer, *Black Boomerang*, 30.

65. Delmer, 30–33.

66. Delmer, 37, 38.

CHAPTER 4. ALL DOUBTS FALL AWAY

1. Lee Richards, "The Rainbow in the Dark: Assessing a Century of British Military Information Operations", *Defence Strategic Communications* 1 (March 2016):

41–66; "Propaganda in War: Ludendorff's Tribute", *The Times* (London), October 31, 1919, 13–14.

2. Walter Lippmann, *Public Opinion* (New York: Harcourt, Brace, 1922).

3. Peter Longerich, *Goebbels* (New York: Random House, 2015), Kindle edition, 80–81.

4. Richard J. Evans, *The Third Reich in Power, 1933–1939* (New York: Penguin, 2006), Kindle edition, 136.

5. Allison C. Meier, "An Affordable Radio Brought Nazi Propaganda Home", *JSTOR Daily*, August 30, 2018, https://daily.jstor.org/an-affordable-radio-brought-nazi-propaganda-home.

6. Ernst Kris and Hans Speier, *German Radio Propaganda* (Oxford: Oxford University Press, 1944), 134.

7. Quoted in Ian Kershaw, *The "Hitler Myth": Image and Reality in the Third Reich* (Oxford: Oxford University Press, 1987), 157.

8. Kershaw, *"Hitler Myth"*, 158. Kershaw quotes a series of SD reports.

9. Kershaw, 158.

10. Kris and Speier, *German Radio Propaganda*, 130–131.

11. Kris and Speier, 59.

12. Victor Klemperer, *I Will Bear Witness: The Diaries of Victor Klemperer, 1933–41* (London: Orion, 2016), Kindle edition, 217–218.

13. Klemperer, *I Will Bear Witness*, 164, 368.

14. Evans, *Third Reich in Power*, 136–137.

15. Evans, 571.

16. Siegfried Kracauer, "1. Exposé. Mass and Propaganda. An Inquiry into Fascist Propaganda (1936)", in *Selected Writings on Media, Propaganda, and Political Communication*, edited by John Abromeit, Jaeho Kang and Graeme Gilloch (New York: Columbia University Press, 2022), 49–55; Peter Fritzsche, *Life and Death in the Third Reich* (Cambridge, MA: Harvard University Press, 2009), Kindle edition, 536–537.

17. William L. Shirer, *Berlin Diary* (New York: RosettaBooks, 2011), Kindle edition, 413.

18. Kris and Speier, *German Radio Propaganda*, 66–72.

19. Kris and Speier, 153–155.

20. Kris and Speier, 156.

21. "Front Report", January 10, 1940, quoted in Kris and Speier, 156.

22. "Front Report", October 10, 1940, quoted in Kris and Speier, 157.

23. Kris and Speier, 164.

24. Victor Klemperer, *The Language of the Third Reich*, trans. Martin Brady (London: Bloomsbury, 2013), 110.

25. Quoted in Kris and Speier, *German Radio Propaganda*, 38.

26. Hannah Arendt, *The Origins of Totalitarianism* (New York: Penguin Modern Classics, 1973), Kindle edition, 461, 460.

27. Arendt, *Origins of Totalitarianism*, 500.

28. "Inside Russia: Traitors and Heroes", BBC Storyville, February 21, 2023. The clip is 29:48 to 31:03. It's from Channel One, Russian TV, directed by Anastasia Popova and Paul Mitchell.

29. Liz Sly and Kostiantyn Khudov, "Europe: Accounting of Bodies in Bucha Nears Completion", *Washington Post*, August 8, 2022, www.washingtonpost.com/world/2022/08/08/ukraine-bucha-bodies.

30. "Inside Russia: Traitors and Heroes", BBC Storyville.

31. "Disinformation to Conceal War Crimes: Russia Is Lying About Atrocities in Bucha", EU vs. Disinfo, April 7, 2022, https://euvsdisinfo.eu/disinformation-to-conceal-war-crimes-russia-is-lying-about-atrocities-in-bucha.

32. "Traditional Values & Authoritarianism. What Makes Russians Support Putin and the War?", Open Mind Institute, November 26, 2022, www.open mindsinstitute.org/reports/traditional-values-authoritarianism-what-makes-russians-support-putin-and-the-war.

33. "Putin Says Russia 'Had No Other Choice' in Ukraine", *Al Jazeera*, April 12, 2022, www.aljazeera.com/news/2022/4/12/putin-flies-into-russian-east-for-ukraine-talks-with-belarusia; "Putin Tells Russian Business People He Had No Choice over Ukraine", Reuters, February 24, 2022, www.reuters.com/world/europe/putin-tells-russian-business-people-he-had-no-choice-over-ukraine-2022-02-24; "Propagandist Who Called for Killing Ukrainian Kids Back on Air", *Kyiv Independent*, November 3, 2022, https://kyivindependent.com/propagandist-who-called-for-killing-ukrainian-kids-back-on-air; Brendan Cole, "Russian TV Says Ukraine No Longer Exists, Compares War to 'Deworming a Cat,'" *Newsweek*, July 19, 2022, www.newsweek.com/russian-tv-ukraine-no-longer-exists-simonyan-russia-1-deworming-1726014; Ishaan Tharoor, "The Russian Rhetoric That Adds Weight to Charges of 'Genocide,'" *Washington Post*, April 6, 2022, www.washingtonpost.com/world/2022/04/06/genocide-claims-ukraine-russia-zelensky.

34. Svitlana Oslavska, "Inside the Basement Where an Entire Ukrainian Village Spent a Harrowing Month in Captivity", *Time*, February 15, 2023, https://time.com/6255183/ukraine-basement-yahidne-held-captive.

CHAPTER 5. INTO THE RIDICULOUS

1. Robert Bruce Lockhart, *Comes the Reckoning* (London: Putnam, 1947), 56.

2. Stephen Bunker, *The Spy Capital of Britain* (Bedford, UK: Bedford Chronicles, 2007), 65–68.

3. Bunker, *Spy Capital of Britain*, 80.

4. Lockhart, *Comes the Reckoning*, 156–157.

5. David Garnett, *The Secret History of PWE* (London: St Ermin's Press, 2002), 31–32.

6. Bunker, *Spy Capital of Britain*, 78, quoting Hugh Dalton, *The Fateful Years: Memoirs, 1931–1945* (London: Frederick Muller, 1957).

7. Conrad Putter, *Rundfunk gegen das Dritte Reich* (Munich: KG Saur, 1986), 106.

8. Adolf Hitler, *Mein Kampf*, trans. James Murphy, https://greatwar.nl/books/meinkampf/meinkampf.pdf, 248. See also Erich Fromm, *Escape from Freedom* (New York: Open Road Media, 1994), Kindle edition, 232.

9. Richard J. Evans, *The Third Reich in Power, 1933–1939* (New York: Penguin, 2006), Kindle edition, 100–101.

10. Evans, *Third Reich in Power*, 136–137.

11. Sefton Delmer, *Black Boomerang* (London: Secker & Warburg, 1962), 41.

12. Quoted in Ian Kershaw, *The "Hitler Myth": Image and Reality in the Third Reich* (Oxford: Oxford University Press, 1987), 157.

13. Kershaw, *"Hitler Myth"*, 162.

14. Kershaw, 163.

15. Michael Balfour, *Propaganda in War, 1939–1945* (London: Routledge, 1979), 316.

16. Kershaw, *"Hitler Myth"*, 164.

17. Garnett, *Secret History*, 41.

18. Garnett, 43.

19. Delmer, *Black Boomerang*, 41.

20. Garnett, *Secret History*, 43–44.

21. Garnett, 43.

22. Delmer, *Black Boomerang*, 42.

23. Balfour, *Propaganda in War*, 142.

24. Delmer, *Black Boomerang*, 44–45.

25. Interview with Peter Seckelmann by A. Sydney Albert, December 4, 1941, TNA KV 2/3667.

26. Delmer, *Black Boomerang*, 49.

27. National Archives and Records Administration, Foreign Broadcast Intelligence Service (hereafter NARA, FBIS), Transcripts of Monitored Foreign Broadcasts, 1941–1946, Chief, Voice of, Transcript of SW Broadcasts, record no. 1000, September 9, 1941, 1:53–2:00 p.m. EST, Translator: H. Parker, RG262.

28. Chief, Voice of, Transcript of SW Broadcasts, record no. 7017, September 16, 1941, 4:52-5:02 p.m. EST, Monitoring Station: Sanda, Translator: H. Parker, NARA, FBIS.

29. Delmer, *Black Boomerang*, 49.

30. Garnett, *Secret History*, 47.

31. Ellic Howe, *The Black Game: British Subversive Operations Against the Germans During the Second World War* (London: Futura, 1982), 113.

32. Untitled progress report giving stories put over by LF in the past week, June 2–9, 1941, TNA FO 898/60.

33. Chief, Voice of, Transcript of SW Broadcasts, record no. 6873, September 13, 1941, Rec. station: Sanda, Translator: H. Parker, 9:53–10:00 p.m. EST, NARA FBIS.

34. Untitled progress report giving stories put over by LF [Larchfield] in the past week, June 2–9, 1941, TNA FO 898/60.

35. Peter Jelavich, *Berlin Cabaret* (Cambridge, MA: Harvard University Press, 1993), Kindle location 1413.

36. Delmer, *Black Boomerang*, 50.

37. Howe, *Black Game*, 113; Garnett, *Secret History*, 42; Delmer, *Black Boomerang*, 50.

38. Chief, Voice of, Transcript of SW Broadcast, record no. 6874, September 14, 1941, NARA, FBIS.

39. Gerhard Paul, *Max Braun, Eine Politische Biografie* (Werner J. Rohrig Verlag, 1987), 201.

40. In 1982 Réne Halkett told his life story to BBC journalist Ian Fell. Fell faithfully transcribed the recordings, and he has been kind enough to share them with me for the purposes of this book.

41. Asa Briggs, *The History of Broadcasting in the United Kingdom*, vol. 3, *The War of Words* (Oxford: Oxford University Press, 1970), 433; Vike Martina Plock, *The BBC German Service During the Second World War: Broadcasting to the Enemy* (Cham: Palgrave Macmillan, 2021).

42. Delmer, *Black Boomerang*, 68; Garnett, *Secret History*, 46.

43. SRN 809, February 23, 1942, TNA WO 208/4143; Harald Welzer and Sönke Neitzel, *Soldaten: On Fighting, Killing and Dying* (New York: Simon & Schuster), Kindle edition.

44. SRM 45, February 10, 1942, TNA WO 208/4136; Welzer and Neitzel, *Soldaten*, location 4473.

45. Report on LF, June 1–4, 1941, TNA FO 898/60.

46. Garnett, *Secret History*, 41.

47. Progress report covering August 12–25, 1941, TNA FO 898/60.

48. UP Minutes of Friday, August 1, 1941, TNA FO 898/69.

49. Rumours R/159 to R/161, TNA FO 898/69.

50. Evidence that GS1 is thought to be in Germany, June 1942, TNA FO 898/60.

51. Evidence that GS1 is thought to be in Germany.

52. Evidence that GS1 is thought to be in Germany.

53. Delmer, *Black Boomerang*, 65.

54. Presentation to George VI and Queen Elizabeth at Woburn Abbey, Beds, 11/1941, Imperial War Museum, IWM Sound 5217; Lockhart, *Comes the Reckoning*, 144.

55. Delmer, *Black Boomerang*, 65.

56. The folio of Frank Lynder's unfinished and unpublished 1984 autobiography was located in the Sussex University archives by Lee Richards. University of Sussex Library, ref SxMs176/3, www.thekeep.info/collections/getrecord/GB181_SxMs176_3.

CHAPTER 6. THAT BEASTLY PORNOGRAPHIC ORGANISATION

1. See Philipp Gassert, "'This Is Hans Fritzsche': A Nazi Broadcaster and His Audience", *Journal of Radio Studies* 8, no. 1 (2001): 86.

2. Gassert, "'This is Hans Fritzsche,'" 81–103, poem about Fritzsche on 90. For more background, see Max Bonacker, *Goebbels's Mann Beim Radio* (Berlin: Walter de Gruyter, 2007).

3. Vike Martina Plock, *The BBC German Service During the Second World War: Broadcasting to the Enemy* (London: Palgrave Macmillan, 2021), 238.

4. Michael Balfour, *Propaganda in War, 1939-1945* (London: Routledge, 1979), 73.

5. Balfour, *Propaganda in War*, 174.

6. "War on the Air, Sefton Delmer Speaks to Germany", *Picture Post*, November 1, 1941, 7.

7. Deutscher Dienst der BBC, Sefton Delmer broadcast to Germany, October 14, 1941, Imperial War Museum, IWM Sound 15014, www.iwm.org.uk/collections/item/object/80014610.

8. Bundesarchiv (German Federal Archives), hereafter BA Berlin, R55/532/132. See also Gassert, "'This Is Hans Fritzsche'".

9. Abhorskript der Rundfunksendung, December 9, 1942, S. 34, BA Berlin, R55/527.

10. Abhorskript der Rundfunksendung, S. 36.

11. See Karen Bayer, *"How Dead Is Hitler?" Der Britische Starreporter Sefton Delmer und Die Deutschen* (Mainz am Rhine: Phillip von Zabern, 2008), 112; and Gassert, "'This Is Hans Fritzsche'".

12. Notes on evidence of reception for week ending October 10, 1941, TNA FO 898/463.

13. Quoted in Bayer, *"How Dead Is Hitler?"*, 113.

14. Ernst Kris and Hans Speier, *German Radio Propaganda* (Oxford: Oxford University Press, 1944), 159-160.

15. Chief, Voice of, Transcript of SW Broadcasts, record no. T-6212, January 20, 1942, 3:53–4:00 p.m., Translators: Eilers and Saul, NARA, FBIS.

16. Kershaw, *"Hitler Myth"*, 174.

17. Quoted in Kershaw, *"Hitler Myth"*, 180.

18. Kris and Speier, *German Radio Propaganda*, 129.

19. Chief, Voice of, Transcripts of SW Broadcasts, record nos. 153-154, December 13 and 16, 1941, NARA, FBIS.

20. Chief, Voice of, Transcript of SW Broadcasts, record no. 169, December 29, 1941, NARA, FBIS; Chief, Voice of, Transcript of SW Broadcasts, record no. 4465, January 16, 1942, NARA, FBIS.

21. Chief, Voice of, record no. 4465.

22. Chief, Voice of, Transcript of SW Broadcasts, record no. 7713, January 23, 1942, NARA, FBIS.

23. Chief, Voice of, Transcript of SW Broadcasts, record no. 179, January 9, 1942, NARA, FBIS.

24. I rely here, as so often, on Lee Richards's research. His detailed description of this and other pieces of sexual propaganda in particular and British clandestine psychological warfare in general is in Lee Richards, *The Black Art: British Clandestine Psychological Warfare Against the Third Reich* (www.psywar.org, 2010), 225–226.

25. Carol Jacobi, *Out of the Cage: The Art of Isabel Rawsthorne* (London: Thames & Hudson, 2021), 138, 144.

26. Richards, *Black Art*, 225–226.

27. Chief, Voice of, Transcript of SW Broadcasts, record no. 172, January 2, 1942, NARA, FBIS.

28. Richard J. Evans, *The Third Reich at War* (New York: Penguin, 2009), Kindle edition, 544.

29. Sender der europ.ischen Revolution, Transcript of SW Broadcasts, record no. T-2581-2582, January 4, 1942, NARA, FBIS.

30. Chief, Voice of, Transcript of SW Broadcasts, record no. 4478, January 14, 1942, NARA, FBIS.

31. Sefton Delmer, *Black Boomerang* (London: Secker & Warburg, 1962), 66.

32. Gustav Siegfried, June 16, 1942, TNA FO 898/60.

33. Kirk Robert Graham, *British Subversive Propaganda During the Second World War: Germany, National Socialism and the Political Warfare Executive* (London: Palgrave Macmillan, 2021), Chapter 4 and other chapters.

34. Erich Fromm, *Escape from Freedom* (New York: Farrar and Rinehart, 1941), 221, 265.

35. Paul Addison, *The Road to 1945: British Politics and the Second World War* (New York: Random House, 2011), Chapter 7.

36. Balfour, *Propaganda in War*, 250; Jonathan Schneer, "Stafford Cripps: The Man Who Challenged Churchill", Wonders and Marvels, www.wondersandmarvels.com/2015/04/stafford-cripps-the-man-who-challenged-churchill.html.

37. Cripps letter to "Anthony", June 12, 1942, TNA FO 898/60.

38. Delmer, *Black Boomerang*, 252.

39. Ellic Howe, *The Black Game: British Subversive Operations Against the Germans During the Second World War* (London: Futura, 1982), 115.

40. Leeper to Bruce Lockhart, June 16, 1942, TNA FO 898/60.

41. Translation of article in *Das Reich*, "Gustav Is Silent", April 26, 1942, TNA FO 898/60.

42. See *Woburn at War*, documentary by Anglia TV, 1987, directed by Graham Creelman.

43. "Audio presentation to George VI and Queen Elizabeth at Woburn Abbey, Beds, 11/1941", Imperial War Museum, IWM Sound 5217, www.iwm.org.uk/collections/item/object/80005174.

44. David Garnett, *The Secret History of PWE* (London: St Ermin's Press, 2002), 42.

45. EH/PID/PWE German and Austrian Intelligence: Recollections of A. R. Walmsley, TNA FO 898/547.

46. Memorandum on our propaganda to Germany by F. A. Voigt, March 1941—Appendix II Secret Broadcasts ("Research Units"), TNA FO 898/181 0238.

47. Leeper to Bruce Lockhart, May 6, 1942, TNA FO 898/60.

48. Crossman to PWE Executive, February 2, 1942, TNA FO 898/60.

49. Extract from National Review, March 1942, TNA FO 898/60.

50. Delmer to Leeper, March 15, 1942, TNA FO 898/60.

51. Leeper to Lockhart, June 16, 1942, TNA FO 898/60.

52. Gustav Siegfried, TNA FO 898/60, subfolder 2020.

53. Eden to Cripps July 1, 1942, TNA FO 954/23.

54. "Effect of Allied Radio Propaganda and German Counter-propaganda", July 23, 1945, TNA FO 898/532—PID Document Section, ref A 15.

55. Robert S. Mueller, "Report on the Investigation into Russian Interference in the 2016 Presidential Election", vol. I, March 2019, US Department of Justice, Washington, DC, https://d3i6fh83elv35t.cloudfront.net/static/2019/04/Mueller Report_searchable_compressed.pdf.

56. Craig Timberg, Tony Romm, Aaron C. Davis, and Elizabeth Dwoskin, "Secret Campaign to Use Russian-Inspired Tactics in 2017 Ala. Election Stirs Anxiety for Democrats", *Washington Post*, January 6, 2019, www.washingtonpost.com/business/technology/secret-campaign-to-use-russian-inspired-tactics-in-2017-alabama-election-stirs-anxiety-for-democrats/2019/01/06/58803f26-0400-11e9-8186-4ec26a485713_story.html.

57. Jacob Davey, "Infiltration Operations: How 4chan Sought to Compromise the Black Lives Matter Protests", Institute for Strategic Dialogue, October 22, 2020, www.isdglobal.org/digital_dispatches/infiltration-operations-how-4chan-sought-to-compromise-the-black-lives-matter-protests.

58. Gareth Browne, "They Planted Porn in ISIS Propaganda, Just for Starters, Then Sowed Chaos and Confusion in the 'Caliphate,'" *Daily Beast*, November 21, 2017, www.thedailybeast.com/they-planted-porn-in-isis-propaganda-just-for-starters-then-sowed-chaos-and-confusion-in-caliphate?ref=scroll.

59. Портал Немезида интересно покопался в телеграмм-каналах, *LiveJournal*, April 18, 2023, https://multivar.livejournal.com/668890.html.

60. Conrad Putter, *Rundfunk gegen das Dritte Reich* (Munich: KG Saur, 1986), 309.

61. "Public Opinion Analysis on Prigozhin 1 Day Before the Coup Attempt", Open Minds Institute, June 24, 2023, www.openmindsinstitute.org/reports/prigozhin-before-mutiny; "Public Opinion Analysis on Prigozhin a Day AFTER the Coup Attempt", Open Mind Institute, June 30, 2023, www.openmindsinstitute.org/reports/prigozhin-after-mutiny.

62. Howe, *Black Game*, 129–130.

63. Evidence of reception, November 1943, part II, TNA FO 898/463, https://arcint.co.uk/page/2552/67.

64. From memoirs of Peter Wykeman at Imperial War Museum, "Memories of Political Warfare, 1942–1945", www.iwm.org.uk/collections/item/object/1030005043.

65. Howe, *Black Game*, 137.

66. René Halkett taped interviews conducted between 1978 and 1982 by his broadcast colleague and literary executor, Ian Fell. Interviews are copyright © Ian Fell.

67. Howe, *Black Game*, 140.

68. Elmar Eisenberger was extensively interviewed by the historians Siegfried Beer and Wolfgang Mutschich in the mid-1980s. They were kind enough to share their archive with me.

69. Howe, *Black Game*, 152–153.

70. Evans, *Third Reich in Power*, 244–245.

71. Evidence of reception, January and February 1945, TNA HS 6/696.

72. Delmer, *Black Boomerang*, 77.

CHAPTER 7. STRENGTH THROUGH FEAR

1. Brunhilde Pomsel, *The Work I Did: A Memoir of the Secretary to Goebbels* (London: Bloomsbury Publishing, 2018), audio edition.

2. Pomsel, *Work I Did*.

3. Pomsel, *Work I Did*.

4. Richard J. Evans, *The Third Reich in Power, 1933–1939* (New York: Penguin, 2006), Kindle edition, 244–245.

5. Goebbels speech on April 19, 1943, quoted in Ernst Kris and Hans Speier, *German Radio Propaganda* (Oxford: Oxford University Press, 1944), 138.

6. Kris and Speier, *German Radio Propaganda*, 138.

7. Kris and Speier, 142.

8. Joseph Goebbels, "Nation, Rise Up, and Let the Storm Break Loose", Calvin University, German Propaganda Archive, https://research.calvin.edu/german-propaganda-archive/goeb36.htm.

9. Goebbels, "Nation, Rise Up, and Let the Storm Break Loose".

10. Pomsel, *Work I Did*.

11. Peter Fritzsche, *Life and Death in the Third Reich* (Cambridge, MA: Harvard University Press, 2009), Kindle edition, 3217–3221.

12. Willi A. Boecke, ed., *The Secret Conferences of Dr Goebbels: The Nazi Propaganda War, 1939–43* (New York: E. P. Dutton, 1970).

13. Michael Balfour, *Propaganda in War, 1939–1945* (London: Routledge, 1979), 323.

14. Balfour, *Propaganda in War*, 325; Ian Kershaw, *The "Hitler Myth": Image and Reality in the Third Reich* (Oxford: Oxford University Press, 1987), 198. See also

Peter Longerich, *Goebbels: A Biography* (New York: Random House, 2015), Kindle edition, 561.

15. Quoted in Balfour, *Propaganda in War*, 325.

16. Quoted in Balfour, 324.

17. See Balfour, 316.

18. Quoted in Balfour, 357.

19. Quoted in Nicholas Stargardt, *The German War: A Nation Under Arms, 1939–45* (New York: Basic Books, 2017), 335.

20. Longerich, *Goebbels*, 545.

21. Louis P. Lochner, ed. and trans., *The Goebbels Diaries, 1942-1943* (Garden City, NY: Doubleday, 1948); Balfour, *Propaganda in War*, 336–338.

22. Balfour, 354; Lochner, *Goebbels Diaries*, 389.

23. Kris and Speier, *German Radio Propaganda*, 141.

24. Pomsel, *Work I Did*.

25. Balfour, *Propaganda in War*, 356. Balfour also notes that the "increase may lie not in their number but their publication".

26. Pomsel, *Work I Did*.

27. Fritzsche, *Life and Death in the Third Reich*, 3228–3230.

28. Evans, *Third Reich at War*, 577.

29. Victor Klemperer, *To the Bitter End: The Diaries of Victor Klemperer, 1942–1945* (London: Orion, 2021), Kindle edition, 333.

30. Klemperer, *To the Bitter End*, 316.

31. Evans, *Third Reich at War*, 574.

32. Post-mortem on Political Warfare, Communication from Reichsfuhrer of the SS, Directing Centre Munich, March 16, 1944, TNA FO 898/240.

33. Ellic Howe, *The Black Game: British Subversive Operations Against the Germans During the Second World War* (London: Futura, 1982), 180.

34. This description of the new studio is drawn from memoirs of Peter Wykeman at Imperial War Museum, "Memories of Political Warfare, 1942–1945", 13-16.

35. Wykeman, "Memories of Political Warfare".

36. Sefton Delmer, *Black Boomerang* (London: Secker & Warburg, 1962), 91.

37. Delmer, *Black Boomerang*, 99-100.

38. See Howe, *Black Game*; Delmer, *Black Boomerang*, 92–95; and Wykeman, "Memories of Political Warfare".

39. René Halkett taped interviews conducted between 1978 and 1982 by his broadcast colleague and literary executor, Ian Fell. Interviews are copyright © Ian Fell.

40. Delmer, *Black Boomerang*, 95–100; Frank Lynder, "Memoirs", 136–142. The folio of Lynder's unpublished and unfinished 1984 autobiography was located in the Sussex University archives by Lee Richards. University of Sussex Library, ref. SxMs176/3, www.thekeep.info/collections/getrecord/GB181_SxMs176_3.

41. Lynder, "Memoirs", 138.

42. Delmer, *Black Boomerang*, 91–92.

43. Howe, *Black Game*, 174.

44. "Aspidistra Grey" by D. S. Delmer, July 21, 1943, TNA FO 898/45.

45. Wykeman, "Memories of Political Warfare", 15.

46. Halkett interview with Fell.

47. Horst J. P. Bergmeier and Rainer E. Lotz, *Hitler's Airwaves: The Inside Story of Nazi Broadcasting and Propaganda Swing* (New Haven: Yale University Press, 1997), 144.

48. Wykeman, "Memories of Political Warfare", 9.

49. Agnes Bernelle, *The Fun Palace: An Autobiography* (Dublin: Lilliput Press, 1996), Kindle edition, 112.

50. Delmer, *Black Boomerang*, 90.

51. See Bernelle, *Fun Palace*; and Halkett interview with Fell.

52. Evidence of reception, April 1944, Rus, Germany, Calais and Atlantik, TNA HS 6/696.

53. Evidence of reception, November 1943, TNA FO 898/463; Evidence of reception, April 1944, TNA FO 898/463; Deutsche Kurzwellensender Altantik, Object, Method, Effect, TNA FO 898/51; Evidence of reception, October 1943, TNA FO 898/463.

54. Bob Bergin, *OSS Undercover Girl: Elizabeth P. McIntosh, an Interview* (Fairfax, VA: Banana Tree Press, 2012), Kindle edition; Bernelle, *Fun Palace*, 113.

55. Post-mortem on Political Warfare.

56. Louis P. Lochner, ed. and trans., *The Goebbels Diaries, 1942–1943* (Garden City, NY: Doubleday, 1948), 535.

57. Talk by Hans Fritzsche, German Home Service, October 23, 1943, TNA FO 898/62.

58. Muriel Spark and Elaine Feinstein, *Curriculum Vitae: A Volume of Autobiography* (Manchester, UK: Lives and Letters, 2014), Kindle edition, 154–157.

59. Lynder, "Memoirs", 159–160.

60. Delmer, *Black Boomerang*, 103.

61. Delmer, *Black Boomerang*, 103.

62. Delmer, 106–107.

63. EH/PID/PWE German and Austrian Intelligence: Recollections of A. R. Walmsley, 18, TNA FO 898/547.

64. Lynder, "Memoirs", 143.

65. Delmer, *Black Boomerang*, 151.

66. Lynder, "Memoirs", 158.

67. Halkett interview with Fell.

68. See Lewis Hyde, *Trickster Makes This World: Mischief, Myth, and Art* (New York: Farrar, Straus and Giroux, 2010), Kindle edition, 10; and Paul Radin, *The Trickster: A Study in American Indian Mythology* (New York: Schocken, 2015), Kindle edition, 77.

69. "The Raven Steals the Light", in *The Raven Steals the Light*, Bill Reid and Robert Bringhurst, eds. (Vancouver: Douglas & McIntyre, 1984).

70. Balfour, *Propaganda in War*, 358.

71. Leonard Miall, "OBITUARY: Professor Michael Balfour", *Independent*, September 27, 1995, www.independent.co.uk/news/obituaries/obituary-professor-michael-balfour-1603240.html.

CHAPTER 8. D-DAY AND THE DEATH DRIVE

1. "How Many Russians Have Died in Ukraine? New Data Estimates Soldier Casualties", NPR, July 14, 2023, www.npr.org/2023/07/14/1187847548/how-many-russians-have-died-in-ukraine-new-data-estimates-soldier-casualties.

2. Jaroslav Lukiv, "Ukraine War: Putin Tells Russian Soldiers' Mothers He Shares Their Pain", *BBC News*, November 25, 2022, www.bbc.com/news/world-europe-63760278.

3. Alexander J. Motyl, "Russia's Cult of Death", *Hill*, February 21, 2023, https://thehill.com/opinion/international/3864092-russias-cult-of-death/.

4. Richard J. Evans, *The Third Reich at War* (New York: Penguin, 2009), Kindle edition, 573.

5. This section on "Krankheit Rettet" is drawn from Delmer, *Black Boomerang*, 129–131; Ellic Howe, *The Black Game: British Subversive Operations Against the Germans During the Second World War* (London: Futura, 1982), 229; and, most importantly, Lee Richards's account of the operation in *The Black Art: British Clandestine Psychological Warfare Against the Third Reich* (www.psywar.org, 2010), 129–138.

6. Sefton Delmer, *Black Boomerang* (London: Secker & Warburg, 1962), 130–131.

7. John Thompson MacCurdy, *War Neuroses* (Cambridge: Cambridge University Press, 1918), vi–vii; John Forrester, "1919: Psychology and Psychoanalysis", *Psychoanalysis and History* 10, no. 1 (2008): 37–94.

8. Interviews with Josh Cohen by author 2020–2023, per email and in person.

9. Sefton Delmer, *Trail Sinister* (London: Secker & Warburg, 1961), 378.

10. Interviews with Cohen.

11. The idea of people being driven by a fundamental attraction to death and destruction, including self-destruction, was first introduced by the Russian psychoanalyst Sabina Spielrein at a session of the Vienna Psychoanalytic Society on November 25, 1911. Spielrein would later be murdered in the Holocaust, and her brothers were victims of Stalin's Terror. Sigmund Freud, *Beyond the Pleasure Principle* (New York: W. W. Norton, 1990), i.

12. Interviews with Cohen.

13. Mark Abrams, "Analysis of Hitler Speech on April 26, 1942", Churchill Archives Centre, Cambridge, Papers of Mark Abrams, www7.bbk.ac.uk/thepursuitofthenazimind/JTM/MarkAbramsAnalysisofHitlersSpeech1942.pdf.

14. Note to support the theory that it would not be unpatriotic even for officers in the army to accept unconditional surrender, TNA FO 898/192.

15. Klaus Kirchner, *Krankheit rettet: Psychologische Kriegführung* [*Illness Saves*] (Erlangen: Verlag D + C, 1976).

16. Delmer, *Black Boomerang*, 130.

17. Kirchner, *Krankheit rettet*, 36.

18. Kirchner, 33–36.

19. Kirchner, 38–39.

20. Carol Jacobi, *Out of the Cage: The Art of Isabel Rawsthorne* (London: Thames & Hudson, 2021), 142.

21. René Halkett taped interviews conducted between 1978 and 1982 by his broadcast colleague and literary executor, Ian Fell. Interviews are copyright © Ian Fell.

22. Delmer, *Black Boomerang*, 131.

23. Transcript of Monitored Foreign Broadcasts, 1941–1946, Station: Catholic Clandestine, Transcript of Short Wave Broadcast, February 28, 1944, 5:15 p.m. EST, NARA, FBIS.

24. Delmer, 133–135; Howe, *Black Game*, 217–218; Richards, *Black Art*, 194.

25. Howe, *Black Game*, 219.

26. Delmer, *Black Boomerang*, 133–135. See also Richards, *Black Art*, 143.

27. Delmer, 141–142.

28. Delmer, *Black Boomerang*, 125–126.

29. Delmer, 145.

30. Robert Bruce Lockhart, *Comes the Reckoning* (London: Putnam, 1947), 307.

31. Delmer, *Black Boomerang*, 145–147. See also Stephen Bunker, *Spy Capital of Britain: Bedfordshire's Secret War, 1939-1945* (Bedford: Bedford Chronicles, 2007), 126-127; Richards, *Black Art*, 164.

32. Delmer, 155–160.

33. Transcript of Monitored Foreign Broadcasts, 1941–1946, Station: Catholic Clandestine, Transcript of Short Wave Broadcast, March 17, 1944, 5:15 p.m. EST, NARA, FBIS.

34. Agnes Bernelle, *The Fun Palace: An Autobiography* (Dublin: Lilliput Press, 1996), Kindle edition, 112–113.

35. Delmer, *Black Boomerang*, 155–160.

36. Victor Klemperer, *To the Bitter End: The Diaries of Victor Klemperer, 1942–1945* (London: Orion, 2021), Kindle edition, 519.

37. Halkett interview with Fell.

38. Lockhart, *Comes the Reckoning*, 307.

39. Delmer, *Black Boomerang*, 161–164.

40. Delmer, 164-165.

41. Delmer, 165.

42. Transcript of Monitored Foreign Broadcasts, 1941–1946, Radio Atlantik, June 6, 1944, 5:20 p.m. EST, NARA, FBIS.

43. Lockhart, *Comes the Reckoning*, 307.

44. This apposite phrase comes from Ian Fell, describing Halkett's feelings about Delmer's text, in email correspondence with author from September 12, 2023.

45. Delmer, *Black Boomerang*, 165–167.

46. Halkett interview with Fell.

CHAPTER 9. VALKYRIE

1. Sefton Delmer, *Black Boomerang* (London: Secker & Warburg, 1962), 172–173.

2. Quoted in Michael Balfour, *Propaganda in War, 1939–1945* (London: Routledge, 1979), 385.

3. Robert Bruce Lockhart, *Comes the Reckoning* (London: Putnam, 1947), 314.

4. Quoted in Balfour, *Propaganda in War*, 386.

5. Quoted in Balfour, 387.

6. Victor Klemperer, *To the Bitter End: The Diaries of Victor Klemperer, 1942–1945* (London: Orion, 2021), Kindle edition, 543.

7. Delmer, *Black Boomerang*, 174, 177.

8. Balfour, *Propaganda in War*, 391.

9. Klemperer, *To the Bitter End*, 543.

10. Klemperer, 547.

11. Quoted in Balfour, *Propaganda in War*, 391.

12. Balfour, *Propaganda in War*, 174–175.

13. Klemperer, *To the Bitter End*, 547–548.

14. Joseph Goebbels, "The Call of Duty", Calvin University, German Propaganda Archive, https://research.calvin.edu/german-propaganda-archive/goeb50.htm.

15. Ian Kershaw, *The "Hitler Myth": Image and Reality in the Third Reich* (Oxford: Oxford University Press, 1987), 215.

16. Quoted in Balfour, *Propaganda in War*, 388–389.

17. Quoted in Kershaw, *"Hitler Myth"*, 217.

18. Klemperer, *To the Bitter End*, 547.

19. Goebbels, "Call of Duty".

20. Balfour, *Propaganda in War*, 396.

21. Delmer, *Black Boomerang*, 183.

22. Delmer, 121.

23. Balfour, *Propaganda in War*, 438.

24. See, for example, Ian Kershaw, *The End: The Defiance and Destruction of Hitler's Germany, 1944–1945* (New York: Penguin, 2011), Kindle edition.

25. Delmer, *Black Boomerang*, 213–214.

26. Delmer, 119–120.

27. Quoted in Kershaw, *"Hitler Myth"*, 221.

28. Quoted in Balfour, *Propaganda in War*, 397–398.

29. Henry V. Dicks, "Personality Traits and National Socialist Ideology: A War-Time Study of German Prisoners of War", *Human Relations* 3, no. 2 (1950): 111–154, https://doi.org/10.1177/001872675000300201. See also Henry Dicks, "National Socialism as a Psychological Problem", 1945, in Wellcome Collection, London: PP/HVD/A/3.

30. Interviews with Josh Cohen by author 2020–2023, per email and in person.

31. Karen Stenner, *The Authoritarian Dynamic* (Cambridge: Cambridge University Press, 2010).

32. Interviews with Cohen.

33. Dicks, "Personality Traits and National Socialist Ideology", 111–154.

34. Henry V. Dicks, "Some Principles of Psychological Warfare Policy", May 1944, Welcome Collection PP/HVD/A/1 and Birkbeck University website, www7.bbk.ac.uk/thepursuitofthenazimind/HD.php.

35. Dicks, "Some Principles of Psychological Warfare Policy".

36. Interviews with Cohen.

37. Nicholas O'Shaughnessy, *Selling Hitler: Propaganda and the Nazi Brand* (London: Hurst, 2016), Kindle edition, 105.

38. Dicks, "Some Principles of Psychological Warfare Policy".

CHAPTER 10. HOW DEAD IS HITLER?

1. Muriel Spark and Elaine Feinstein, *Curriculum Vitae: A Volume of Autobiography* (Manchester, UK: Lives and Letters, 2014), Kindle edition, 147.

2. René Halkett taped interviews conducted between 1978 and 1982 by his broadcast colleague and literary executor, Ian Fell. Interviews are copyright © Ian Fell.

3. Sefton Delmer, *Black Boomerang* (London: Secker & Warburg, 1962), 196–203.

4. Victor Klemperer, *To the Bitter End: The Diaries of Victor Klemperer, 1942–1945* (London: Orion, 2021), Kindle edition, 649.

5. Klemperer, *To the Bitter End*, 650.

6. Klemperer, 652.

7. Klemperer, 654.

8. Klemperer, 674.

9. The conventional estimate of 25,000 killed can be found in Richard J. Evans, *Lying About Hitler: History, Holocaust, and the David Irving Trial* (New York: Basic Books, 2001).

10. German (RU G9) Rumours, G9 Report, February 14, 1945, TNA FO 898/72.

11. Klemperer, *To the Bitter End*, 664.

12. Klemperer, 678.

13. (RU G9), Rumours, March 1, 1945, TNA FO 898/72.

14. Klemperer, 680.

15. Quoted in Marlis G. Steinert, *Hitler's War and the Germans, Public Mood, and Attitude During the Second World War* (Athens: Ohio University Press, 1977), 304–305, 307.

16. Steinert, 306.

17. Joseph Goebbels, "This Is How We Will Defeat the Soviets!", Calvin University, German Propaganda Archive, https://research.calvin.edu/german-

propaganda-archive/goeb90.htm; Peter Longerich, *Goebbels: A Biography* (New York: Random House, 2015), Kindle edition, 673–674.

18. Longerich, *Goebbels*, 674.

19. "OTD—Josef Goebbels' Diary—13th March 1945", People's Mosquito, www. peoplesmosquito.org.uk/2015/03/13/otd-josef-goebbels-diary-13th-march-1945.

20. Steinert, *Hitler's War and the Germans*, 309.

21. Quoted in Ian Kershaw, *The End: The Defiance and Destruction of Hitler's Germany, 1944–1945* (New York: Penguin, 2011), Kindle edition, 258.

22. Klemperer, *To the Bitter End*, 720.

23. Longerich, *Goebbels*, 683.

24. Asa Briggs, *The History of Broadcasting in the United Kingdom*, vol. 3, *The War of Words* (Oxford: Oxford University Press, 1970), 692; Vike Martina Plock, *The BBC German Service During the Second World War: Broadcasting to the Enemy* (Cham: Palgrave Macmillan, 2021).

25. Delmer, *Black Boomerang*, 218.

26. Delmer, 218–219.

27. Klemperer, *To the Bitter End*, 759.

28. Quote in Harald Jähner, *Aftermath: Life in the Fallout of the Third Reich, 1945–1955* (New York: Knopf Doubleday, 2022), Kindle edition, 16.

29. Delmer, *Black Boomerang*, 239–241.

30. Delmer, 232.

31. Delmer, 233.

32. Delmer, 233–235.

33. Quoted in Karen Bayer, *"How Dead Is Hitler?" Der Britische Starre- porter Sefton Delmer und Die Deutschen* (Mainz am Rhine: Phillip von Zabern, 2008), 154.

34. Quoted in Bayer, 163.

35. "The Hour of Sefton Delmer", *Die Tat*, September 5, 1945.

36. Delmer, *Black Boomerang*, 252–253.

37. Quoted in Bayer, *"How Dead Is Hitler?"*, 167.

38. Richard Ashby Wilson, *Incitement on Trial: Prosecuting International Speech Crimes* (Cambridge: Cambridge University Press, 2017), 28–29.

39. Eugene Davidson, *The Trial of the Germans* (Columbia: University of Mis- souri, 1966), 541–546.

40. Wibke Kristin Timmermann, "Incitement in International Criminal Law", *International Review of the Red Cross* 88, no. 864 (2006): 823–852.

41. Sefton Delmer, *Die Deutschen und Ich* (Hamburg: Nannen-Verlag, 1962), 681–682.

42. Davidson, *Trial of the Germans*, 550.

43. Timmermann, "Incitement in International Criminal Law".

44. Gregory S. Gordon, "The Forgotten Nuremberg Hate Speech Case: Otto Diet- rich and the Future of Persecution Law", *Ohio State Law Journal* 75, no. 3 (2014).

45. David Garnett, *The Secret History of PWE* (London: St Ermin's Press, 2002), 386.

46. Victor Klemperer, *The Lesser Evil: The Diaries of Victor Klemperer, 1945–1959* (London: Weidenfeld & Nicolson, 2021), Kindle edition, 284, 532.

47. Quoted in Bayer, *"How Dead Is Hitler?"*, 184.

48. Delmer, *Black Boomerang*, 255–256.

49. See, for example, Jähner, *Aftermath*, 317.

50. Quoted in Bayer, *"How Dead Is Hitler?"*, 192.

51. Delmer, *Black Boomerang*, 256.

52. Quoted in Jähner, *Aftermath*, 362.

53. Quoted in Jähner, 363.

54. Hannah Arendt, "The Aftermath of Nazi Rule", *Commentary Magazine*, October 1950, www.commentary.org/articles/hannah-arendt/the-aftermath-of-nazi-rulereport-from-germany.

55. Delmer, *Die Deutschen und Ich*, 680.

56. Quoted in Bayer, *"How Dead Is Hitler?"*, 198; *Daily Express*, March 22, 1954, 4.

CHAPTER 11. HOW TO WIN AN INFORMATION WAR

1. Max Hunder, "At Least 1,000 Civilians Hiding Under Ukrainian Stronghold Steel Plant in Mariupol—City Council", Reuters, April 18, 2022, www.reuters.com/world/europe/least-1000-civilians-hiding-under-ukrainian-stronghold-steel-plant-mariupol-city-2022-04-18.

2. *Salò, or the 120 Days of Sodom*, directed by Pier Paolo Pasolini, 1975.

3. Interview by author with Open Minds Institute, 2023.

4. Jim Rutenberg, "How Fox Chased Its Audience down the Rabbit Hole", *New York Times*, April 6, 2023, www.nytimes.com/2023/04/06/magazine/fox-dominion-jan-6.html.

5. Sarah Cook, "Beijing's Global Megaphone", Freedom House, 2020, https://freedomhouse.org/report/special-report/2020/beijings-global-megaphone.

6. My thanks to the internet scholar Rennee de Resta for first making this point to me.

CHAPTER 12. ORDINARY ORDINARY

1. NPFPP 16823, Sefton Delmer's MI5 file, dated October 4, 1954, TNA KV 2/3715-78A, note by G. R. Mitchell, October 1, 1954.

2. Sefton Delmer, *Black Boomerang* (London: Secker & Warburg, 1962), 260–270.

3. See Karen Bayer, *"How Dead Is Hitler?", Der Britische Starreporter Sefton Delmer und Die Deutschen* (Mainz am Rhine: Phillip von Zabern, 2008), 235; Sefton Delmer, "Children in Blue Get That Nazi Look", *Daily Express*, September 29, 1954, 4.

4. Jacobi, *Out of the Cage*, 142, 149.

5. Quoted in Nicholas Rankin, *Churchill's Wizards: The British Genius for Deception, 1914–1945* (London: Faber & Faber), Kindle edition, 418.

6. Delmer, *Black Boomerang*, 8–12.

7. Quoted in Bayer, *"How Dead Is Hitler?"*, 260; R. H. S. Crossman, "Black Prima Donna (Review of D. Sefton Delmer, *Black Boomerang*)", *New Statesman*, November 9, 1962, 676–677.

8. Bayer, *"How Dead Is Hitler?"*, 259–260.

9. Günter Bohnsack and Herbert Brehmer, *Auftrag Irreführung: Wie die Stasi Politik im Westen machte* (Hamburg: Carlsen, 1992), 167.

10. Jason Burke, "Secret British 'Black Propaganda' Campaign Targeted Cold War Enemies", *Guardian*, May 14, 2022, www.theguardian.com/world/2022/may/14/secret-british-black-propaganda-campaign-targeted-cold-war-enemies-information-research-department; Paul Lashmar, Nicholas Gilby, and James Oliver, "Slaughter in Indonesia: Britain's Secret Propaganda War", *Guardian*, October 17, 2021, www.theguardian.com/world/2021/oct/17/slaughter-in-indonesia-britains-secret-propaganda-war.

11. Author's telephone interview and online interview with Libby Ainsley, October 27, 2023.

12. Siegfried Beer, *ÖsterreicherInnen in den westlichen Armeen und Geheimdiensten*, in *Widerstand in Österreich, 1938–45: Die Beiträge der Parlaments-Enquete 2005* (Graz-Wien, 2007), 215–219.

13. Lee Richards, *The Black Art: British Clandestine Psychological Warfare Against the Third Reich* (www.psywar.org, 2010), 225–226.

14. Permission to include David Jay and René Halkett's "Armour" (1981) courtesy of Ian Fell.

15. Interview on BBC Radio, *Open House*, October 20, 1966.

16. See *Woburn at War*, documentary by Anglia TV, 1987, directed by Graham Creelman.

17. Bayer, *"How Dead is Hitler?"*, 282.

18. Sefton Delmer, *Trail Sinister: An Autobiography* (London: Secker & Warburg, 1961), 11.

INDEX